CONTINUE TO MARCH

by
1st Sgt. Robert G. Lay
U. S. Marine Corps, Ret.

First Edition

Print ISBN: 978-1-54399-346-2

eBook ISBN: 978-1-54399-347-9

CONTENTS

CHAPTER 1

IN THE BEGINNING

The year 1935 marked the middle of a decade of misery for millions of people around the world. While the winds of war blew across Europe and China, blinding, choking dust storms blew across the heartland of America. Adding to America's misery was the aftermath of the stock market crash in October 1929, which left millions of Americans jobless and many banks and giant corporations bankrupt. Soup lines became commonplace in America's cities, while thousands of impoverished farmers from Kansas, Oklahoma, and the Texas panhandle streamed westward to find work—their crops having burned up by drought and the soil literally blown away by the wind. While Adolf Hitler and Benito Mussolini consolidated power in Europe, Senator Huey P. Long, the "Kingfish," imposed a virtual dictatorship in Louisiana—in both instances abrogating the rights of millions of people. The "Kingfish" was assassinated in September 1935, and history shows that the world would have been a better place had Hitler and Mussolini met the same fate.

I was born in the middle of this anguished decade on Sunday, September 22, 1935, in Bourbon County, Kansas. The old home place was four miles west and one-half mile north of Fulton, Kansas, on the north side of the Little Osage River. I was the third of six children born to Glen Filmore Lay and Nellie Mae (Chaney) Lay. Their first child, Betty, was born in 1929. A second child, a girl, was born in 1930 and died at birth. My younger sisters were Margaret, Dorothy, and Judy.

Betty remembers me as a very mischievous little brother whose primary purpose and joy in life was teasing her and making her life miserable. Happily, in our adult life we became very close friends and found much solace and comfort in one another when tragic times fell upon our family. Betty clearly recalls the day of my birth. She says that I was born late in the afternoon on a gloomy, cloudy day, which probably accounts for my mischievous ways. I was born at home, as were my sisters. A doctor from a nearby small town came to assist in the deliveries.

I was a healthy baby at birth, but at two months old I caught whooping cough and very nearly died of that disease, which swept across the country that year. It's always been said by my family that I would have certainly died had it not been for the great love and determination of my maternal grandmother, Lydia Chaney. Grandma Chaney sat by my side, night after night, to keep me from choking to death during the frequent coughing spasms. According to records kept by the Kansas Historical Society, there were fifty-three reported deaths from whooping cough in Kansas alone that year. The records also indicate that there were likely many more unreported deaths. Betty recalled that Momma and Grandma Chaney were constantly worried that I was going die as a baby.

Maternal grandmother Lydia Chaney, Momma Nellie, Melinda, Me (five months old) and Betty. 1936

After the whooping cough episode, the great dust storms rolled in again the next spring. Betty remembers Momma and Grandma Chaney soaking bed sheets in water and hanging them on the inside of the windows to keep the dust from coming into the house. No matter what they did, the dust still managed to find its way inside. It came in around the windows and formed little sand dunes on the windowsills. Dust floated through the air in the house. It got into the water and food and left a gritty feeling in our mouths. There wasn't anything that anyone could do during those dust bowl years except to try to survive. It was just another one of the miseries people back then had to endure.

I recall very little of these early years, and by the time I was old enough to remember things like that, the dust storms had subsided, and by 1939-1940 the farmers were beginning to recover and see some fruits of their labors.

The old home place was on about twenty-five acres of Osage river-bottom land. The small wood-framed house was situated about a quarter of a mile from the banks of the river that snaked its way through the timbered bottomland. Dad had built our house himself from used lumber saved from an old barn. A neighbor had given him the lumber in exchange for Dad's help with tearing down the barn. He hauled the lumber about a mile to our home site with a wagon and a team of horses and built the house on a foundation of cement and stones picked up from the fields and along the riverbank.

The house had four rooms: a kitchen, living room, and two bedrooms. On the south side was a screened-in porch that ran the width of the house. Dad kept a couple of tables on one side of the porch on which to lay the meat for winter. Every year, he would wait until late fall to butcher a fat hog. After a day of butchering, he would cut the hog into smaller portions for curing. Rubbing the meat with a curing salt prevented it from spoiling. The cool temperatures and the curing salt insured that the meat would keep for as long as it was needed.

Inside, the plaster walls of the house were covered with wall-paper, and the wood flooring had been overlaid with linoleum. Although the rock foundation was held together by cement, it failed to completely block the winds of winter that swept in from the north-west, rattling the empty cornstalks still standing in the field west of the house and blanketing the river, the small streams, and the pond with a thick coating of ice. There was no insulation in the walls or beneath the floor. Sometimes the winter winds, swirling around and under the house, would cause the linoleum to rise slowly up and down like a huge beast, breathing heavily. A glass of water on a table by the bedside would often develop a thin glaze of ice by morning because the wood burning stove in the living room was our only source of heat.

Momma cooked on a small wood cook stove in the kitchen, and in the winter we could always find a big teakettle of hot water sitting on top of it. Calls of nature were responded to at an outdoor privy about fifty yards from the house, which we simply called the toilet. That situation was bad enough in mild weather, with the smell and the flies, but it took a lot of grit and much discomfort to force a body out of a warm bed at night in the dead of winter to go out to that toilet. In fact, a slop jar, or chamber pot, was allowed on the coldest winter nights for the women, but no self-respecting man would dare to stoop to that level! In the outhouse, an old *Sears and Roebuck* or Montgomery Wards catalog were the usual substitutes for real toilet tissue.

Gathering the materials and building the house must have taken my Dad many hours of hard, grueling work, especially considering that he had no power tools but only basic hand tools. For water, he dug a well and lined it with native stone. Water was drawn out with a bucket and rope. When I last visited the old place in the late summer of 2008 with my son Mark, the old well was still there, but the concrete covering and rock lining had long since cracked and fallen in. The old house, having stood empty for many years, had burned down in the mid-1960s.

When I last visited the old place in the late summer of 2008 with my son Mark, the old well was still there, the concrete covering and rock lining having cracked and fallen in. The old house, having stood empty for many years, burned in the mid 1960s. Rose bushes, purple and white irises, and yellow daffodils, which Momma planted in the 1930s, still bloom every spring on the old place. I wasn't there at the time, but the family said that Momma cried when the old house burned. None of us could fully understand then how many of her memories went up with that smoke. Though later owners have farmed the surrounding land, for some reason the place where the house stood and the yard and garden area remain intact, though overgrown with weeds and brush. Mark wrestled around in the tangle of vines and brush and found a piece of the old mingled cement and stone from the original foundation. We each took a stone for a souvenir of the old home place.

My very earliest memories of childhood are centered on this old home place. I was a skinny kid, with brown eyes and light brown hair that rarely saw a comb, and I probably looked as if a cow had licked me at the hairline of my forehead. Wearing my bib-overalls, no shirt, and deeply suntanned, I remember going barefoot in the summertime, walking down the old dirt road, and watching the thick dust puff up between my toes. I remember running as fast as I could across the pasture, hurdling milkweeds and thistle, thinking that I surely must be the fastest kid in the whole world!

I remember Grandma Chaney taking me fishing down on Lost Creek. We'd often come home with a catch of perch and bullheads strung on a forked stick. Grandma would clean the fish, roll them in cornmeal and flour, and fry them up for supper.

Another good memory is one of walking with Grandma Chaney a mile or so across the fields and down a couple of hedgerows, taking a shortcut to the home and camp-meeting grounds of a local holiness preacher. I remember everyone getting down on their knees in the preacher's living room and praying for a long time about something. The loud praying was sort of scary for me, and I remember hoping that God would never get mad at *me*!

I'll always remember Grandma Chaney as a saintly, quiet, mild-mannered, white-haired woman. Always wearing her old apron, she was constantly busy about the house or out doing chores. She lived with us most of the time, but sometimes she would go stay for a while with her other daughter, my aunt, Melinda Newcomb, in Fort Scott, which was the county seat of Bourbon County.

I still have an old black-and-white photo of Dad hauling wood on a winter day, and I remember him looking just like that from when I was a little boy. Standing there, with a team of mules and an old wagon, he's dressed in a heavy, old woolen coat with his collar turned up against the wind, and the earflaps of his cap pulled down around his ruddy, whiskered face, as he blew plumes of breath into the frigid air.

I remember Mama working in the garden in the summer, cleaning vegetables in the back yard and chopping the heads off a couple of chickens to fry up for supper. Even today, the smell of ham and beans cooking brings back images of a big pot of simmering goodness on the old wood burning cook-stove. It seemed like I could never get enough of those beans and cornbread suppers! I'd eat until I felt I would surely burst.

Sometimes my Grandma Lay (Iva [Wilson] Lay) would come up from Neosho, Missouri, to visit for a few days. Grandma Lay was a thin, angular, spirited woman, with long, graying black hair. Her husband—my grandfather, Amos Hueston Lay—died in 1938. I only saw my grandfather once, and that was just before his funeral. He was laid out on a daybed in the home for viewing and visitation. I will always hold this picture of him in my mind. He looked like he was sleeping peacefully, still a handsome figure of a man, wearing a suit, a vest, and a mustache in the style of the day.

Grandma Lay was born and raised on the border of Kansas and Indian Territory, long before Oklahoma became a state. She was a lively, outgoing woman, tidy and meticulously clean, I remember how she always made us kids wash our hands before supper. She liked to tease, and she enjoyed either telling or hearing a good joke or story. Her tales of the hardships that she had lived through were indeed hair-raising. Grandma Lay lived to the ripe old age of ninety-three.

The banks of the Osage river near our house were lined with cottonwood, elm, walnut, hickory, and oak trees, which served as home and playground for numerous squirrels, raccoons, opossums, owls, and a great many other birds and small animals. There was an abundance of cottontail rabbits, which we hunted as a food source in the winter. Dad had an old single-shot .22 caliber rifle with the rear sight missing.

When I was maybe only four or five years old, I recall sloughing through the snow, following Dad as we went out hunting rabbits in the hedgerows and brush piles. Even without that rear sight on his rifle, he always took pride in shooting the rabbit in the head. Dad said he didn't want any gut-shot rabbits to eat. Later, in my early teens, when I was trusted to go hunting alone, I knew that I would be admonished if I brought home a rabbit or squirrel that wasn't killed with a clean headshot.

My family was very poor when I was a kid, and I don't recall things getting much better as I grew into adulthood. By the same token, though, I don't remember that we suffered much or ever felt deprived—probably because practically everybody else we knew was just as poor (although I believe we were much closer to the bottom of the economic ladder than most).

In spite of that, my childhood memories are happy ones, and many years later, after having lived in and around several big cities and experiencing modern freeway traffic, air pollution, and high crime in the city, I've come to believe that I was truly blessed to have been born and raised on a farm in rural Kansas. Unlike thousands of people in the cities at that time who depended upon soup lines for food, we seemed to always have enough to eat. Most of our food was raised on the farm, with vegetables from the garden, which Momma canned for the winter months, and a hog, which dad butchered in the fall. We also ate a lot of rabbits in the fall and winter. Believe me, when I tell you that rabbit parts, rolled in flour, fried golden brown, and served with biscuits and gravy, makes for a savory, delicious meal!

Dad and Momma were robust, tough, hard-working people, accustomed to hardships and rough times. Though I don't recall either of them ever attending church, they certainly lived by Christian principles and the Ten Commandments. Those were the days when a man's word was his bond. Contracts and agreements were usually sealed with a handshake, and sometimes even that wasn't necessary. If a man said he would do such-and-such, he'd do it, and that was that. Being honest is a principle I learned early on and I tried to practice it as much as possible for the rest of my life.

The same behavior was expected from us kids. If we said we were going to do something or be somewhere at a particular time, that was what was expected, and we had better follow through with it! There was also just a normal expectation that you'd never tell a lie. I remember as a kid getting several good spankings for either trying to lie or hiding the truth about something. Getting a spanking from Dad was a brutal experience, and I learned my lesson very early in life about such things.

I honestly believe that these kinds of expectations served me well throughout the rest of my life. My goal was always to try to build and maintain a reputation in my adult life of a being a man of my word.

The Lay Family, Osage River Valley Home, 1941. Dad, Mom, Betty, Bob, Margaret and Dorothy.

CHAPTER 2

FAMILY HERITAGE

I can trace my dad's family all the way back five generations to my great, great, great grandfather, Isaac Lay, who was born somewhere between 1759-1767. We have no records that identify the parents of Isaac or that state exactly where he was born. However, there are land records stating that he and his wife, Catherine (Bradley) Lay, raised a large family in Burkes County, North Carolina. At some point they moved to Scott County, Virginia, where Isaac died in 1810. Isaac Lay's descendants migrated to Eastern Tennessee, and then later into Missouri, where my dad was born in 1902 in Newton County. Though we can find no record of Isaac's ancestors, family tradition has always held that his parents migrated from Alsace-Lorraine, a French-German province. Catherine Lay was Irish and was believed to have descended from one of the earliest American families.

**My paternal grandfather and grandmother, Amos and Ivy Lay, my father
Glen and his sister Fontella. 1904**

Dad was a tall, lean, handsome, rawboned man, with long, strong, sinewy arms. Over the years, his skin took on a leathery appearance, tanned from a lifetime of hard work in the fields and on bridge construction crews as a young man. He had dark brown, deep-set, steady eyes and black hair that had just begun to turn gray when he died at age eighty in August 1983. Dad always wore bib overalls and a denim or flannel shirt. He preferred a straw hat in the summer and a bill-cap with earflaps in the winter. He loved to hunt, but he made it very clear that although he loved the activity of hunting, he always hunted for food or for fur, not just for sport. He loved hunting rabbits in the snow, but the form of hunting he loved the most was raccoon hunting at night during the fall and winter months.

My dad always owned a "coon dog," whether it was a Black and Tan or a Blue Tick hound dog, or some combination of both. At that time in rural Kansas, a good coonhound was counted among a man's most prized possessions, and during coon-hunting season, those dogs were the center of most of the conversations whenever and wherever men would gather. Coon hunters were prone to brag about their dog's ability to trail a coon, and they also admired the dog's persistence in pursuing the chase. A dog's ability to trail a coon has to do with its sense of smell, i.e., how good of a "nose" does it have? The coon hunters we knew loved to tell stories of particular chases—stories that were greatly embellished, perhaps even invented, that demonstrated how good a "nose" their dog had.

My dad had a dry sense of humor, and he loved a good joke or story. He was known to spin a few stories of his own from time to time. For example, several years after Dad had died, my sister, Dorothy, then a home healthcare nurse, had as a patient an old gentleman who had known Dad for many years.

He told Dorothy of a time years ago at the rural country store in Mantey, Kansas, when he, Dad, and several other guys were standing around the pot-bellied stove warming themselves on a cold winter day. He said that Dad kept shuffling and stomping his feet until one of the men asked him, "What's wrong? Did you freeze your feet out coon hunting?"

Very seriously, my dad said, "Yes, I did freeze my feet last night."

When the man asked him how he'd done it, Dad said he had frozen them standing in the snow holding a flashlight so that Nellie could see while she was chopping wood!

Dad taught me how to hunt, how to recognize animal signs in the woods, and how to aim and shoot a rifle at a really early age. He was very adamant about how to handle a weapon properly, how to safely climb through a fence while carrying a rifle, and how to carry the gun with its muzzle always pointing in the air or at the ground. He told me never to load or unload a gun in the house, nor to keep a loaded gun indoors. I remember him telling me over and over again to never play with guns as if they were toys, and to never, ever point a gun at anything you don't intent to shoot.

Dad also taught me how to recognize the different species of trees and wild berries, and sometimes he'd use a story or joke to teach me a lesson. I recall one time when we were out hunting in the woods, and we sat down on an old log to rest. Dad brushed away some dead leaves to make a little clear spot on the ground. He took a small stick and punched two identical holes in the ground, side by side. He said, "Now, boy, listen to me." He pointed at one of the holes and said, "That is a hole in the ground; do you understand?"

I said, "Yes."

Then he pointed at the other hole and said, "That is your butthole, you understand?"

I nodded, yes, I understood. Dad waited a few seconds then asked me, "Now, where is your butthole?"

I pointed to the hole in the ground that Dad had said was my butthole. With his trap now laid, Dad leaned back, laughed, and said, "Boy, you sure are dumb! You don't know your ass from a hole in the ground. Now, where is your butthole?"

A light slowly came on in my head, and I sheepishly pointed to my backside. Dad then said, "Now, let that be a lesson to you, boy, don't believe everything people tell you!"

I'm so thankful for my dad! Dad taught me a lot about life and hard work. He was the best man I've ever known. I worked side by side with him throughout my childhood and adolescence. I followed him many miles though the fields and timber, hunting rabbits, squirrels, and raccoons at night. I can still clearly recall the stark beauty of a cold, crisp, moonlit winter night, so silent you could hear the falling snowflakes as they landed softly on the dry leaves that were still clinging to the scrub oak trees. Sometimes we would just stop where we were, listening to the sounds of the night or waiting to hear the bellowing of the coonhound when he picked up a scent on a fresh trail. I can still picture the ice on Lost Creek, glistening like quicksilver in the pale moonlight. The creaking sounds of the branches on the leafless trees as they bent gently with the wind, casting flickering shadows on the sparkling ice, created the illusion that the ice was flowing.

A warm bed never felt so good as it did after a long walk in the woods on a winter coon hunt, especially after a big slice of Momma's homemade bread and butter and a glass of fresh whole milk just before bed. Hunting raccoon at night taught me not to fear the dark. This confidence served me well throughout my life, especially during my years in the Marine Corps and while serving in Vietnam.

Momma was a stoutly built woman, with large arms and legs, and I think she always felt she was too heavy. She was very strong, with an indomitable spirit. Her peaceful, gentle disposition revealed a touch of class not expected from someone raised in such an impoverished, rural environment. Momma was a classy lady.

Momma and Dad. 1928

Born in 1910, Momma had been raised on the banks of the Little Osage River, about a half-mile from where I was born. Her dad, Addison T. Chaney, died when she was only six. Her youngest sister, Opal, died tragically the following year from burns received when her dress caught fire while she was playing with matches. It was only a year later that the family house caught fire and burned to the ground, destroying nearly everything they had. Grandma Chaney, Momma, and her little sister, Melinda, moved into a small building they had used as a granary and set up housekeeping. There was a small loft that they used for sleeping. They lived in that granary all summer and through the next winter, while Grandma pleaded in vain with the insurance company for funds to rebuild the house. Eventually, they moved into a small house in Fulton, but Grandma still retained ownership of the old property.

My maternal Grandmother Lydia Chaney, with Momma (left) and her sisters Opal and Melinda. 1913

Momma had to work hard to help her widowed mother scrape together a living for herself and little Melinda on the seven acres of land owned by Grandma Chaney. These seven acres were bordered on the south by the Osage River, and the nearby shallow crossing was known in those times as the Chaney Ford. They had a garden, along with some chickens and pigs. Grandma Chaney worked as house-keeper, a field hand, and whatever other work was available. It was a hardscrabble life that really didn't change much as Momma grew into adulthood and eventually had a family of her own.

My mother was a very pretty woman, with dark brown hair and eyes, and a natural, easy smile. She had a pleasant, engaging person-ality and always projected sincerity and compassion. She was one of the most positive people I have ever known. I never heard her say a bad word about anyone. During times when some unfortunate thing would happen, such as when the river flooded and washed away the pumpkin patch, or a valuable milk cow died, or a hail storm destroyed the cornfield, and my dad would be discouraged, cursing his hard luck, Momma would gently say, "Now Glen…," as she softly touched his arm, and would then go on to offer words of encouragement.

Raising five children on a small farm in Kansas during those times was no easy task, and it's no exaggeration to say that Momma was engaged in hard labor all her life, except perhaps during the later years, after they had retired, sold the farm, and moved into the small town of Fulton.

This may have been one of the happiest times of her life, as she had many lifelong friends who would frequently stop by to visit or call to chat on the phone. Momma loved to write letters. She had beautiful penmanship and frequently corresponded with her many family members and friends. She never failed to send out cards on birthdays, anniversaries, Easter, and Christmas. After I left home to make my own way in the world, no matter where life took me, I always wrote to Momma or sent a post card. I don't believe I ever failed to send her a nice card for Mother's Day and for Christmas. I found several of these cards among her possessions after she passed away.

After Dad died in August 1983, Momma's health began to fail. She suffered constantly with severe pain in her legs and feet. It was especially hard for her when she had to give up driving. She hated to have to depend on others to take her shopping or to doctor appointments. Three years after Dad passed away, she was forced by circumstances to give up her home in Fulton and move to a small h ouse in Fort Scott, Kansas, so she could be closer to my sister, Margaret, who helped care for her.

Momma tried her best, but she didn't do well in Fort Scott. Although she kept her little house clean and neat and continued to fix her own meals, she missed her home in Fulton and being close to her old friends. She became very lonely and depressed, especially during her last winter in the little house. She tried to hide her loneliness and act bravely, but she always cried when we'd visit and it came time to leave, or when we had to say goodbye on the telephone.

In September of 1988, my Momma was hospitalized by a sudden heart attack. She was in serious condition. Within hours, we children had gathered at her bedside. The doctor informed her that she had to either consent to go to St. Luke's hospital in Kansas City, where she could get a pacemaker, or remain where she was—and likely die. The doctor said that he needed a decision by early the following morning.

All of us kids talked and prayed with Momma that evening, encouraging her to have the surgery, but she said that she had lived a long, happy life, and she didn't want the pacemaker. We all told her how much we loved her and that we wanted her to live as long as she possibly could, but that we would leave the decision up to her.

Momma knew that having the surgery and a pacemaker would mean giving up the little house and what independence she had left. She would have had to live with one of us children or go into a nursing home. She said that she just preferred to go peacefully now, but that she would consider and pray about it overnight. At some point during the night, she changed her mind and decided to go through with the surgery and get the pacemaker.

The next morning, she was transported by ambulance to St. Luke's hospital in Kansas City. She didn't do well. They told us that her heart was too weak and too damaged. Momma died six days later at St. Luke's. I believe that she had just lost her will to live and couldn't face another long, lonely winter, being what she probably considered a burden to us kids. And perhaps she just wanted to go and be with Dad.

I believe that a person never fully recovers from the loss of one's mother. I know I never have, and to this day, when I think of my sweet Momma, my eyes still fill up with tears.

CHAPTER 3

STARTING SCHOOL

Going back to my childhood, when I was six years old, I began my education in a rural one-room schoolhouse simply named White School. Momma had also attended White School for several years when she was a child. The school was nearly two miles from our house, and Betty and I walked there every day. It was an easy, fun walk when the weather was nice, and a couple of other farm kids joined us along the way. When the frigid winter days set in, the walk wasn't nearly as much fun! I recall on at least a couple of occasions Dad hitching a horse to a homemade wooden sled and taking us to school through the deep snow.

As with many rural schools at that time, we had one teacher for all eight grades. There was a large chalkboard at one end of the room, along with the teacher's desk, and a big pot-bellied stove at the other end. Several bookshelves were attached to one side of the rear wall, which served as the school library. A small building near the entrance was used to store coal, which was necessary to heat the school in the winter. A farmer who lived across the road from the school had somehow acquired the duty of starting the fire in the stove early every morning and making sure that it was shut down in the evening. On opposite sides of the schoolyard were two outhouses, one for the boys and one for the girls. All the buildings were painted white, I suppose in keeping with the name of the school.

I think that recess must have been my favorite time in school, because I have almost no recollection of studies or classes. I do remember when I was in the first grade that a simple coloring assignment revealed that I was colorblind, though I was never officially diagnosed until years later. The teacher gave me a drawing of a horse to color and I colored the critter orange! She asked why I had colored it orange, and I said it was because my dad had a horse the same color! She smiled at me, and said that she didn't think so.

In the spring of 1944, when I was eight years old, we moved to another farm just a mile west of the place where I'd been born. Our new home was situated on about seventy acres that were almost equally divided between pastureland and cultivated land. A small tree-lined stream named Lost Creek ran through the middle of the property and emptied into the Osage River about a mile downstream. Two years later, Dad bought an additional fifteen acres of mostly timbered land that bordered the property on the east. The new place had a house, a huge old barn, and two other smaller buildings, one of which became our chicken house.

This house was pretty unusual. The former owner had built it himself. The story goes that he had begun to build the house with the intention of making the whole thing completely underground, but he ran into bedrock about four feet down, which forced him to modify his plan. He built forms and poured concrete to create a rectangular structure with about four feet underground and four feet above ground level. He topped it with a gabled roof and piled dirt around the outside walls until only about two feet of wall was visible. Inside the structure, an adult had to stand up to see out through several small windows that were positioned just above the top of the dirt berm. There was a front entrance and a side entrance, both of which required going down four or five steps.

Overall, from a practical point of view, the house wasn't too bad of an idea. It stayed cool in the summer and warm in the winter. It was also a safe place to be in the event of a tornado, which was always a concern in Kansas in the early spring and summer. However, in addition to being the ugliest house in that part of the country, the walls inside were often damp and had a musty smell. During rainy weather, water ran down the entrance steps and puddled there, or it ran into the house. In the downstairs, or underground part of the house, was the kitchen and dining area, a living room, and a bedroom. Three bedrooms occupied the upstairs, and, as with our former house, there were no toilet facilities, nor a bathroom of any kind, nor even running water. Our light source consisted of a single kerosene lamp. Dad and Momma always feared that someone would accidentally knock it over and start a fire. It wasn't unusual in those days for houses to burn down due to fallen or broken kerosene lanterns.

The property directly west and south of the house was fairly flat, cultivated land that was bordered by hedgerows of Osage orange trees. To the north and east was rolling pastureland. Across Lost Creek, one could see more cultivated land, an alfalfa hayfield, and more timberland. I spent most of my early days and throughout high school exploring every square foot of the territory on both sides of Lost Creek for a couple of miles. I think I knew every brush pile, hedgerow, and hollow tree where a squirrel, rabbit, or raccoon may be hiding.

CHAPTER 4

THE TEENAGE YEARS

My teenage years were spent doing what most boys who grew up on a farm do. Whether winter or summer, there were always chores to deal with every morning and evening—jobs like helping feed the chickens, hogs, and horses, and helping with milking the cows. In the fall and winter, I would split and carry in the evening's wood supply. When it was summer, I helped Dad haul hay and store it in the barn, and I hoed weeds from the cornfields and garden. My sister Betty recalled recently that when we were kids, she and I and got into a fight over something, and, as punishment, Momma fixed us a mason jar of water and sent us both to the cornfield to hoe weeds. In fact, I mostly recall summer as a time of work, even though we always seemed to find time to swim in Lost Creek or in a neighbor's pond on those hot summer days.

In early summer, Dad and I hunted young squirrels to eat (the meat of adult squirrels was too tough to be eaten easily). Momma would roll the squirrel parts in flour and fry it like chicken. Then she'd make a thick gravy from the drippings to pour over mashed potatoes or biscuits. It was definitely a Sunday meal that we looked forward to.

I recall that some of the Frank Chaney family (Frank was Momma's half-brother) would sometimes come over for a Sunday morning squirrel hunt, which would be followed by a big feast of fried squirrel, biscuits, and gravy.

The Chaneys were a large family of six big, tough boys and one pretty little girl. Their next-to-youngest boy, Gene, who was about two years younger than I, was one of my best friends, and we spent a lot of time hunting together and doing all the ornery things boys do! Gene had somehow acquired a pretty good set of boxing gloves, and there were many times when he and I would put on those gloves and fight. We'd fight until we were exhausted, and then we'd sit under a shade tree to rest, only to get up and go at it again.

Although I was a bit older and taller, Gene was really tough and always gave me a hard time. I think we both envisioned ourselves becoming famous boxers someday. In fact, a boxing career was something I often daydreamed about. In the summer I'd pack an old gunnysack with hay, hang it from a tree in the yard, and fight that bag like a boxer in training. Dad would laugh at my silliness, and once he jokingly remarked that when he was a kid he used to hang up a bag like that, except that he filled his bag with rocks instead of straw!

When I was about twelve years old, my Uncle Elmer, Dad's youngest brother, taught me the basic chords on the guitar. I remember being absolutely thrilled when Uncle Elmer would visit and bring his guitar and play and sing for us. He was a pretty good guitar player and singer, and he even played several times on a local radio station in Pittsburg, Kansas. I would always pester him to teach me more on the guitar. I didn't have one myself, so I borrowed one from a neighbor for a while.

I finally saved up enough money to buy a cheap guitar through the *Sears and Roebuck* catalog. I somehow acquired some sheet music to several popular country western songs of the time. After

I got that guitar, I spent much of my leisure time learning to play and sing along. When I was in the eighth grade, I won first place in the school's community talent contest, playing and singing a popular "hillbilly song," as country music was called at the time. Thus began my lifelong love of the guitar and music in general.

Me and my Guitar.

In the fall of 1949 I entered Fulton High School and remained there through my sophomore year. Although I earned passing grades those first two years of school, I don't remember having much interest in studying more than just enough to get by. I was much more interested in teasing girls and acting tough in front of a small group of other boys with similar attitudes. Often, during the lunch hour, instead of eating in the lunchroom, we'd walk down to the local pool hall and spend our lunch money shooting pool and having a beer and some peanuts for lunch. We thought smoking was cool, and we were always trying to find enough money for another pack of cigarettes.

Early in my freshman year, a fighting incident occurred. On a dare, during lunch hour, I initiated an action that led to a fistfight with an older student, a junior, who fancied himself a boxer. He could always be seen jogging during the lunch hour and shadowboxing around the schoolyard while my friends and I went to the pool hall. I don't recall the blow-by-blow scenario of one particular fight, but I do remember that it occurred in the front yard of the town's mayor, and that I left the fight unscathed, while my opponent was on the ground nursing a very bloody nose. Although I was far from being a bully, no one ever pushed me around after that.

I was an average student and enjoyed my time at Fulton High. I won a spot on the basketball team and was elected class president during my sophomore year. My parents weren't as pleased as I about my experience there, and they apparently felt I was headed for trouble if I continued to attend. Beginning my junior year, I enrolled at Prescott High School in Prescott, a small town five miles north of Fulton.

Prescott was a more peaceful, conservative community than Fulton, which had a long reputation of being a rough-and-rowdy small town. My parents thought there would be less opportunity for me to get into trouble at Prescott, and they were right. My sister Margaret also started school that year at Prescott as a freshman. Margaret was a pretty and popular girl and was chosen as cheerleader of the basketball team; I played on the first team both my Junior and Senior years. These were happy, fun times.

One of the best things that happened to me at Prescott High School was that I became acquainted with a locally well-known musical family in the area, the Gene Shroyer family. Kenneth, the oldest boy of the Shroyer family, my classmate at Prescott High School, played the accordion. His younger brother, Jack, played the mandolin, and their father, Gene, played the fiddle. Kenneth's mother played the piano. They were all very talented musicians, and I was thrilled when they invited me to bring my guitar and play along with them.

I began to spend as much time as possible playing country and old-time music with the Shroyer family, sometimes staying overnight at their house and jamming all evening. We mostly played old-time fiddle tunes, bluegrass, and country music. Several times I played with the Shroyer family at community functions, such as a square dance, or pie suppers. My musical relationship with them is, and has been, an important part of my life now for more than fifty years.

Also, during my years at Prescott High, I had another classmate, Jack Bortzfield, who also played guitar and sang at about my skill level. We often spent the night at my house or his, playing and singing the popular tunes of the day. He and I both dreamed of being big country music stars (though we were far from possessing that much talent).

Nevertheless, during the summer after we graduated from high school in 1953, Jack and I landed a spot on radio station KNEM in Nevada, Missouri. Calling ourselves the "Bob and Jack Show," we played a thirty-minute program two days a week for several weeks during the late summer that year. I don't remember getting paid for our efforts, but just having the opportunity to play on the radio was reward enough and made us feel good!

It was always a thrill when someone would mention that they'd heard us on the radio. Come to think of it, I don't recall that anyone ever actually said that they had really *enjoyed* the show—just that they had heard it. Honestly, we really weren't very good, and one day after the show, the manager told us not to come back anymore—that they were changing the format of the station and we no longer fit. Of course, we were disappointed at losing the opportunity, but that experience gave us just a little taste of what it might feel like to be an entertainer—and I loved the feeling.

CHAPTER 5

MY FIRST JOB

During the summer of the year that I turned sixteen, I got a job as a laborer on the county road crew. Dad also worked there as a laborer and was certainly influential in me getting hired. I also worked sometimes on Saturday during the school year. The pay was 85 cents per hour, and I felt lucky to have the job. I was the only kid on the crew, and I worked alongside Dad and the other men, digging ditches, building culverts, cutting brush, and whatever else I was assigned. The road boss, who was a hard, stern taskmaster, told me when he hired me to not expect any favors just because I was a kid, and that he expected me to do the same work as the men on the crew. He kept his word, and I didn't disappoint him.

Occasionally, it was necessary to use explosives to break rock, or take out a tree or stump, and for a little while I was assigned to work with a man they called simply "the dynamite man." Since I was the youngest guy on the crew and could run the fastest, they gave me the job—once the charge was set—of lighting the fuse and then running a safe distance away. I thought it was exciting and got to learn the fine points of how to use dynamite, such as the quantity needed for a particular job and where and how to pack the charge. Sometimes we intentionally put in more dynamite than was necessary to do the job, but the boss watched us pretty closely as he knew what we were up to. But it was quite a sight when we packed in the extra to watch a tree rise straight up in the air about four or five feet!

For several weeks that summer, the road boss assigned me to work down in the county rock quarry. It was considered to be the hardest of all the jobs because it meant going underground in this large hole where rock was being dug up with a bulldozer or blasted loose with dynamite. My job was to help them load the rocks, by hand, into a dump truck that hauled them to the rock crusher to make gravel. If the rocks were too large to lift, I broke them into smaller pieces with a sledgehammer. The road boss told me that he put me on this job because I was young and strong and he figured that I could better handle the intense heat and dust.

My partner down in that hole was a tall, stout, middle-aged black man with graying hair. Everyone knew him as Big Jim. Big Jim was a kind and gracious man with a quiet and sometimes brooding disposition. I had attended grade school and played softball with two of his sons, so we had a lot to talk about while we broke and loaded rock.

After a while, I began to suspect that Jim had been assigned to work in the hole for a different reason than I. Since Big Jim was perhaps the oldest and probably one of the more senior men on the crew, I would have thought that he should have been given one of the easier jobs. I finally became convinced that the reason Big Jim was working in that hole was because he was the only black man on the crew. I remember feeling pretty sad and troubled when I came to that conclusion. But there were other things that happened to Big Jim that summer that bothered me even more. The other men on the crew teased and harassed him constantly, doing stupid things like putting a snake in his lunch bucket, a frog or snake down the back of his overalls, or telling racial jokes in front of him. It seemed like they came up with a new trick every day to play on Big Jim.

He was a gracious man and tried to take all the teasing good-naturedly, laughing it off, but I worked closely with him, and I could sometimes see the hurt in his dark, bloodshot eyes, his bowed head, and the slump in his shoulders after a particularly mean joke or prank. Jim never protested to his tormentors or complained to the boss. To do so would probably have led to the immediate loss of his job.

Big Jim has likely now gone on to a better place, but I think such injustices probably followed him throughout his life. For me, the memory of that long-ago hot summer, working with Big Jim and loading rocks is a fond, even though a sad, memory—fond because I really liked Big Jim and grew to respect and admire him, and sad because of the way that he was treated. To be perfectly honest, I also I felt a bit guilty because I never said anything or tried to do something about it.

CHAPTER 6

HIGH SCHOOL

My senior year of high school was a busy and enjoyable year. There were only twelve students in my senior class. I played center on the basketball team. We had a good year, winning most of our games. When spring rolled around, and track and field practice began, I joined the track team. I wasn't much of a runner, but I was able to throw the discus further than anyone else in school. My boyhood friend and neighbor, Donald Paddock, who was a couple years older than I, had taught me how to throw the discus. I didn't have a real one, so I made my own by filling a small metal wheel from an old toy wagon with cement. The makeshift discus was about the same size as a real one, but it weighed considerably more. I had a throwing circle marked off in our cow pasture out behind the old chicken house, and I spent many summer evenings and Sunday afternoons out in that pasture throwing that little cement-filled wagon wheel. When I got my hands on a *real* discus, it felt considerably lighter. You can imagine how happy and excited the coach was on the first spring day at school when we went outside for track and field practice, and I did a couple of discus throws. I did well in that sport and ended up winning several gold medals, including first place at the regional track-and-field meet, held at Ottawa, Kansas, that spring.

High School, Senior Picture 1953

As graduation time grew closer, and our senior year was nearly finished, the conversations among my buddies and me often centered on what we were going to do after graduation. For some, it was a foregone conclusion that they were going to stay on the farm and carry on the family tradition. A couple of guys said they were going to join the service, and there were many foolish arguments about which was the best branch of the military. Of course they ended up arguing in favor of the particular branch in which their father, uncle, or brother had served. I knew very little about any branch of service myself, but I kind of leaned toward the Marines, because I'd heard that they were the toughest. I also seriously considered going to college in the fall, but I had no idea how much it cost or where I would get the money.

I didn't date much in High School. I had a schoolboy crush on several girls but didn't take any of them seriously. Getting to know a lot of girls and making a bunch of friends was a little difficult in those days. First, of course, there was the issue of money, which was something I didn't have much of. Because of the remoteness of where we lived, there weren't many available girls. In addition to that, I didn't even have a car until I was a senior in high school. With the money I earned during the summer between my junior and senior years, I purchased a 1941 two-door sedan, which would be a classic and valuable car if I owned it now. Although it was a pretty neat car, it was a bit unreliable. I couldn't afford decent tires, so I had to rely on used ones, which went flat pretty often, leaving me stranded on some remote back road. One night, the inevitable happened after going to a movie with pretty girl from school. We parked for a little while on the way home on a remote road. When it came time to go home, my car wouldn't start! We had to walk about three miles to one of our friends' homes and wake them up after midnight to ask for a ride home. Her parents were really worried, and with good reason. I never dated her again.

My sister Margaret had a childhood friend, a girl her age, who lived about a mile from us on the north side of Lost Creek. She was blonde and very cute, a bit bashful, with a perky spirit. I was closer to her than with any other girl during my youth. It seemed like I was always chasing her, but she was always just a step ahead of me. The fact that her father's intent was to keep her away from me didn't make things any easier. We did manage to have some close moments in spite of his best efforts. I still remember how many times I'd walk up Lost Creek to an area that was almost directly behind her house. Sometimes, I'd sort of hang out in that area, hoping that she'd take a walk back through their pasture, but no such luck. For a little while, our friendship was very sweet, but it never evolved beyond the hand-holding and tender-looks stage.

When I joined the Marine Corps, I left no girlfriend behind to pine over me. And I'm actually glad it worked out that way. Because of that, I was able to focus all my energies on my training and becoming a Marine. My friend eventually married an upperclassman. They went on to become very successful and raised a nice family. Later in life, after we had both retired, I would see her at our high school reunions, and it was a lot of fun remembering our younger years. She turned out to be a very classy lady, which didn't surprise me at all.

CHAPTER 7

WESTERN KANSAS WHEAT HARVEST

Shortly after graduation, it became painfully apparent that there were no serious jobs to be had, and certainly no career opportunities—unless you wanted to be a farmer or cattleman. My boyhood friend Donald, who was also at loose ends that summer, conceived a plan to go to Western Kansas to help in the wheat harvest. It was something that young men often did during the summer, because the pay was much better than anything we could find anywhere in our area. Donald had a late forties' model, four-door De Soto. One day, in early June, he and I set off for the wheat harvest in western Kansas. During harvest time in the Midwest, the wheat ripens first in Oklahoma, then the ripening moves slowly northward into Kansas, then to Nebraska, and, by late summer, ends up in North Dakota. Our general plan was to join the harvest in southern Kansas and follow it north as far as Phillipsburg in northwest Kansas. We would be able to stay with some of Donald's family who lived there.

We got off to an early start one bright, sunny morning and pointed the old DeSoto westward. We headed west on US Highway 54—two naïve, gangling, country boys on our first trip away from home. By early afternoon, we pulled into the little town of Caldwell, just a few miles south of Wichita. We parked on Main Street and had just started walking down the sidewalk when a farmer, wearing bib overalls and a straw hat, stopped us. He said, "You boys looking for work?" When we answered in the affirmative, he said that he would hire one of us, and he knew a neighbor who would hire the other! We got directions to the farm, and that evening I was settled in with the farmer and his wife, while Don stayed at the adjoining farm.

I had a sleeping room upstairs in the old, white, wood-framed house, and I don't recall that they had any other family living with them. Surrounding the house were several outbuildings, an old barn, and several large, circular, metal grain bins. There was also a windmill that pumped water into a metal watering trough for the livestock.

Wheat fields surrounded the farm as far as you could see. The farmer had also fashioned a makeshift shower directly under the windmill. It was nothing more than a wooden enclosure to provide privacy and some crude plumbing, and it had a shower nozzle. The water wasn't heated, of course, but for a boy who was accustomed to no shower facilities whatsoever, it was a luxury! Besides, it was summer in Kansas, with daytime temperatures usually in the upper nineties to a hundred or above and the evenings were not much cooler.

It took about a week to finish this farmer's harvest. I spent most of my days either shoveling wheat from the old truck into a grain auger or driving the truck out into the wheat fields to collect the wheat from the combine when its hopper was full. I would wait in the truck at the edge of the field while the combine chewed its way back and forth across the field, like some hungry, noisy, green monster, surrounded by a cloud of swirling dust, insect parts, and wheat husks.

When the hopper was full, the farmer would stop the combine and give me a wave. I'd fire up the old truck and go bouncing across the field to collect the wheat. When I had a full load, I headed for the house and, with a big scoop shovel, unloaded it into the grain auger, which lifted the grain and dumped it into the top of the storage bins. Usually, by the time I got back to the field, the hopper was full again I also drove several loads of wheat to the grain elevator in the nearby small town. It was hard physical work, and the days were very hot and long.

I worked mostly shirtless, with a straw hat, leather boots, and jeans. My skin was browned the color of an old leather wallet and as I was as slim as a hungry coyote. I remember drinking huge amounts of water during the day, and I thoroughly enjoyed the large meals the farmer's wife would serve everyday at noon. There was always fried chicken, pot roast, or pork chops, with mashed potatoes and gravy and all the trimmings, along with huge glasses of iced tea. Since our day began at daylight, by noon we were more than ready for a big meal.

I don't recall doing anything for entertainment, like going to a movie or a dance while I was there. There really wasn't time for play or leisure. Work had to come first. When wheat is ready to harvest, there's just a small window of opportunity to get it out of the field and into storage. Any unnecessary delay could lead to disaster for the crop. For example, a tornado could show up and flatten the wheat to the ground; a sudden, violent Kansas thunderstorm, or a hailstorm, could completely ruin the entire year's crop. When the harvest was finished, my job was done. The farmer paid me cash for my work, thanked me, and I was ready to move on.

As good fortune would have it, Donald was also finished with his work at the other farm, so we bid our friends farewell and headed north and west to a farm near the small town of Pratt. We worked there together for a few days, doing essentially the same kind of work as with the previous farmers. When the harvest was completed, we again headed west on Hwy 54.

It was dark when we drove into the old cattle town of Dodge City. We ate a hamburger at a small restaurant on the eastern edge of town and decided to head north toward Phillipsburg. By midnight, we were both dead tired, so we pulled off the road into a freshly cut wheat field, spread out a couple of old blankets, and went to sleep under the stars in the wheat stubble, rolling up an old shirt for a pillow. I don't believe we even thought about getting a motel, nor do I believe any motels would have been available in that remote part of Kansas at the time. Besides, we wouldn't have wasted precious money on just a place to sleep!

The next day, we drove north through the heart of wheat country, the endless flat fields of golden-green ripening wheat undulating under a blazing sun, like gentle ocean waves. Occasionally, we passed by small cattle ranches and other row crop farmers with fields of soybeans, milo, or corn. Less than a hundred years before, this had been the land where hunting and war parties of Comanche, Cheyenne, and other Indian tribes roamed, and where William F. (Buffalo Bill) Cody hunted buffalo and led US Army Calvary units on the chase. It was the land of the huge blue sky, truly awesome in its brilliance and scope, and the occasional white puffy clouds, that looked for all the world like soft cotton candy drifting lazily along.

By late afternoon, we had reached Phillipsburg and settled in with Donald's aunt and uncle. They lived on a shaded street in the small town in a large, rambling wood-frame house. They were kind, accommodating people, and we felt very comfortable. We soon found work with a couple of local farmers and spent our days in the wheat fields. I don't recall exactly how long we stayed in Phillipsburg, but I'm guessing that it was about two weeks.

Because Donald had family there, we made friends with some of the local kids they knew and had a few social opportunities. One Saturday night we drove to a dance in a small town just over the border in Nebraska. I met and danced all evening with a charming young lady. She was very pretty and was as attracted to me as I was to her. We both fell into a "puppy love" state that evening. For teenagers, "love" can be so intense and painful, especially when there's no time to really develop it. We made promises to see each other again. Of course, that never happened, and my feelings and yearning for her followed me home and hung on far too long.

I also remember another occasion during that time on a Sunday afternoon when we went swimming at a popular swimming hole on a small lake. It was at this party that I had a near-drowning experience that scared me so badly that I've carried a fear of drowning for the rest of my life. I don't know why I thought it would be cool to swim across the lake while most people were swimming or hanging out on one side where there was a beach area and picnic tables. I fancied myself a pretty good swimmer, but for some reason, when I got about halfway across, I suddenly felt weak and found it difficult to keep my head above water. I began thrashing around and took water into my lungs, which caused me to come close to panicking. No one on shore noticed that I was having trouble, and my calls for help were either not heard or were ignored. I knew that I'd have to save myself. I was finally able to focus and gain control of myself.

I floated on my back for a few minutes and then slowly swam back to shore. I didn't tell anyone about the incident, but I felt the stinging from the effects of the water in my lungs for days afterward, and I still remember that feeling of fear and near panic until this day. For that reason, I've always been extra cautious around any swimming event. And I learned, from circumstances later in life, that to continue to live and succeed under desperate situations, I'd need to focus intensely on only the important things of the moment and use all my mental and physical strength to live and succeed and overcome when necessary.

When we wrapped up our wheat harvesting experience and returned home in early July, I had saved more than four hundred dollars, which seemed like a lot of money to me. But I knew what I had been saving for, and I spent nearly half of my summer's earnings on a new, electric Gibson guitar, which I purchased from Ruddick's Music Store in Fort Scott. My dreams of becoming a country music star were alive and well! However, I had little or no knowledge of just how to make that dream come true. I think I also realized that I was not blessed with a magnificent voice or even any special musical ability. I could play the guitar, and I could carry a tune, but I wasn't anything great.

As the summer of 1953 rolled into fall, I became more and more restless, struggling with the question of what I was going to do with my life. It seemed that there were little or no opportunities available, unless one had a burning desire to be a farmer or cattle rancher, and I knew for certain that wasn't for me. My thoughts about going to college were dashed after a visit to small community college in Fort Scott, where I discovered that the cost of tuition and books was far beyond my financial means. It was at this point that my idea of joining the military began to solidify.

One day in late September, I was helping Momma dig a bucket of potatoes. I'm assuming that our conversation must have been about what I was going to do, because I distinctly recall the moment, and Momma saying something like, "I hope you're not planning on laying around here all winter and letting your Dad support you." That may sound a bit harsh, but it wasn't said in a mean way—just low key, as part of our conversation. It did, however, stir up a sense of urgency within me to find something useful to do with my life, and joining the military seemed to be the way to go. Once that decision was made, I wanted to go as quickly as possible.

CHAPTER 8

JOINING THE MARINES

I remember going to the U.S. Post Office building in Fort Scott, where all the armed forces recruiting offices were located. A high school friend from Fulton, John Thomas Durbin, was with me. The first recruiting office we stopped at was the Navy. A man in a sailor suit talked to us about the Navy and told us that if we passed the test it would be several weeks before we could leave for training. He sat us down in his office and got us going on the written exam.

As we were taking the test, the sailor excused himself for a few moments and left the room. While he was gone, a United States Marine appeared in the doorway. He was tall, muscular, and dressed in the magnificent Marine Corps dress blue uniform. It was the first time I had ever seen a Marine, and I was very impressed by the handsome uniform. He stood in the doorway, hands on his hips, and said, in a deep voice, something like, "And what are you boys doing?" We told him we were thinking about joining the service, whereby he asked, "Why don't you join a man's outfit, the Marines?" One of us asked him how soon we could leave, and he replied that we could leave tomorrow if we wanted to—if we passed the test. We needed no further persuasion. The powerful image of this Marine recruiter in dress blues and his confident manner is still burned into my memory to this day.

John and I immediately abandoned the Navy exam before the Navy recruiter returned and followed the big Marine down the hallway to his office, where he had us sit down in a room and gave us what was likely the very same screening test. After taking the test, the recruiter told us that we had both passed and showed us some exciting pictures in a pamphlet, featuring Marines on exotic beaches with pretty girls, and Marines assaulting a beachhead, and describing how the rugged training would make us into men.

Within an hour or so, we had filled out all the necessary papers and were signed up to join the Marines.

We were scheduled to depart in a few days. When we left the Post Office that day, I walked a little taller and a little prouder: *We joined the Marines! Wow! Aren't we something?* Little did we know the full impact of what we had done or what lay ahead. In truth, we had set in motion a series of events that would shape our lives for as long as we lived.

On the day I left for boot camp, Dad drove me to the old Trailways bus station in Fort Scott. It was September 15, 1953. Momma, Grandma Chaney, and my three sisters, Margaret, Dorothy, and Judy, all came to see me off. I can still see the face of Grandma Chaney sitting in the back seat, her long, grey-white hair tied in a bun at the back of her head, tears running down her cheeks. Momma was crying also, but Dad was somber.

The Marine recruiter was there to see us off. He congratulated us on joining the Marines and gave us a powerful handshake before John and I boarded the bus for Kansas City. When the big bus pulled away from the station, I remember feeling a bit choked up, and I can still see in my mind the image of Dad standing beside the old Chevy in his bib overalls and straw hat, lifting his hand for a final wave.

Arriving in Kansas City that evening, like dozens of other young men and women entering the military service during that era, we stayed overnight at the old hotel under government contract for such purposes, and we ate supper using our government meal tickets. After supper, John and I, along with a group of other enlistees, just as the hundreds who had gone before us, found our way to the nearby strip-tease joint. It was, for me, and likely for many other naïve farm boys, the first time I ever saw a completely nude adult female. We sat in bug-eyed, open-mouthed, sweaty silence as a bevy of well-endowed, attractive women danced, squirmed, and humped their way through the evening show. It did indeed seem that my decision to leave the farm and see the world as a Marine was going to offer all the excitement I had anticipated.

The following day at the Armed Forces Examination and Entrance Station, the day's activities, including a physical examination, mental testing, and a swearing-in ceremony, are now but a blur in my memory. I recall how self-conscious I felt standing in a long line of naked men, each taking our turn to stand in front of a Navy doctor or Corpsman who was seated. We had to stand directly in front of the man, while he examined our privates and had us turn our head and cough, first to the left, then to the right. At the time, I didn't know what it was all about, but I was glad when it was over.

Then we all had a laugh when we were given a little bottle and told to go into the bathroom and pee in it. When a couple of guys couldn't pee, another guy said he had plenty and volunteered to fill their bottles for them. They replied, "Hell, no one will ever know the difference!" The guys involved all passed the physical, so I guess no one was ever the wiser.

When the physical exams were over, we were taken into a room where we all stood up, raised our right hands, and were sworn into the Marine Corps. Later in the evening at the huge Union Station train depot, a grizzled old Marine in the dress green uniform, with a lot of stripes on his sleeve, herded us through the depot and saw us board the train. John and I were part of a group of about a dozen new enlistees, now considered Marine recruits. I felt proud, but I was soon to learn that we were considered by other full-fledged Marines—those who had survived boot camp—to be the lowest form of life on earth: Marine recruits, lower than whale shit at the bottom of the ocean, our Drill Instructors informed us.

Our destination was the U.S. Marine Corps Recruit Depot, San Diego, California, where we would experience twelve weeks of boot camp. One of the men in our group was named as the man in charge, and the old top Sergeant seeing us off gave him the written travel orders and our meal tickets. He gave us stern instructions to behave ourselves, and act like gentlemen on the train, or we would suffer severe consequences.

As the train rumbled westward through the night, I remember drifting off to sleep listening to the clickety clack of the wheels on the rails and the lonesome sound of the train whistle in the night as we passed through small whistle-stop towns. The next morning we were in New Mexico, and I watched in wonder as the panorama of the great Southwest unfolded before my eyes. (I still have in my possession an old postcard that Mama had kept, which I had sent her from Clovis, New Mexico. It was dated October 16, 1953. On the back, I told Momma that we were having a good time and told her not to worry.) Once again, the image in my mind of Momma crying as we said our goodbyes at the bus station hung heavy in my heart.

But, indeed, we were having a good time, acting like big shots— tough Marines, going off to war to fight for our country! How foolish we must have looked to the older generation of passengers, some of whom were probably veterans. The next day, as we neared our destination, we began to get more serious, and a bit of anxiety began to creep into our hearts when some passengers told us, "You'll be *sorrry!*" Other passengers, when they learned who we were and where we going, would just shake their heads in pity with a knowing smile. One grumpy old fellow gave us a quick once-over, peered over the top of his glasses, and blatantly predicted that half of us wouldn't make it through boot camp, and then he turned back to reading his newspaper. By the time we reached San Diego, we had become very quiet, and I think we had all come to realize that perhaps what awaited us was not what we had first imagined. In truth, we were in for the most shocking experience of our young lives—an experience that no Marine ever, ever forgets: the arrival at boot camp.

CHAPTER 9

BOOT CAMP

When we stepped off the train at San Diego, we were suddenly confronted, seemingly out of nowhere, by what appeared to be two screaming madmen in khaki uniforms. They were both shouting orders at the same time, "GET IN LINE AGAINST THE WALL!! NO TALKING! NO LAUGHING!! STAND CLOSE ENOUGH THAT YOUR NOSE IS TOUCHING THE BACK OF THE MAN'S HEAD IN FRONT OF YOU!! WHAT ARE YOU LOOKING AT, IDIOT? DON'T LOOK AT ME, SHITHEAD! KEEP YOUR EYES STRAIGHT TO THE FRONT!"

These madmen, deeply suntanned, in their perfectly creased khakis, General MacArthur-type frame caps with the glistening black bill pulled down low over their eyebrows, were pacing back and forth in front of us in a terrible rant, with demeaning obscenities streaming from their mouths. If a recruit didn't move fast enough, he was immediately confronted by a screaming mouth right up in his face, spewing droplets of spit, sweat, and angry, intimidating insults. I didn't move fast enough to get up against the wall and was grabbed by the shoulders and slammed against it. I slid to the ground but hurriedly picked myself up and scrambled back in line. Within a couple of minutes we were all standing silent and motionless, aside from some nervous twitching, awaiting our next torture. To borrow an old Marine term I was to learn later, I was scared shitless! A quick roll call was made, and a big green military truck pulled up. It had a canvas cover over the back and a wooden bench on each side. One of the madmen barked an order, and we quickly scampered aboard to the sounds of the madmen shouting, "Hurry, Hurry, HURRY! Move, MOVE, IDIOTS!

With a grinding of gears, the truck lurched forward while we held on for dear life during the ten-minute bouncing ride to the recruit depot. The truck proceeded to a gateway arch, manned by two uniformed men with white helmets and white web belts with black pistol holsters. After we passed through the archway, the bus stopped in front of a stucco-colored building that faced an enormous asphalt-covered parade field. The field was surrounded on three sides by the same stucco-colored buildings, with palm trees lining the streets. It looked beautiful, especially because I had never before seen such buildings and landscape.

As we nervously peered out from the rear of the truck like scared caged rabbits, we could see several groups of men in baggy, drab-green uniforms, caps pulled low over their eyes, responding to the shouted orders of sharp, khaki-clad men, wearing wide web belts adorned with big shiny brass buckles. It appeared they were learning to march.

But there was no time for sight-seeing or gawking, because as soon as the truck stopped, the same two madmen appeared and began shouting at us to get off the truck and to form a line in front of the building, again one behind the other, with nose touching the man's head in front. It was much closer than I had ever wanted to be to another man.

At this point, a scene I will never forget is embedded in my memory. On the steps and around the doorway that we faced were perhaps eight to ten individuals dressed in dark green, loose-fitting uniforms buttoned clear to the neck and with the same colored caps pulled down tightly over their hairless heads. They were down on their hands and knees, vigorously sweeping the sidewalk and steps with hand brushes. When one of the madmen barked an order, they instantly stopped what they were doing and fled like scared rats up the steps and disappeared through the doorway. I remember feeling pity for these guys and assumed they were prisoners of some sort. I was glad I wasn't in their situation!

Looking back, my naiveté is amazing! I *was* in their exact situation—I just didn't know it yet! I was soon to realize that these were recruits, and they were just a few hours ahead of us in the training cycle. They had already gotten the big haircut and received their initial issue of uniforms. They were temporarily quartered, as I would be, in this building awaiting assignment to a platoon to begin their training.

My first few days as a Marine recruit passed as a blur of seemingly chaotic activity. Every waking moment one to three Marine Corps Drill Instructors, whom I had previously mistaken as madmen, were either shouting orders at us, teaching us how to wear the uniform, how to put sheets and blankets on a mattress, how to walk, talk, and what was expected of us. There were new words to learn, new terms to describe things, in this entirely new world over which I had absolutely zero control. A floor was now called a deck, a wall was a bulkhead, the toilet was a head, and the bed, a rack. There was no talking without permission from a Drill Instructor (DI). No recruit was to *walk* anywhere, anytime. A recruit must *run* everywhere they go. And a recruit couldn't go anywhere or do anything without permission. My entire life, every waking moment and movement, was controlled by the Drill Instructors.

The initial shock of Marine Corps boot camp is an experience that all Marines remember for the rest of their lives. It is highly likely that all Marines, no matter whether they serve one hitch or go on for a forty-year career, look upon their time spent in boot camp as the experience that changed their lives, for the rest of their lives—their first watershed moment, which would never be forgotten.

My experience was no exception. I began as a very naïve, awkward, backwoods Kansas country boy, and was transformed into a very proud, self-confident, basic Marine, who could be further trained to fight any enemy of our nation, anywhere in the world, on a moment's notice—and win.

It was by no means an easy transformation. It took many hours, even weeks, of tough, often brutal training. The Drill Instructors of that time in the Corps had great flexibility in the way they carried out the training schedule. Although physical abuse and maltreatment of recruits was unlawful at that time (as it is to this day), either no one was watching back then, or else those in authority didn't care or perhaps agreed with the abuse. I know there were plenty of old-time Marines who believed that a certain amount of physical contact (and sometimes a plain old ass-kicking) was necessary to build real Marines.

Whatever the case, the three Drill Instructors assigned to my platoon were true believers in every sort of physical abuse and hazing. Nevertheless, right or wrong, they produced a platoon of well-disciplined, tough, motivated Marines. They lit a fire in my belly that has burned brightly now for more than a half-century and is responsible for any successes I've achieved in my lifetime. Two of the three DIs assigned to my platoon, number 407, were Korean War vets and had several rows of ribbons over their left breast pocket. The faces and character of these men has been sealed permanently in my memory.

Although every day of boot camp seemed to be just a struggle to stay alive and get through the day, the one bright spot for me was when we were each issued our weapon, the M1 Garand rifle. I had been around firearms all my life and had fired them since I was eight or nine years old. I fondled that rifle with awe and quickly memorized every part. I could take it apart and put it back together again in less than half a minute. I looked forward with great anticipation to the time when we would go to the rifle range for two weeks to learn to fire it.

When we finally did go, I didn't disappoint my family's expectations of me, and I even lived up to my own. On our last day at the rifle range, we fired for the record, which was the score that would follow us throughout our tour of duty in the Marine Corps. At the end of the last day, when all the scores were tallied, I had fired the highest score of anyone in my platoon, earning me the badge of Expert Rifleman to wear on my dress uniforms. I was also given a certificate recognizing the honor and received a new steam iron, which came in handy for many years of pressing my uniforms. I was very proud of that badge and still have it to this day.

After the rifle range training, we returned to our Quonset huts at the Marine Corps Recruit Depot in San Diego. By this time, we had only had three weeks left until graduation. We all felt pretty proud and salty. We were very much motivated now to complete our training and get on with our assignments at our first duty station. There was a good deal of excitement among us but also a great deal of stress, as our Drill Instructors even now continued to hold the threat of possible failure over our heads. They made us believe that any infraction of the rules or failing an inspection would result in our being set back, making us unable to graduate with our platoon, or, worse yet, labeled a failure, discharged, and sent home. The anxiety was maddening.

Throughout the training, there had only been a brief period of a few days when I gave any serious thought to calling it quits. This occurred in the early weeks after we'd received our initial clothing issue. One of my new combat boots was hurting my foot and had caused large blisters and pain shooting up my ankle and leg. We were told that this was normal and that it would probably take a week or more for these heavy boots to feel comfortable. They said that it wasn't uncommon to have blisters on our feet.

Well, a week or more passed, and the blisters and pain on the one foot only got worse. When I finally gathered enough courage to bring it to the attention of the Drill Instructors, the pain was awful, and getting through each day was increasingly difficult. It was becoming a serious issue for me. When I brought it to their attention again, they just raged at me for being a "candy ass" and threw me out of the DI house. By this time, I was feeling very discouraged and even harbored thoughts of quitting. I laid awake a couple of nights, feeling sorry for myself and not being able to sleep because of the burning pain in my foot. One night, I made a decision about what I should do. I decided that I couldn't just quit. How would I ever face my family and friends if I came back home a failure because of blisters on my foot? No, I told myself, I couldn't do that. I realized that I had to face up to it and save myself if I was going to survive this ordeal. I told myself that my name was *Bob Lay*, and that I had come from a long line of tough people, and these bastards were not tough enough to make me quit!

I didn't realize then that there would be a number of other occasions later in my life when I would be knocked down by my circumstances and would have to tell myself the same thing again.

After Taps and "lights out" one night, I stayed awake, and, on my rack, with my flashlight under the blanket, I inspected my blistered foot. It was bad. Some of the blisters looked like infection was setting in. I also brought my boots under the blanket and inspected them carefully for the first time. It was only then that I discovered what should have been obvious a couple weeks earlier; one boot *was one size smaller than the other*!

The next day, I mustered the courage to again bring this to the attention of the Drill Instructors. This time they took it seriously and sent me to sick call to have the blisters treated and get a signed slip from a doctor, much like a prescription, that I could take to the clothing issue building and get new boots that were the same size. Well, this didn't work out so well. At sick call, a Navy Corpsman briefly examined my blistered foot and told me the blisters were no big deal—that I was just being a pussy and to get the hell out of his Sick Bay.

I limped back to our training area, very discouraged and on the verge of tears. I reported back to the Senior Drill Instructor, explaining to him what had happened. As I spoke, I could see the anger rising by the expression on his face. He scared the hell out of me when he jumped up and threw his

chair against the wall! Thankfully, though, he wasn't mad at me. He told one of the other Drill Instructors that he was going to Medical and asked me to follow him. Back across the huge parade deck we went, with me following him, limping along as fast as I could, trying to keep up.

On our arrival at Medical, the Drill Instructor left me in the hallway to wait while he went into the office. After a few minutes, he came out and told me that we were going to see the Chief Medical Officer, a high-ranking Navy officer. We entered the room, and

I reported to the officer seated behind a large desk, as I had been directed. He told me to stand at ease and tell him what had happened that morning when I reported to Sick Call. I told him exactly what had transpired. He instructed me to sit down and take off my boot. He examined my foot and then told me to put my boot back on. He picked up his phone and called someone. Shortly after that, approximately five Corpsmen came into the room and lined up on one side of the office. The Medical Officer asked me to point out the Corpsman who had seen me that morning and had told me to get out without being treated. I easily pointed out the culprit. The Medical Officer dismissed the Corpsman, pulled out a pad, and wrote an authorization for a new pair of boots. He then directed us to the treatment room, where the Drill Instructor waited while all my blisters were treated. The DI then took me to clothing issue, presented an authorization slip, and I was issued a new pair of boots. We returned to our barracks. The Drill Instructor excused me from any training for the rest of the day.

When I look back on that time and incident, I realize that I learned an important lesson in leadership—a lesson that has served me well for the rest of my life whenever I've been placed in positions of leadership. The lesson is this: Take care of the people you are responsible for leading, and they will take care of you and your mission. That Marine Drill Instructor taught me an important lesson in leadership: he may have been harsh on me, and maybe even brutal, but that was what was required to get the job done. At the same time, he wouldn't allow anyone else to treat his men badly.

Finally, graduation day, January 4, 1954, arrived! Even on this special day, our Drill Instructors never complimented us or told us that they were proud of us. To me, it just seemed like they were glad to be rid of us. To tell the truth, for me the feeling was mutual. I was promoted to Private First Class because I had been the high-scoring shooter of our platoon. Several other recruits were also promoted, due to their outstanding performance in training. It was a very happy day.

The day before graduation, we had each been called to the DI house to receive and sign for our written orders. This was when we first found out what we would be doing in the Corps and where we would we stationed. When, at the beginning of our training during our forming period, we had an opportunity to ask for a choice of duty, I had requested to be a Rifleman in the Infantry. To my great surprise, the Marine Corps classified me as an Engineer. I received orders to Marine Corps Engineer Schools at Camp Lejeune, North Carolina. Specifically, I was ordered to attend an eight-week course in Water Supply and Purification. My orders gave me ten days leave and five days of travel time to get to North Carolina. It was a surprise, and somewhat mystifying, but it sounded exciting. Besides, this meant that I would get to travel completely across the United States and to live in North Carolina! Although at first I was a bit disappointed (I had wanted to be a Rifleman), the more I thought about it, the happier I became. I was anxious to be on my way!

On Graduation Day, everything took place so quickly that I can't remember in sequence what happened. I know that we got up earlier than usual, shaved, showered, and put on our dress uniforms. Then came the final packing of all our belongings in the sea bag, except for some personal hygienic items and a change of underwear and socks that were put into a small handbag. There was an inspection by the Drill Instructors, and we shouldered our sea bags and marched to the huge parade ground, where several other platoons were already staging for the graduation ceremony.

Then, just like many generations of Marines before us, we passed in review before the reviewing stands, where families and guests of the graduating Marines watched in solemn, often tearful, pride. We passed in review to the music of the Depot Marine Corps Band, which played *The Stars and Stripes Forever*. When they struck up the *Marine Corps Hymn*, I'll never forget the chills that went up my spine and the tears that flooded from my eyes. To this day, when a band strikes up the *Marine Corps Hymn*, I still get that same thrill and remember the pride we all felt on that occasion.

Finally, we stopped and faced the reviewing stands, and the Drill Instructors dismissed us. It was over! Boot camp was finally over, and we were free to depart! It was an exhilarating feeling but also a bit intimidating, because there was no one to tell us what to do! So, while a lot of the newly minted Marines mingled with their families, I and a number of others made our way to the buses that awaited us at the edge of the parade ground. The buses were there to take us to either the San Diego bus station or train station, or to Camp Pendleton, California, about twenty miles north of San Diego, to begin Infantry Training School. I climbed on the bus and bid boot camp goodbye. It was truly the most unforgettable moment of my life.

January, 1954.

The bus dropped me off at the Trailways bus station in down-town San Diego. I bought a one-way ticket to North Carolina. Soon I boarded the huge bus and grabbed one of the front seats so that I could see where we were going. I wanted to see and experience every-thing that I could! Soon, the bus driver fired up the diesel motor and we were on the highway on the outskirts of San Diego, heading east. I leaned back in one of those huge, comfortable seats and excitedly watched the magnificent desert landscape roll by. It was going to be a great journey! I would be so happy to see Momma and Dad and my school friends. What a happy time this was going to be!

Over the next couple of days, as the bus rolled eastward, I had a lot of time to think about what I had just been through and where I was going. I remember thinking, *Yes, this is what I want to do with my life. I want to be a Marine, one of our country's warrior class, whose sole job is to defend our country. Let others be farmers, merchants, factory workers, businessmen, whatever. I would be a Marine, carry a weapon, and travel around the world; a United States Marine I would be.* As far as I was concerned, there could be no higher calling.

CHAPTER 10

FIRST DUTY STATION

The old farm had never looked so good, but let's face it—Kansas is ugly in January—bleak, windy, cold, and snowy. For me, it was somewhat like going from the Technicolor world of Southern California to a black-and-white frozen world in Bourbon County, Kansas. Nevertheless, it was wonderful to be home, and I was so excited to see Momma and Dad and my sisters. I couldn't wait to tell them all the stories about boot camp. I still remember that warm hug and those happy tears from Mom, the handshake and the quick, half-hug/chest-bump from Dad. It was fun showing off my uniform and my Expert Rifle badge and describing how I had outshot everyone in my platoon at the rifle range. I know that Dad was proud of me, because, after all, he was the one who had taught me to shoot!

I visited my old high school, Fulton High, in my dress-green Class A uniform, expecting to impress all my old classmates. I was disappointed, however, as hardly anyone recognized me! They all seemed consumed by their own interests, so I kept my visit short.

Lesson learned: you can't go back! Home is never the same again. You can't live on old memories. You must "continue to march" in life; keep your chin up, and welcome all of life's challenges. Over the years I've developed a way to deal with tough challenges. I say to myself, "God has blessed me with the ability and the opportunity to demonstrate that I can do (this or that)." (Truth be told, sometimes I need to repeat this over and over.)

I soon began to feel a bit restless at home and was getting excited about going to Camp Lejeune, North Carolina, the largest Marine base on the east coast. The fact that there was still no indoor bathroom or hot water at home and not much to do in Kansas in the winter helped me in my decision to cut short my leave and head to North Carolina on a Trailways bus!

When I arrived at Camp Lejeune, I was assigned to report to Courthouse Bay, a satellite base within the main base and the home of the Marine Corps Engineer Schools. I was assigned to Schools Company, and a few days later began to attend Water Supply and Plumbing School. It was a small class, with perhaps a dozen students.

First Duty Station, Camp Lejeune, North Carolina, Engineer School.

I have no idea how the Marine Corps determined to assign me to this kind of technical training, as I had requested the Infantry. Nevertheless, I threw myself into learning the information. Essentially, the school taught us how to locate and process a potable water source for Marines operating in the field under any kind of weather and for either small or large units. I studied hard and came out first in my class.

My first fistfight in the Corps occurred at Schools Company. There was a fad going around of goosing people in the ass and hollering loudly, causing the recipient to jump, which was actually very funny. After a while, a person might become "goosey," and would jump and holler if there was even a hint of someone goosing him. I had warned my classmates not to try this on me. I told them in no uncertain terms, "If you goose me, you're going to have a fight on your hands!" Well, of course, one fellow ignored my warning, and in class formation one day, he goosed me. I quickly spun around and smashed him in the face with a hard right hand. He went down. I jumped on top of him and continued punching him. The fight was broken up quickly, but he had a bloody nose, and I had a bruised right hand. We were both put on report and had to go see the Company First Sergeant. The First Sergeant gave us two hours of extra duty for two weeks, cleaning and painting some water supply unit vehicles. This work had to be done after regular working hours and on the weekend. I never got goosed again.

The Marine Corps had a policy of allowing graduating students to choose, based upon their class standing, their choice of a base that had an opening for someone with these skills, which, in this case, was a Water Supply person. The one who is first in class gets his choice, then the second, and so on. In this instance, there was an opening at Marine Corps air station at Opa-locka, Florida, which is a suburb of North Miami. I had never been to Florida and barely knew where Miami was located on a map. Much later in life, I came to realize that this base was considered one of the best assignments in the entire Marine Corps and that I was a very lucky guy.

In April of 1954, I took a train to Miami. I remember getting off the train and seeing a small rectangular sign on a pole that simply said "Miami." I took a taxi to the base, though I had no idea where it was located. The taxi driver charged me four dollars, which I thought was a very good deal, because he took me onto the base and right up to the building where I was to report.

When I reported in, there was some confusion about what they were going to do with me. Where was I going to work? My training in water supply, which included water purification, appeared to be only useful when a unit was in the field. The problem was soon solved, however. They assigned me to thirty days of Mess Duty, which is the absolute *worst* assignment in the Marine Corps! Mess men live in a separate barracks and are required to get up at an ungodly hour, as in 03:30, and must work seven days a week until perhaps 21:00 or later. The work entails serving meals and then cleaning the entire mess hall thoroughly afterward, washing all the huge cooking pots, and doing any other tasks that went along with feeding hundreds of men three times a day. Mess men are looked upon as virtual slaves for the thirty days they are assigned. Thankfully (I thought), the Marine Corps could assign a person to only thirty days during a year. I later found out that this limit was commonly exceeded.

When my thirty days of mess duty was over, I reported back to the First Sergeant. He greeted me by saying, "Oh, it's you again, the guy with the weird MOS." Again, the question came up; what were they going to do with me? My MOS (Military Occupational Specialty) was number 1121, which indicated that I was a Plumbing and Water Supply Man. The First Sergeant quickly resolved the problem by assigning me to thirty days on Interior Guard Duty.

After serving *that* thirty days, I again reported back to the First Sergeant, and the same problem arose. This time, however, he said they had decided that the only place where there was any water that needed purifying was at the swimming pools and the base water plant. There were two swimming pools; an officers' pool and an enlisted servicemen's pool. I was soon to see that both pools were big and beautiful, surrounded by gorgeous flowers and palm and palmetto trees. What an assignment! I could hardly believe my good luck!

I was told to report at the officers' pool to a man named Harold Painter. Mr. Painter was a civil service worker who was the manager of both the pools and the water plant. He maintained an office in the pump room of the officer's pool and kept precise logs of everything that needed to be done: when the pool needed to be cleaned, the various water tests that had to be done several times a day, and determining how much of the chemicals, such as chlorine, needed to be fed into the water to keep it pure and clean. It was very cool (temperature-wise) down in the pump room, which made it a good place to hang out.

Mr. Painter was a friendly, easygoing, middle-aged guy, and I took a liking to him right away. I found that my duties consisted of cleaning up around both swimming pools, sweeping up any debris left from the previous day, and adding the chemicals to the water for purification. Of course, my uniform of the day was swimming trunks. Just about every day I'd find money (change) on the bottom of the pool. Swimmers would routinely put small change in the pocket of their swim trunks and then lose it when swimming. It was also not unusual to find bottles of booze with a couple shots still in them. I couldn't let that go to waste! Frequently, the officers would have an evening cocktail and swim party, leaving a lot of debris for me to clean up. However, on these nights they typically would also lose a lot of change in the pool—anywhere from $5 to $10 altogether. Mr. Painter and I would usually split the money, but quite often, he just let me have it all.

The weather in Miami was nearly always beautiful—sunny and warm. I still could hardly believe my good fortune. In fact, I believed that I must be the only guy in the Marine Corps with such good duty! I remember thinking, *Wow, this sure beats humping the hills of Camp Pendleton, or wading in the swamps of Camp Lejeune as a Rifleman in an infantry company,* as I had foolishly requested!

CHAPTER 11

GETTING MARRIED

When I first checked into this unit, an old Master Sergeant told me that I would find that I had more liberty and places to go than I had money for. I soon found that to be true. Miami and Miami Beach at that time in the mid-fifties was one of the vacation capitals of the world, mostly for the rich and famous. There were many beautiful women looking for a good time, but they were also looking for a man with lots of money. At that time, a Private First Class in the Marine Corps made about $78 a month. I soon realized that a just a few drinks in the clubs and lounges in Miami and Miami Beach would quickly deplete my monthly allotment. I needed to find other places and ways to recreate.

On one of my excursions, I came upon a youth center sponsored by a local Pentecostal church in North Miami. It was within easy access from the base, and they welcomed me warmly. On certain days of the week, they sponsored dance parties, entertainment shows, and offered refreshments. Absolutely no liquor or smoking was permitted, which was fine with me, as I didn't smoke or drink at that time.

It was at one of these dances that I met a girl named Connie. She was petite and cute, with dark brown hair and eyes, and she possessed a high passion and a quick temper. We were strongly attracted to each other right from the beginning, and, after a short whirlwind courtship, we decided to get married.

(I should mention that this was against the advice of all of our families and friends. We didn't own a car or have a place to live or even any savings in the bank. It wasn't the best situation under which to take a wife!)

In retrospect, it's easy to look back after several decades and see how foolish we both were. We were soon to learn, as countless other have, and through considerable emotional pain, that a passionate attraction for one another as teenagers doesn't automatically pave the way to a successful marriage. And if children are born into this marriage, it's even more tragic—for the couple, the children, and often others as well.

Connie and I were married on Saturday, August 13, 1955, in a garden wedding at her mother's house. We could hardly wait to set up housekeeping in a small trailer in a trailer park in North Miami. With the gifts we received at our wedding shower, along with some household items handed down by her family, we had everything we needed to set up a cozy home, including a console TV that we "inherited" from her mom and dad. Not many people owned a TV at that time, and we were ecstatic about it! Our little black-and-white 10-inch TV could only get two or three stations. but we were thankful. I joined a carpool to the base and set out to become a good husband and a "brown bagger"—someone who carries lunch to work in a brown paper bag.

Connie and her family were deeply involved with a Pentecostal church, Revival Tabernacle. We went there with her family, attending Sunday morning and evening services. Connie was treasurer of the church Sunday school. We became friends with another couple about our age and often socialized together.

Since I had no church home, I was soon baptized at that church. The baptism took place during a revival meeting in a large tent, and was led by a traveling minister named Jack Coe, who was quite well known at the time. He was in Miami on a traveling crusade to help people get saved by accepting Jesus as their Savior. I was baptized at one of his services in a large tank of water along with hundreds of other repentant Christians in that huge tent.

Some in the community, however, didn't appreciate the revival activities, and complaints ensued. Reverend Coe was subsequently arrested and charged with practicing medicine without a license, because, as a part of his services, through the "laying on" of hands in the "power of Jesus," people were claiming to have been healed.

The local newspapers carried the story and showed pictures of Brother Coe in the Miami jail, which may actually have worked to his advantage, because the publicity was good for his ministry. The charges were soon dropped, and Brother Coe moved on to another city.

Connie's family consisted of her mother, Peggy Smith, her stepfather Tony, and one younger half-brother, also named Tony, and her sister, Gilda. Gilda was two years older than Connie. We also were acquainted with and accepted by her birth father Mr. Rafford and stepmother, Hazel.

Very early on, some incidents stand out in my mind as red flags—issues that affected our relationship. The first one was when I discovered her diary lying open on a shelf in the bathroom. I hadn't even known that she kept a diary. I couldn't resist the urge to read what she'd written. That was a big mistake. What I read made me very angry, but most of all, it hurt me emotionally. I had placed her on such a high pedestal, believing her to be a very religious girl from a really good family. I was honestly impressed by her family and by her, and how nice they were to me. Unbelievably, she had written in her diary about a relationship she'd had with a Marine before she met me. She described in detail the thoughts and emotions she'd had. I was angry and hurt that she had never told me about this before because I believed that I was her first love. I went into our bedroom, woke her up, and confronted her. At first, she was angry that I had read her diary, and then she began to cry, finally admitting that she'd lied about me being her first serious relationship.

Neither of us slept much that night, and I brooded over it for a long time. I tried to understand the situation from her point of view. She said that she'd fallen in love with me right away but was scared that if I knew about the previous relationship, I might break it off, and she'd never see me again. I understood, to some extent, and forgave her.

The second incident was really a silly matter, but nevertheless it revealed something about both of our characters. We were walking home from her mother's place one evening, which we often did. We got into an argument over something that I don't even remember what it was. It must have seemed very important then, however. We were arguing in the street when she decided to go back to her mother's house for the night. I told her no, she was coming home with me. The fight escalated quickly, and I actually began to drag her down the street by her arm. She was crying and screaming, *"Let me go! Let me go!"*

"You're my wife, and you're going home with me," I said. Thinking back on the situation, I can see how ridiculous it was. Somebody called the police, and suddenly, two Miami police officers pulled up. One of them grabbed me from behind, and the other one grabbed her, separating us. One of them asked, *"What is going on?"*

I told them, "This is my wife, and I want her to go home with me, and she is trying to go back to her mother's house."

The officer said, "It appears she doesn't want to go home with you!" He informed me that I could not physically force my wife to go with me. She could go where she wanted. He also informed us that we were disturbing the peace, and that if we didn't stop, they were going to arrest us and take us downtown to jail. We promised we would stop fighting and go home There were no further problems that evening, but that incident revealed that we both had quick tempers.

In spite of some of these early feuds, Connie and I were happy during those early days of our marriage. She soon became pregnant and we were excited as we looked forward to a baby. Her family hosted a baby shower, and we received a number of very nice gifts, which we really appreciated. We knew we were going to need a car with a baby soon to be born, so we began to save up to buy a vehicle. We couldn't afford much of one!

One day, with $200 cash in our hands, we took a city bus to an area where there were many used car lots. Almost as soon as we got off the bus, we noticed a car parked in front of a private home with a "For Sale" sign on it. We went to look at the car and were soon the new owners of a 1941 four-door Pontiac, with a straight-six motor. The cost? Exactly $200! The car was very clean. It had belonged to a mechanic, who had kept it tuned and well serviced. We drove home in our new Pontiac and proudly showed it to my wife's family. Now we could drive to church and not have to bum rides with them!

In April 1956, I received orders to be transferred to another unit temporarily to participate in a large training operation that involved a number of large units from the east coast. This operation would last three months. It involved Marine Corps infantry units that were practicing making amphibious assaults on islands around

Puerto Rico and was supported by Marine Air Wing units from Cherry Point, North Carolina, and Miami. Both Connie and I were upset about these orders, which would separate us for nearly three months during a critical time of her pregnancy. I tried through all available channels to get out of going, but to no avail.

It was a very sad day when I had to leave. Along with the other men, I boarded an old World War II LST ship for the five-day cruise to Puerto Rico. We were packed like sardines on the old ship, and anyone who has ever ridden on one of these old flat-bottomed tin cans will attest to the torture of riding one. It was swelteringly hot, and many of us spent nearly the entire trip seasick. It was so good to see dry land again! Unfortunately, when I stepped off the landing ramp, the first thing I did was to sprain my ankle! It was a bad sprain, and I ended up riding from the beach to our living area on a stretcher in a jeep while the rest of the unit walked. I had to use a crutch in order to be mobile for about three weeks.

The living area had some old permanent buildings and a water supply with showers. We utilities support people had very little to do. The unit I was with provided radar support for aircraft that supported the infantry units.

In 1955, while stationed at Marine Corps Air Station, Miami, Florida, I was deployed to Roosevelt Roads Naval Station, Puerto Rico for three months.

Of course, having little to do made the time pass very slowly. Connie and I wrote to each other several times a week. During this separation, she made up her mind that she couldn't tolerate my decision to remain in the Marine Corps. She said she couldn't stand the long separations. I, on the other hand, wanted very much to remain in the Marine Corps, so I knew this was going to be a major point of contention when my enlistment period ended in October, which was only a few months away.

Finally, the operation was over. I returned by ship to Miami and was transferred back to my home unit. I caught a ride with some people going my way, and I can still recall the moment when they dropped me off at the trailer park where we lived. As I walked down the lane toward our trailer, dragging all my gear, Connie suddenly appeared, running toward me. We had a sweet and tearful reunion. She'd gained a lot of weight, and her belly was pretty big. She told me that her doctor thought the baby might be born around the first week of July.

When she began to have labor pains, I drove her, in our old Pontiac, to St. Francis hospital in Miami Beach. On July 11, 1956, we became the proud parents of a beautiful baby boy. He weighed more than 8 lbs. and we were thrilled. We had wanted a boy! We named him Bobbie Lay, Jr., and were as happy as any other couple with a new baby. We would never have dreamed that one day we would be involved in some bitter, painful disputes that would eventually tear our marriage apart and lead to a divorce.

On October 15, 1956, my enlistment expired, and I was honorably discharged from the Marine Corps. Leaving the Corps was against my better judgment and certainly not what I wanted to do. We decided to drive to Kansas so my family could meet Connie and see the baby. We thought we'd probably only stay for about a week and then return to Miami, where I would have to find a job. We traded in our old Pontiac for a 1951 Oldsmobile. It was a very nice car, and we looked forward to the trip to Kansas.

CHAPTER 12

KANSAS OR BUST

We left Miami, bound for Kansas in our "new" Oldsmobile, looking forward to a fun adventure. Everything was going smoothly until we were traveling through Arkansas. The car started running roughly, and smoke was coming into the interior. We were also leaving a smoke trail behind us. I stopped at a service station to see if it was something I could fix, but I was only able to determine that there was an engine problem. There wasn't much we could do but to keep going and see how far we might make it.

We continued at a much slower speed, keeping the windows down to let the smoke out. The car was really burning oil, so we had to stop every fifty miles or so and add another quart. We finally made it to my folks' place, with the windows rolled down to let the smoke out and with smoke pouring out of the exhaust.

Our reunion with Mom and Dad was great, and we excitedly introduced them to their new grandson. The living conditions at the farm in Kansas were a real shock for Connie. My parents were still without indoor plumbing and heated the house only by a wood stove. Connie had grown up in a modern home in Miami.

The outhouse was probably the most difficult adjustment for her. On her first trip there, which was just after dark, I walked with her and waited outside. Suddenly, a cow let out a low "*moo-oo-oo!*"

When the cow mooed, Connie screamed and ran out, pulling her panties up as she ran into my arms, yelling, *"WHAT WAS THAT?"* She had never heard anything like this sound before, and it scared her nearly to death. No amount of coaxing could get her back into that outhouse. We had to buy her a chamber pot that she could use in the bedroom.

Every day that we were there presented a new challenge for us—things like sterilizing and preparing baby bottles without running water in the house. Water had to be drawn in a bucket from cistern, which was located outside. Heating the water required using a teakettle and pans on a wood stove. My mother helped Connie the best she could. Then there was the issue of taking a bath and keeping clean without indoor facilities.

Recently discharged from the Marine Corps, October 1956. I and Connie visited folks in Kansas. Pictured: Me, Bobbie, Dad and paternal grandmother Iva Lay.

One of the main issues that we faced was whether to repair our car or trade it in for another one. I'd definitely have to get a reliable car before we could head back to Florida. My Uncle Raymond Newcomb, who lived about a mile south of Fort Scott, offered to help me repair my car. Raymond was a skilled mechanic and had all the necessary tools. I drove the car to his place and into his back yard, where he helped me pull the motor out and tear it down. We found the problem. One of the pistons had a hole in the top, which accounted for the burning oil and smoke. We installed a new piston, reassembled the motor, and got the car running again. However, we knew that other operating systems were probably also damaged, so, although the car now was operable, I couldn't trust it to make another trip back to Florida. I traded it for a really nice, low-mileage 1951 Chevy.

Meanwhile, because Connie was having such a hard time living out on the farm and trying to adjust to that difficult lifestyle, we decided that she and the baby should take a bus back to Miami and temporarily move in with her mother. I would stay with my parents and find a job to earn enough money for my trip home. I took Connie and Bob, Jr., to the bus station and said a tearful goodbye, not knowing when I would see them again.

Jobs were nearly nonexistent in Kansas at that time, especially in the winter. In nearby Fort Scott, there was a poultry slaughterhouse that always seemed to be looking for employees. I took a job there, working on the line, which meant that I was one guy in a long line of other people performing one part of the cleaning of either a chicken or a turkey that hung upside down by the feet as it moved slowly along the line to the final disposal of the bird.

My first job was to stand in the line of moving birds and, with a sharp knife, cut out the bird's anus and throw it into a large tub.

I was occasionally moved to another position on the line, doing a different part of the complete procedure. This job was worse than any job beyond my imagination! I was able to tolerate it for about a week, when one day I found myself thinking (as I watched the slaughtered, stinking chickens moving along in front of me) that I had been a *Sergeant in the Marine Corps*! I asked myself, "What am I *doing* here?" So, when the boss came by at about 5 PM and told me that he wanted me to work overtime, helping the cleanup crew to empty these large tubs of chicken guts and parts, I looked at him and said, "No, I can't do that. I'm scheduled to be off at five, and I was planning on leaving and not coming back. I quit!"

I went back to Dad and Mom's place. I knew that at this time of year, which was December, I could earn some pocket money hunting and selling rabbits. There was a place in Fulton that was a buying center for rabbits. I never knew what the rabbits were used for—human food or pet food. I was just happy that there was a place I could sell them! So, for the rest of December, I stayed with Mom and Dad. I hunted rabbits and also hunted for a job. The Christmas season wasn't very fun that year, and Christmas Day was memorable to me only as being terribly sad.

On Christmas Day, the family gathered at Mom and Dad's for a Christmas feast. I loved being there with the family, but I missed Connie and little Bobbie so much. They were all I could think about. After dinner, I felt very sad and knew that I needed to get away from everyone. I took my rifle and told them I was going rabbit hunting. I walked through the pasture and some timbered land along the banks of Lost Creek, the stream that ran through Dad's property. My heart was heavy. I didn't feel like killing a rabbit or anything else that day. Tears were flowing from my eyes as I wandered aimlessly around the fields and hedgerows, thinking about my wife and Bobbie. Here it was, my son's first Christmas, and I wasn't with him. Did he get any presents? Was he safe and well? Did Connie and her family have a happy Christmas? I didn't know.

CHAPTER 13

BOTTOM OF THE WELL

It was extremely cold—probably near zero—with a wind chill that was even lower than that. As I took stock of my situation, a deep sadness settled over me, and I broke down. I found an old log and sat down. Light snow and sleet began to swirl around in the air. I sat there a long time, alone—just me and Jesus—and I prayed to Him for strength and guidance. I found myself thinking, *Here I am—twenty-two years old, and all the money I have in this world is in my pocket, and that's only a few dollars. I have no job, my wife and baby son left me and are living with her mother in Miami, and they're also broke—and there's no foreseeable way that I can improve my situation.*

I sat there on that old log and let the tears flow. I finally stopped when the cold wind began to chill my shoulders. I dried my tears, and I began to think about my time in the Marine Corps. I had made Sergeant in my first three-year enlistment, and I thought, *No Sergeant in the Marine Corps would act this way! He would stand up tall and face his problems, no matter how difficult and disabling they might be.*

Then I recalled an old marching command, "Continue to March," used in "close order drill" in the Marine Corps. I thought, *This is what I need to do with my life—continue to march, and start going forward again;* always "continue to march" and never quit, no matter how hard things might be.

Sometime right after the New Year, an opportunity presented itself. It was as if Jesus had answered my prayers. The *Fort Scott Tribune* ran an ad, seeking employees for a new Safeway store that was opening soon, right on the south edge of Fort Scott. I answered the ad and was called in for an interview. They hired me as a stocker/checker, working one of the cash registers and stocking shelves. Happily, the pay would be enough to rent a small apartment and buy groceries for three people! I was very fortunate to have been hired, because the store manager told me that there were a lot of applicants. He said he had selected me because he saw on my resume that I had been a Sergeant in the Marine Corps, and he knew that to become a Sergeant in the Marine Corps, "you must be a pretty good man." Well, I made up my mind that I wasn't going to disappoint him. I was hired and helped to stock the new store. I really liked the job, and my outlook on life brightened considerably.

I had soon saved up enough money to rent a small upstairs apartment in Fort Scott, and I asked Connie to join me. Connie and Bobbie, Jr., came by train to Fort Scott, and we set up housekeeping in the apartment. It was so good to see my baby boy again and hug my wife! She could be real sweetheart and very loving when she wanted to.

Spring was in the air, the weather got warmer, flowers were beginning to bloom, and so did our marriage. One blot on the situation, though, was that we pretty much had to keep to ourselves and not visit my family very often, as some dispute between Connie and some of my sisters remained unresolved, and there were still a lot of raw feelings.

We began to attend a Pentecostal church and made friends with another couple about our age. We did a little socializing with them and settled into a routine, not knowing how long we were going to be living in Kansas.

It turned out to be not much longer. In June 1957, after much discussion and "what if's," we decided that we should move to Miami. This would give us four months longer to save enough money to make the move. We both agreed that we didn't want to settle down in Kansas because of the brutal winters and scorching summers.

Four months passed quickly, and soon we were ready to go. By the time we left, most of the sore feelings between Connie and my family had been resolved, and we left on good terms.

The actual move to Miami went well. The '51 Chevy made the trip without any problem. We stayed with Connie's mother for a few days while we located an apartment. I got a job at a 7-Eleven food store in north Miami. This proved to be a dead-end job, and working twelve-hour, back-to-back shifts for six and sometimes seven days a week was too much to expect. I began to look for a job that would make use of my training in the Marine Corps. Incredibly, I found that exact job!

I applied for and was hired as a Water Treatment Plant Operator at the South Broward County Water Treatment plant. The job involved performing chemical tests of the water at various stages of the purification process. Most of these skills I already knew from my water supply training in the Marine Corps. The other plant operators taught me the rest of the things I needed to know. They would not, however, pay me as a state-certificated operator because I didn't have a license. To get that, I would have to take an exam to become a licensed operator. It proved not be an easy and quick process, but I did get the wheels turning. I'd have to take some evening classes before I could take the test. Although that may sound doable, with my hectic schedule and dealing with what was going on with Connie,

I delayed enrolling in the classes. It would have meant a significant pay increase for me if I'd been able to do that.

Sometime during the late summer, Connie decided that she wanted to get a job so that we could have some extra money to begin saving to perhaps buy a house. She soon found a job as a checker in a grocery store. She rode the city bus to work and back, and her mother took care of Bobbie when I was working. It was a hectic schedule, and I wondered how long we could last at this pace.

CHAPTER 14

CONNIE WALKS OUT

One day, Connie failed to come home at her regular time. She worked the late-night shift and it was past midnight when she finally got in. She made up some kind of story, but this began to happen more frequently, until she wasn't able to find reasonable excuses. I began to think the unthinkable—that my wife was seeing another man. Was another man sleeping with *my wife*?

When I tried to question her about it, she'd just brush it off or throw a little tantrum. I accepted the excuses she offered just to get her to quiet down. Thus began the pattern of my giving in to her to appease her. I didn't like to fight, argue, and get all upset. I would eventually learn that when a man lets himself accept this role of always giving in to the woman's demands, she will ultimately lose her respect for him as a man, and. consequently, lose her desire for him.

Things got even more complicated. During the late fall and summer of 1957, Connie and I moved twice, trying to find a better apartment. However, the last time we moved, we did so at the request of the apartment management. Neighbors had complained about loud voices and shouting coming from our apartment. It was an embarrassing and shameful thing for me—to be evicted because other people didn't want to live near us. We had sunk to a new low. It became more difficult to find another apartment, because apartment managers would do a background check and quickly discover our rental history—which wasn't a pretty picture. Finally, we found a small trailer to rent in a trailer park.

During this time, we fought continually, and she kept lying about where she had been and what she'd been doing. She completely stopped doing any housework. It was strange, but I guess I began to actually accept that she was being unfaithful and was possibly seeing more than just one guy.

The events of this time period are somewhat of a blur, and I can only recall a few of the incidents I can or want to remember. I was working at the water plant, and I liked my job. The only bad thing about it was the 45-minute drive from where we lived. The old Chevy was doing fine, but I needed tires badly, and I didn't have the money to buy new ones. I never knew if I was going to make it to work and back without a flat tire. I also knew that I had sunk to a new low when I had to ask the janitor at the water plant for a loan to buy tires. He was a kindly, middle-aged man, and was happy to loan me the money. I paid him back over the next two paydays. He knew about my problems because I had talked to him about what was going on with Connie and me. In fact, looking back, it was probably therapeutic for me to have someone like him to talk to.

As for me, during this time—and all during the time we were married—I never drank any alcohol, I didn't smoke, and I remained true and faithful. We had stopped going to church, but I remained true to the tenets of the church. I didn't, however, know how to deal with the situation we were in. How am I, as her husband, supposed to react when one these incidents occurs? She'd come home after being gone several days, apologize for everything, ask me to forgive her, and take her back. I would always say yes. Then this "make up and get a new start" would only last several days or a little over a week. One day, after she'd been gone for several days, she came home to our trailer with her suitcase, and we had a reunion. She looked terrible: she was dirty, her hair was dirty and uncombed, and she was just generally disheveled, as if she'd been up all night. And, she probably had.

We hugged and renewed our affection and love for each other. She asked me what she could do. I told her that she could clean up the kitchen and wash the dishes, as there was a two-day accumulation, and the dishes had begun to stink.

Now, in this small trailer, the kitchen was tiny, and cleaning it was a task that would take only perhaps ten to fifteen minutes. She said no, she was *not* going to do it, because they weren't *her* dirty dishes.

That was the final straw for me. I'd been having a really hard time. I was working, taking Bobbie to her mother's, picking him up, stopping at the grocery store to grab a few groceries, wash clothes, and then try to find some time to play with Bobbie. When she said that, I went into the bedroom where she had just laid down to rest and told her to get up and help me do the dishes.

Of course, I realize now that this was *not* the way to handle this situation. A husband shouldn't *order* his wife to do something. But I didn't think of that at the time. She began to scream at me. Before I knew what I was doing, I reached out and slapped her across the face. I was as surprised as she. I immediately knew that I had done wrong, so I apologized, profusely. But it was too late. She started to cry loudly, got up, grabbed her suitcase, and left the trailer, saying she would never come back. I was so glad that Bobbie was at his grandma's house and didn't witness this.

About an hour later, I heard a car pull up to our trailer. Connie and a man I had never seen before came to the door of the trailer and knocked. *What was she doing? Was she bringing someone to beat me up, or what?*

I opened the door, and he introduced himself and said something about wanting to talk to me about how I was treating Connie. He was on the top step, and she was just behind him. Now, I suppose if the guy had it all to do over, he probably wouldn't have done that. My temper flared, and I lost it, so to speak. I reached out and grabbed him by the front of his shirt and jerked him into the trailer. He tried to fight back, but I was much stronger than he was and it was kind of like fighting a child.

In my anger, I remember saying something like, "I want to show you just what kind of woman she is." I told him that while she was shacked up with him, our house was filthy, and I pointed to the dirty dishes, and told him that the place hadn't been cleaned, that she couldn't find time to take care of our little boy, who was at his grandmother's, while I was trying to work a full-time job, and do everything else, while she was screwing him, and doing whatever.

He began saying, "I'm sorry, I'm sorry, I didn't know she was married at first." I had no intention of hurting him, but I wanted to scare him so much that he would never do anything like this again. My last act was to physically throw him out the door. He fell down the steps when I shoved him, and Connie jumped out of the way. She was crying loudly, and some neighbors began to gather around to watch. What a terrible scene! I told him that if he ever came back here again, he would be very sorry.

They left, and I sat down on the sofa and tried to compose myself. I realized that my life was spiraling out of control. I began to think about going back into the Marine Corps. I knew that one way or another I had to make a change.

For the second year in a row, the holiday season was one of emotional pain for me. On Christmas day, I went to her mom's house and had dinner. Connie was there, but we just politely ignored each other. Bobbie received some gifts, and to all outward appearances, it looked like a happy family Christmas. But inside there was some kind of demon gnawing at my soul. I wrestled with what I could do to rescue my life from a path where I might seriously hurt myself or somebody else and maybe get sent to prison. The Marine Corps was looking more and more like the best path to take.

When New Year's Eve rolled around, I had to work the late shift, from 3 PM until 10 PM. It was nearly eleven when I got home to our trailer. Bobbie was staying with Connie's mother. It felt very lonely. There was evidence that Connie had been there and removed the rest of her possessions. I found a note on the counter. It said that she had made up her mind: she was leaving me for good. She wouldn't be back.

It was the first time she had said something definitive about her long-term plans. In spite of all our problems and doubts about our future, a note like this wasn't the kind of news a person wants to hear on New Year's Eve.

I knew that I didn't want to spend New Year's Eve alone, so I decided to just go somewhere, anywhere. For the first time since I had met Connie, I went down the street to a local bar. The place was in a party mood, and the patrons were doing a good job of "ringing in the New Year." The crowd was singing and drinking toasts to each other. I took a seat at the bar and ordered a draft beer. I had forgotten how good a glass of cold beer could taste. I stayed until after the New Year was welcomed in, and had several more beers. I knew that I should go home, because I was scheduled to work on New Years' day. I made it safely home and slept like a man sleeps who is really tired and has a buzz on. Looking back, I think for the first time in a long time, I felt good. It was nice to be around people who were having fun and laughing.

CHAPTER 15

BACK IN THE CORPS

Sergeant Bob Lay, U.S.M.C. Eternal Vigilance is the Price of Freedom. I reenlisted in the Marine Corp, 1958. Camp Lejeune, N.C.

One of the first things I did after the first of the New Year in 1958 was to go to the Marine Corps Recruiting Station to talk about reenlisting. It now no longer mattered whether Connie approved or not. I needed a way to support my son, provide him with health insurance, and find someone to care for him. I learned that I could reenlist for four years, but since I'd been out of the Marine Corps for more than a year I would have to give up my rank of Sergeant and go back in as a Private First Class (PFC). I told them that I was okay with that—I just wanted to be a Marine again.

After reenlistment, I would be sent to Camp Lejeune, North Carolina, for duty. Bobbie would receive free health care, and I could designate Connie's mom as the person who would receive a monthly allotment for his care. That sounded like just what I needed at the time. I would have an opportunity to regain my dignity dressed in the uniform of the U.S. Marines, even though I would be wearing the stripes of a PFC rather than a Sergeant. I thought, *Okay, then, I'll just become the best PFC in the Marine Corps!*

A few days later, I talked to Bobbie's grandmother about taking care of Bobbie when I re-enlisted, and mentioned that it might even involve long-term care. She seemed to like the idea, and it helped a lot that she would receive a monthly allotment check to help pay for his care. I told her that I would also send her extra money as often as I could. She assured me that she really loved little Bobbie and would make sure that he had the best care she could provide.

We left Connie out of this decision, because to all appearances, she didn't care enough about him to try and find someone to care for him. I figured that she'd be happy that I wouldn't be around to interfere with the lifestyle she seemed to have chosen.

I'm aware that as I describe these events, I may sound somewhat cold and detached. The truth of the matter is that this woman, in spite of all her infidelity and faults, had an iron grip on my heart that I wouldn't be able to completely shake for years. It seemed that all she had to do was stand in front of me, look up at me with those flashing dark eyes, tell me that she loved me, and ask me to forgive her—and I would just melt. Maybe if I devoted myself to being a good Marine, I would gain a little more backbone and overcome this weakness. My plan and my hope was that I could accept the Marine Corps as my new love.

After the final considerations for Bobbie's care, I took the last necessary steps to reenlist in the Marine Corps for four years. I was scheduled to leave for North Carolina on January 31, 1958. I stayed in the trailer until it was time to go, packing a small handbag with only my shaving gear, a couple of pairs of socks, underwear, and some civilian clothes. I also had a sea bag with all my old uniforms in it. The rest of my personal belongings I put into a couple of large boxes and stored them in the trunk of the old Chevy. I gave my notice to management that I would be vacating the trailer. I tried to maintain the status quo and have no more confrontations with Connie before I left. I didn't know where she was most of the time anyway. I notified the water company that I would be leaving, but I worked at the water treatment facility until the day before I left for North Carolina.

I parked my old Chevy at Mrs. Smith's house and told her that she and her family could use it. I wasn't worried about Connie driving it, because she'd never learned to drive. I took a city bus to the recruiting station on the day I was scheduled to leave. It was *heartbreaking* to say goodbye to little Bobbie! Of course, he didn't know what was happening, but I knew that I was doing the best thing for him. I promised him that Daddy would come back for him someday—and I meant that promise with all my heart.

Now I found myself on my way to a new adventure. I would be a Marine again! No more scrounging for jobs or working on the line of a chicken-slaughtering plant, filling in as a grocery clerk or a water plant operator. Yes, sir! I would be a United States Marine!

CHAPTER 16

INFANTRY TRAINING

I arrived at the main gate of Camp Lejeune, North Carolina, on a Marine Corps green bus that I'd caught at the Jacksonville train station. I had forgotten how much I liked this place! A large crimson sign with gold lettering stating, "Home of the 2nd Marine Division," welcomed us to Camp Lejeune. A small booth with two smartly dressed Marines greeted us and waved us through. I couldn't help but feel a bit of nostalgia as we proceeded on to Mainside, along a wide, four-lane boulevard, bordered by deep green shrubs, evergreens, and scrub oak trees on either side of the manicured roads, where the main headquarters buildings and barracks were located. I hoped I would be sent to Courthouse Bay, where I had been stationed in 1954 at Marine Corps Engineer Schools while going to Water Supply school.

The bus let me off in front of a large red-brick building, and I was pointed to the place where I was to report. I was excited, but I couldn't help feeling a bit anxious, because I didn't know for sure what I'd be doing. I was also wearing only the stripes of a Private First Class and not a Sergeant, a fact that had begun to weigh on me. As a PFC, I would be subject to the orders of a lot more people than I would as a Sergeant.

Inside the building was a sign directing me where to report. I turned my orders in at the desk, as indicated. A Marine took my orders, stamped them with a date stamp, and told me to stand by while he conferred with another Marine. He came back and told me that I would be going to Camp Geiger to the Infantry Training Regiment, for a four-week Infantry Training Course. I was shocked, and it likely showed. I politely told him that I was an Engineer, a Water Supply specialist, and not infantry. He seemed to take offense at that, as if I were questioning his authority. Then he told me that all prior-service Marines coming back in, having been out of the Corps for over a year, were required to repeat the Infantry Training course in order to snap us out of our civilian ways and refresh our knowledge of military subjects.

It appeared there was no recourse, so I thanked him and accepted my fate. The Marine directed me to a bus stop and told me that a bus would be coming soon, bound for Camp Geiger. He gave me back my stamped orders with an attached sheet ordering me to Infantry Training Regiment. My heart just dropped. I knew this school had the reputation of being a very tough one. Marine Infantry! Even though I was healthy, I was very much out of condition, not having run or participated in any cardio or strength training in a number of years. I knew I was in for some hard times. Could I make it? *Well, yes,* I told myself. I could take anything they could throw at me. I hoped.

When we reached Camp Geiger, I immediately saw row after row of Quonset huts, WW II era. This was where the troops in training are billeted. Camp Geiger is the Marine Corp's infantry training school on the east coast. The goal of the school is to produce the best-trained infantry Marines possible, who could move quickly to any hot spot in the world and defeat any opponent's infantry. This is a big order. For the individual Marine, it means spending many days and nights training in all the Marine Corps weapons units, such as machine guns, mortars, artillery, and individual weapons, like the rifle, pistol, bayonet, along with all sorts of infantry tactics: attacking a fortified position, nighttime tactics, map reading and navigation, and hand-to-hand combat—day and night, among other skills. Oh, and I almost forgot—crawling under barbed wire while a machine gun fires just inches above your head; not to mention that this training schedule is never cancelled due to weather. Rain or snow, day and night, the training goes on.

Quonset huts are not exactly the best places to live, but at least they provide shelter from the weather. In the middle of each hut, there was one oil-burning heating unit. Of course, this meant the people in the middle of the hut got too hot, while those on either end were cold. *Too bad, Marine! That's the way it is!*

The bus let me off at the hut where I was to report. I went inside to check in and was immediately evicted by a loud-mouthed, arrogant Staff Sergeant. He told me I was to *never* to come through that door without knocking first. I accommodated him and knocked again, then entered. I was still in my civilian clothes, and he didn't like that. He continued to harass me and ordered me to get a Marine Corps haircut the first thing. I left my gear right there and went to get a haircut. I came back, and the Staff Sergeant didn't like the way it was cut, so he told me to go get another one. I told him that I didn't have enough money for another haircut. That really pissed him off, and he told me that the next time he saw me, I'd better have a regulation haircut. (I made a mental note in a special place in my mind to remember this guy and maybe, someday, somewhere, our paths would cross again, and I would kick his ass.)

Right away, I realized that I was nothing more than a trainee to him—just a name and a warm body. It didn't matter that I had been a Sergeant. All he saw was who I was right then.

After getting checked in, I was directed to a building where I would be issued all new uniforms; then I would have two sea bags to drag around with me. I was received my uniforms and made my way, walking, and dragging the heavy sea bags to a Quonset hut to report to the First Sergeant of the training unit. I checked in and immediately met the First Sergeant, who looked and acted very much as you may imagine a Neanderthal man would look and act in uniform. He berated me for ten minutes about not being able to "make it in civilian life," calling me a "retread," the name I had just found out was what they called a person who had been discharged and had to re-up because they "couldn't make it" on the outside.

Next, I was directed to one of the Quonset huts where I would be billeted. I found the hut and selected a rack. I quickly got dressed in my new green utilities and new combat boots. It actually felt good to be back in uniform again! The new boots were a good fit, but I also knew to expect some blisters breaking them in.

I made up my rack and found my way to the chow hall. I had forgotten how good Marine Corps chow could be! The rest of the day was spent squaring away my gear and getting ready for my first full day back in the Corps.

The next morning, I was awakened at 05:00 by someone who came into the hut, turned on the light, and shouted, "Reveille! Reveille! Out of the rack!" I had slept well and was feeling pretty good. I went to the chow hall, ready for breakfast. It was great! After eating, shaving, and getting squared away, I reported to the Quonset hut that had been designated as the Company office. There I was told that I would be part of a unit that would begin training in a few days.

The unit would be composed of two platoons of Marines who had just graduated from boot camp at Parris Island, South Carolina, and when they arrived, I would join them. The actual training schedule would begin a couple of days later. I was also told that I would be designated as the unit Platoon Guide, because I was the senior Marine in the unit, with a seniority date as a PFC going back to January, 1954, when I had graduated from boot camp.

I wasn't all that happy about it, because the Platoon Guide was the one who would carry the training unit designation on a pennant flag on a pole. I'd have to carry this guidon staff pole wherever we went and would need to know the manual of arms for carrying it. I would also be considered the senior person in the unit besides the Troop Handlers, and I would have a leadership role as a platoon guide. In general, I wasn't particularly enthusiastic about any of this, because it only would make the training period a bit harder for me. I accepted my assignment, however, and told myself that I would do the best I could.

The next morning, my second at Camp Geiger, following morning chow, I reported to Neanderthal man, as I had been told to do. I had thought that I might get a couple of days off to square away my gear until the others arrived from Parris Island. That apparently was not to be the case. After chewing my ass out about something, my "boss" put me on "police duty" all day. I wondered if it might be in his job description to chew out everybody who came into his hut, or if it was just for me.

Being on police duty was nothing like being a police office in the city. Police Duty in the Marine Corps was another name for picking up trash—everything that doesn't grow and isn't nailed down. I was dragging around a long canvas bag slung over one shoulder, a lot like a cotton picker in the old South, and using a stick with a nail in one end, which was otherwise referred to in the Corps as a "dive-bomber" stick used for stabbing trash to put into the bag.

So, I spent my first official day walking around Camp Geiger, dragging the bag, and policing the base. Oh, and yes—Neanderthal man checked on me a couple of times, driving around in his own car just to find me and see what I was doing. It was a very humbling duty, indeed. Had I done the right thing? Had I reached my new low? I realized that I was just a notch above a recruit. The next couple of days were spent on working parties and having to do all sorts of rotten jobs. But at last, the freshly minted Marines from Parris Island arrived.

The next day, we formed the training unit, and I took my position as the Platoon Guide. There were about 120 Marines. It felt good to be back in uniform and a part of a unit of Marines. We were issued our field gear, which at that time was called 782 Gear. We also were issued an M1 Garand rifle. I loved my M1 rifle! It was the rifle used throughout WWII and Korea. We were briefed on the training that was scheduled for next month. It sure didn't sound like fun. We were told to prepare a field marching pack, and that reveille would be at 04:00 the next morning. Tomorrow would be training day one.

Things happened quickly the next morning. It was very cold, near freezing. If you didn't already know this, North Carolina gets cold in winter. I'm glad they finally issued me a field jacket with a liner. I needed it! We boarded buses and went to the training area. I saw a large circular area in the piney woods, which was alleged to be three miles around. In the center of the circular area, I could see some training obstacles, a mockup village, and other barbed wire obstacles. We started on a run around the circular area with rifles at port arms. "Port arms" is a position where you hold the rifle with both hands, pointing at an angle across your chest. I had to carry my rifle slung around my back as I carried the guidon at port arms.

It didn't take long for me to tire. My strength gave out pretty quickly. First, my leg muscles began to tire, then I started straining for breath. I was the first one who began to drop back. After all, these other Marines had just graduated from boot camp at Parris Island. It wasn't long until I was completely out of it. I couldn't go any further and had to drop out. I was embarrassed and ashamed, but I'd done the best I could. I ran until my legs just wouldn't hold me up any longer.

The others continued on until the end. They sent a jeep to pick me up. I was brought back to the unit and promptly fired as Platoon Guide. Instead, I was given a position at the end of the formation. And this was only the beginning of the first training day! Now they all knew that I was going to be a problem. And *I* knew I was the problem! But I would do the very best I could. Failure simply wasn't an option for me.

The first couple of training weeks passed quickly, and I struggled with every obstacle and every run. Each day was a struggle to just barely make it. I would collapse on the rack as soon as we got back to the hut. The days passed in a blur, but my muscles began to feel stronger, and my stamina increased.

We went through a period of wet, cold weather. Training continued no matter what the weather brought. I was often in a wet, cold, muddy uniform all day. I thought for sure that I was feeling stronger, but I caught a cold, which quickly became serious. I was sent to sickbay to have it checked out. They examined me and gave me cough medicine and aspirin and sent back to full duty. I didn't improve, but got weaker. I was still coughing, and it was much worse.

Again, they sent me to sickbay, and this time I was given bed rest for a couple of days, along with more aspirin and cough syrup.

Now, bed rest at Camp Geiger wasn't what it is in civilian life. Bed rest for me just meant that I didn't have to go to training those days. I still had to get up at reveille, go to chow with the unit (individuals were not allowed in the chow hall. You had to be with a unit.) As I look back, I think this was First Sergeant Neanderthal's rule. I was told that if I didn't eat in the chow hall I could stay in the hut and heat some C-Rations warmed in a bucket of hot water, because heating food with a heat tab wasn't allowed in the hut. I had to carry a bucket of hot water from the showers a hundred yards down the street. The heating unit ran out of fuel, and the hut got cold. My rack was the first one near the door, and a lot of cold air came in around the door. I couldn't muster the energy to go to get more fuel.

After my two days "bed rest" and C-Rations, I went back to training. The weather remained cold and wet. My cold went from bad to worse, and I developed a high fever. My cough was really bad. I tried to push on, but I was too weak to keep up in the training. I was determined to push on.

One evening in the hut, I suddenly got dizzy and passed out. Two Marines half-dragged me out of the hut, and, with one arm around each of their shoulders, they helped me to sickbay, which was close by. I remember the two Marines helping me to walk and find the place to check in. When we arrived at sickbay, I saw a Navy Corpsman sitting with his feet up on the desk, watching TV. He looked up in a nonchalant way and asked if we had checked out with our First Sergeant, showing little interest in my condition. I think I was examined—I don't remember. The Corpsman sent me to the US Naval Hospital at main side on Camp Lejeune. I do remember riding in an ambulance, which was using red lights and siren, speeding through Jacksonville, through the main gate, and on to the hospital.

I have only sketchy memories about the first few days at the hospital. I do, however, remember some quick scrambling among the staff, at first, and being in an oxygen tent. I remember seeing a Navy nurse for the first time. She was in her dress white uniform, an officer. I'd never seen a Navy nurse before. Very impressive! I was feeling really sick, with a high fever and aching body, coughing a lot, and being helped to the head to relieve myself. It hurt so much when I coughed! I was diagnosed with pneumonia, and acute pleurisy and was in critical care for several days. After my fever subsided, I began to think that I just might survive. But, believe me, before that, there were more than a couple of times that I thought I was going go die. And, do you know what? For a while, I was okay with that.

As I lay there in bed one day, thinking about my situation, I concluded that I was pretty much at the lowest place in my life. I was completely broke—I didn't even have any pennies or a little change in my wall locker. My marriage was in total shambles. I knew that my wife was sleeping with another man. I had no home for my little boy, and I didn't know when I would ever see him again. There were no family or friends to visit me at the hospital or to associate with after I was released. I didn't even have change to make a phone call to my family in Kansas.

To make things worse, it was during this time that I received a call from Connie. She told me that our car, the old Chevy, had broken down, and they had to leave it sitting on one the main streets in Miami. Of course, "they" meant her and her boyfriend. She said the police had it towed to an impound lot and were charging $9.00 a day to hold it. She said they didn't have money to bail the car out and have it repaired. She wanted me to send money. I told her I had no money. She never asked how I was doing or anything about my situation. In closing, she reemphasized that she and I would never get back together again. I thought, *That's okay with me*, but it saddened me nonetheless. I closed my eyes and whispered prayers to Jesus.

It was after this phone call that I awoke in the middle of the night feeling very sick and was unable to go back to sleep. I began to softly whisper the Lord's Prayer while I closed my eyes, and I tried to visualize the face of Jesus. I said the Lord's Prayer over and over again. I prayed to God to give me strength to survive and to give me wisdom to carry on with my life. Again, as the time before when I was sitting out in the cold on a log on that Christmas day, I think had an epiphany. I felt like God was near, and a warm feeling began to creep over me, like being slowly immersed in warm water. I saw the face of Jesus looking straight at me, and nodding, as if indicating that He would take care of me. I must have drifted off to sleep. The next morning, I awoke, feeling better than I had for a long time. I felt a fire of enthusiasm in my belly and a new motivation to get well and get out of the hospital. I thanked God.

I began to improve rapidly and was placed in a larger room with several other patients. A few days later, I was moved to a room with one other person. I soon became acquainted with my roommate and learned that he was a Marine First Sergeant. At first I thought, *Oh shit, in the same room with a First Sergeant! My life is going to be miserable.*

Well, to my pleasant surprise, he seemed more like a fatherly figure or an uncle to me. We became acquainted and spent some time playing checkers and just talking. He didn't tell me much about himself, but he asked a lot of questions about me. He had served in WWI in the Pacific and in Korea, but he didn't seem to want to talk a lot about it. He wasn't married, and he lived in the bachelor staff barracks.

Meanwhile, I began to heal rapidly, and after about two weeks I was ready to be released. I was told that I would be sent back to Infantry Training School. All the clothing I had with me was what I had on when I was admitted, which was my underwear, socks, utility uniform, and combat boots—no cap. It was a cold, windy day when I was released, and a field jacket sure would have felt good as I stood at the bus stop, shivering, while waiting to catch a bus back to Camp Geiger.

When I arrived at Camp Geiger, I checked in at the same Quonset hut as I had when I first arrived. I was hoping I would be assigned to a unit that was at the same point in training as I had been when I went into the hospital. That didn't happen. I was assigned to a training unit that still had nearly three weeks left until graduation.

I checked into my new training unit, determined to do the best I could. It was better weather now, and spring was just around the corner. I was happy to be out of the hospital. I went to supply and picked up all my clothing and gear, where it had been stored since I had been in the hospital. I was also happy that the troop handlers of this new unit seemed more friendly and willing to give me every opportunity to succeed. I progressed rapidly and actually enjoyed most of the training. Time passed swiftly and soon we were ready to graduate from Infantry Training School, a milestone event for me. I had also gotten paid for the first time since I'd reenlisted. A person always feels better with a little money in their pocket. This meant I would be able to send some money to Mrs. Smith for Bobbie's care.

Finally, the day arrived when our unit graduated from Infantry Training School. I felt like a Marine again and recognized that old fire in my belly. I was issued orders to Marine Corps Engineer Schools at

Courthouse Bay. This was where I had been stationed in 1964, going to Water Supply school. I was very pleased with this assignment.

When I checked in at Engineers' School, I was assigned to Headquarters Company. When I turned in my orders, I was happy to see the guy who had been my roommate at the hospital. He was the First Sergeant of the unit! He saw me in the office when I was checking in and called me into his office, welcoming me into the unit. He said that if he could help me in any way, I was just to let him know. I could hardly believe that things were going so well for me! I believe that I nearly died when I was in the hospital. It had been a close call. It seemed like my life had been in a nosedive for so long. I thanked God for answering my prayers.

I reported to the Utilities Section for duty and learned that I was assigned to the Refrigeration School. My daily duties at first were to be a kind of handy man: keep the office and classrooms clean, make coffee, and run errands. Although these kinds of duties were below those of a Sergeant I remembered that I was just a Private First Class. I was determined to be the best PFC in the Marine Corps.

I called Mrs. Smith to see how Bobbie was doing. She told me that everything was all right and that he seemed happy. She didn't know where Connie was. I told her that I would be taking out an allotment from my pay to send to her for Bobbie's care and that the Marine Corps would also add money to supplement it. I told her that I would also get Bobbie an ID card, which I did, and sent it to her. I told her that after awhile, when I was settled, I'd come to see her and Bobbie. I also called the Miami Police Department and inquired about the status of my car, the old Chevy that had been abandoned by Connie and her boyfriend. I found out that the car had been sold at auction to pay the storage bill. I asked what had happened to the items in the trunk. (When I reenlisted and left Miami, I had packed everything I owned—personal items, clothing, etc., in the trunk.) The police told me that those items had probably been donated to a charity. So, it seemed that I really did, indeed, lose everything I owned, and almost my life.

After a few weeks had gone by, one day my supervisor at Refrigeration School asked me if wanted to attend the Refrigeration and Air Conditioner school, as a new class was starting soon. I jumped at the chance! I was transferred to Schools Company and went through the eight-week course. I liked the subject matter and came out at the top of the class. I then received orders back to Refrigeration Schools section, where they had requested that I be returned.

My superiors were very happy with me, and right away assigned me duties as an Assistant Instructor. With these duties, I would assist the primary instructors, helping with classroom duties such as making sure the room was always ready. I would ascertain that any handouts or other training aides were available and anything else that the Instructor needed. Sometimes I would fill in for the primary instructor. I wore a red and gold armband, identifying me as an Assistant Instructor. I was proud of my new assignment. I was told by the senior instructors to learn everything I could about every aspect of all the subjects, because I may be assigned as a primary instructor someday.

I lived in the barracks, where, during the evenings and weekends, it could get pretty lonely. Going anywhere required a big effort. Courthouse Bay was not on a main highway and was about fifteen miles from Mainside, or from anywhere for that matter. Just from the barracks to an intersection on a highway was a mile. Anyone stationed at Courthouse Bay without a car had a pretty lonely existence. To go to the closest town, Jacksonville, required hitchhiking or catching a ride with someone to Mainside, and then taking a bus to Jacksonville.

Jacksonville was a typical military town. Droves of young Marines wandered up and down the streets searching for the seemingly nonexistent "good" girls to get acquainted with. It seemed on the weekends and holidays, all the parents would keep their daughters at home so they wouldn't be preyed upon by these "animals" who were roaming the streets of Jacksonville. The streets were lined with pawnshops, uniform stores, music stores, and clothing stores.

The bars could only serve beer—no whiskey or other hard drinks. They were packed with young Marines, drinking themselves into a stupor while trying to score with one of the women who worked there. The main job of those gals was to separate these young Marines from their money. All of these places had one or more bouncers to break up fights and to literally throw the troublemakers out the door. One trip to Jacksonville was enough for me.

CHAPTER 17

FINDING A CHURCH

I went to the USO several times. There I could find snacks, free coffee, a library, pool tables, television, and other games. But it seemed to me that the USO was also the kind of place where the lonely people hung out. It only made me feel lonelier when I was there. I concluded that I needed to find a more interesting way to spend my time—maybe something more productive.

I remembered how I had enjoyed going to church in the past, and decided that maybe I should look for one here. The Jacksonville telephone book listed a Pentecostal church like the one I had attended in Miami. I determined that I was going to check it out. One Sunday morning I got up early, dressed in the best clothes I had (which were pretty shabby), and found my way to this church in Jacksonville. It was located about a mile from the bus station downtown—an easy walk for a young Marine.

I arrived in time for their 10 AM Sunday service. First, there was congregational singing, and then we all broke up into groups and went to Sunday school classes, where I was introduced to everyone. Then the main service began. The pastor delivered a powerful sermon followed by more singing. A young man played guitar, and a young woman, his sister, sang several songs before the altar call. They were really good!

When the services ended, people seemed to spend a lot of time visiting before they left to go home. The pastor made it a point to seek me out and welcome me, telling me how glad he was that I had come. He invited me to their Wednesday evening prayer meeting. Several other folks introduced themselves and asked me to please come back. I hadn't felt so loved and wanted in a very long time.

From then on, if I didn't have duty, I always went to Sunday services and often to the Wednesday evening prayer meetings. During the Christmas season, I went caroling with a group from church. We went from house to house in the community, standing in the yards, singing Christmas songs. I was also invited by a young woman from the church to go on a hayrack ride, which I did. This same girl invited me to come home with her and her family after Sunday services to have dinner. Her name was Sharon. I accepted her invitation.

Not long after that, when Sunday services were finished, we piled into their old car. The group included Sharon, her mom and dad, her older sister, and two younger children. It was a tight fit! We went to their house out in tobacco country. I felt honored to have been invited to share a delicious home-cooked meal with this wonderful family! I spent the afternoon taking a walk with Sharon and then just hanging around, playing with their cats and a dog. Late in the afternoon, her father took me back to Jacksonville, where I caught a bus to the base.

After this, from time to time, I'd accept their invitation and go home with them after church and enjoy another home-cooked dinner. It felt so good to get away from the barracks. The friendship I developed with Sharon never blossomed into a romantic relationship. I was looked on as more of a family friend than as Sharon's boyfriend. Besides, I was technically still married to Connie and just wasn't interested in that kind of relationship, nor, of course, was she interested in a guy who was still married and had a child.

CHAPTER 18

A NASTY FIGHT

It was during the time when I was seeing Sharon that I got into a fight. It left me badly injured, but not with anything permanent. What happened was that I had fixed up one of the Marines I knew with Sharon's sister, who was a couple years older than Sharon. Her name was Emily. His name was Bill Rice. He was a handsome, aggressive sort of guy from South Carolina. He'd been in the Marine Corps for about five years but was still a private. He had a bad habit of getting into fights, and he'd been reduced in rank a couple of times for fighting. He actually said that he *liked* to fist fight! This was back in the days when most people fought with just their fists—not with guns or knives.

Bill took a liking to me, and I enjoyed his high spirit. We had taken these sisters to church several times and had a lot of fun. He had a fairly decent car, a 1949 Ford. One Wednesday evening, he and I got dressed up and went out to the tobacco farm to take Sharon and Emily to prayer meeting. It was a nice summer evening. While the girls finished dressing, Bill and I sat on the front porch swing chatting. While we were there, a car came up the road with three guys in it. They slowed down in front of the house, and one of them stuck his arm out the window and gave us the finger, shouting, "Fuck you, Marines!"

Apparently, the local boys didn't like us Marines coming around and dating the girls in that area. Well, naturally, when we saw that and heard their insult, it was too much to ignore. Marines just couldn't overlook that, especially not a fighter like Bill. He jumped up and said, "Come on, Bob! Let's go get 'em!" He flew off the porch and went running for his car. I followed him. We didn't even think to tell the girls where we were going.

We pulled out behind right behind them. When these guys saw us gaining on them, they got scared and took off at a high speed. We gave chase and tried to stop their car by passing them, then slowing down and not letting them pass us. They tried to pass us on the other side, nearly ending up in a ditch. They were really getting scared now. We chased them relentlessly for several miles. When they finally pulled over, they were at a service station that had an adjoining bar. Perhaps they had planned this, knowing that a number of their buddies were probably inside.

They screeched to a halt in front of the bar, Bill and I skidded in right behind them. Bill jumped out and said, "Bob! I'll get the driver and you get the other guys!" We ran over to their car and commenced fighting these punks who had insulted us, and the U.S. Marine Corps. We were going to kick their ass!

We were doing a pretty good job of that when suddenly a number of their buddies came running out of the bar and jumped us. Now we were in a fight for our lives. Somebody hit me on the head with a beer bottle, leaving a large gash. I was knocked out for several minutes. When I came to, I was lying in a puddle of water in the driveway, and they were kicking me and punching me when I tried to stand up. Bill had his back to a car and was surrounded by several guys who were punching him. I fought like a demon and was finally able to get up and go help Bill.

We managed to get away from them and jumped into Bill's car. We pulled out with guys still trying to punch us through the windows. We sped off, but then we turned around and went back by the tavern. The gang was still outside. We flipped them off as we drove past the tavern on our way back to the girls' house.

The family had no idea where we had gone. When we returned, they were pretty shocked. We were both wearing suits, which were now soaked with blood, water, and mud, and were probably ruined. I had a nasty cut above my left eye, a large gash on the back of my head, a broken nose, which was still bleeding some, numerous cuts and bruises, and several broken ribs on my right side. Bill also had several cuts and bruises. The girls came running out crying, very upset by our appearance. Their first thought was that we had been in a car accident.

Obviously, our plans to attend prayer meeting were cancelled. We both were in need of medical help. Instead of going to church, we went back to Courthouse Bay to the medical clinic to get patched up. The clinic was required to complete a written report of our visit. They also had to send a copy of this report to our unit. The report required an explanation for these injuries. We didn't want to get in trouble, so we both told the medical people that we had fallen down a stairway in Chinquapin, North Carolina, at 18:00 hours.

Of course, the medical people didn't believe it, but they wrote what we had told them. Both of us were beaten up pretty badly. It's possible that if we hadn't been strong enough nor skilled in the Marine Corps hand-to-hand combat training, those guys might have killed us. Perhaps they'd be more careful in the future about whom they pick a fight with. But at least I think we taught this gang a lesson about picking a fight with Marines.

The next day, Bill and I were called to appear before the Company Commander, Captain Elmer E. Long. Captain Long was a real old-timer, and sort of a hero on the island, having fought against the Japanese in the South Pacific during WW II. He'd been captured and had spent several years in a Japanese prison camp. Elmer was a salty old guy, with ribbons and decorations running all the way up to the left shoulder seam on his shirt. Wow! He smoked cigars and wore his frame cap indoors often. It was against regulations to wear a cover of any kind indoors, unless you were armed. But who was going to tell Elmer to take it off?

The First Sergeant told us to go into Captain Long's office and report, as ordered. We marched in and reported. Captain Long told us to stand at ease. He was wearing his frame cap and nursing a stinking cigar. He had the clinic medical reports in front of him. He looked up and was somewhat amused at the sight of our injuries. I had black stitches hanging out of my left eyebrow, stitches across the bridge of my nose, with dried blood around the stitches. I also had a huge white bandage on the back of my head that looked like half of a soft ball, and the imprint of the heel of a shoe on my face. I also found it difficult to stand up straight up for long, and I limped a bit because of the fractured ribs on my right side. Bill was covered in bandages also.

Captain Long took a puff from his cigar, looked up from the reports and said, "So, you guys fell down a stairway last night in Chinquapin, North Carolina?" We both replied, "Yes, sir, we did."

The Captain leaned back in his chair with an amused look on his face. In his thirty-plus years in the Corps he had probably seen a large number of injured Marines. After a bit, he said, "It looks like there was someone down at the end of that stairway who beat the shit out of you."

We both looked down and sheepishly said, "Yes sir, there were about a dozen of them."

The Captain asked, "Well, I want to know; did you make a good show of yourselves?"

We replied, "Yes sir, we did."

He then went on to ask if any police were involved, and we told him no. He asked if there would be any police report from any law enforcement agencies showing up at the base. Again, we told him no. Then the Captain said, "It looks like you guys have been punished enough." He dismissed us and told us to report to our work unit.

My work at the Refrigeration School was still going well. I continued my assignment as an Assistant Instructor and was still gaining the respect of the senior staff at the school. Then, in February 1959, I received an order to Formal Schools Instructor course at another location on Camp Lejeune. It was an intense course, providing instruction and training regarding how to teach formal classes and had been recognized and approved by Headquarters, U.S. Marine Corps. The course study included how to deliver a lecture-type class, a lecture that included a demonstration, and other teaching skills, e.g., using a chalkboard effectively, how to use a pointer, how to incorporate the use of visual aides, and other fine points of maintaining composure in front of a class. The course was often referred to as "charm school." I actually enjoyed the class, and did well. Now, I would feel confident as a teacher in any type of instructional situation.

When the class was finished, I returned to my home unit at the Refrigeration School. Shortly after I got back, I was officially assigned to work as a Primary Instructor on the subject of Refrigeration Theory. I was delighted with this assignment! I was the only Corporal Instructor in the Utilities Schools, which included the Water Supply School, Electrical School, Construction School, and Refrigeration School. The rest of the Instructors were all Staff Non-Commissioned Officers, and were at least two ranks above me.

After getting this assignment, I studied until I was completely confident that I knew precisely how liquids and gasses would react when exposed to varying pressures and temperatures or when concealed in a closed refrigeration unit, therefore making refrigeration possible. No other instructor wanted to teach Refrigeration Theory, because they said it was too difficult to teach. That was good for me, because I was the only person who would and could teach this course of study. With this assignment I was now eligible to receive additional pay every month, because I was doing what the Marine Corps considered to be a critical Military Occupational Specialty.

CHAPTER 19

HITCHHIKING BACK TO KANSAS

During the remainder of 1958 and into 1959, I made several trips to Miami to see Bobbie and Mrs. Smith. I hitchhiked there on two of these trips. Also, during the summer of 1958, I hitchhiked to Kansas to visit my parents. I hadn't seen them for nearly two years and was very homesick. Hitchhiking was the only way I could get anywhere, because I didn't have the money for any commercial transportation. It was relatively easy to hitch a ride if one was traveling in uniform in those days.

I dressed in my class-A summer uniform, took ten days leave, and headed west on Hwy 24 for Kansas. I wasn't having any trouble catching rides, and by late afternoon, I had made it to the little town of Spindale, North Carolina. I was standing in the center of town near the city square with my thumb out, when an old four-door Buick pulled up beside me and stopped. There were two rather rough-looking women, a bit older than me, in the car. The gal in the passenger seat, a blonde, asked if they could give me a ride. I accepted, and jumped in as she scooted over. The driver was a slim, dark-haired woman.

As the driver gunned the car and pulled away, one of them asked me where I was going. I told her, and she asked if I was in a hurry to get there. I said no, not necessarily. She then asked if I wanted to have a drink with them. I said, "Okay, I could sure use a cool beer after hitchhiking all day."

One of them explained that this was a dry county, and it was against the law to sell liquor of any kind. However, they knew where we could buy some beer and whiskey. With that, she gunned the old Buick, and out into the country we went. We soon started up a twisting, gravel mountain road. Around the curves she went—too fast, I thought. The rear wheels were kicking gravel over the edge, as higher and higher we went. We pulled into the driveway of a shabby old house that had a dilapidated barn, a couple of outbuildings, and a bunch of chickens running around.

A bevy of scary-looking, barking dogs greeted us. The gal that was driving honked the horn, and an old man in bib overalls came out of the house to greet us. It was apparent that the women and the old man knew one another. He leaned down toward the car and peered at me with a questionable look. The driver informed him that I was a friend of theirs, and I was okay. She told him that she wanted to buy some beer and a jar of moonshine—corn whiskey. The man went back to the house, and returned with a gallon jug of homemade beer and a quart-size fruit jar of whiskey. I offered to pay for the liquor, but they said no, they'd buy it. We were offered a taste before we paid. It tasted good to us. The swallow of moonshine felt particularly strong, and it burned my throat going down. But it tasted sweet and good, and, if I remembered correctly, how good moonshine was supposed to taste.

One of the women paid the man and away we went down the mountain to Spindale, going toward to the driver's house. On the way, we stopped at a grocery store and bought some sliced lunch meat, sliced cheese, and a loaf of bread. When we got to the house, they made sandwiches, and we sat around watching an old black-and-white television, eating sandwiches, and drinking warm home-made beer, which was very dark and had a strong flavor.

I began to have reservations about having accepted the ride they offered, but I couldn't resist the temptation to stay when the blond woman began to cozy up to me. Before long, we were doing some serious necking. I was thinking that maybe it would be okay if I stayed for just a little while, and then I'd have them take me back to town and to the main highway out of there.

But it didn't work out that way. The women invited some friends over, and they had also brought beer and whiskey. They had an old guitar, which was in decent shape. I tuned it up and played. I sang everything I knew, and that party lasted until the wee hours of the morning. I had forgotten how hard moonshine can hit you. It hit me hard.

There's no point in reviewing all my sketchy memories of this wild party, which really lasted all the way from Saturday into Saturday night, and then until early Sunday morning. Now I had used up two days of my leave, and I wasn't even out of North Carolina! I gathered up my belongings and tried to make myself as presentable as possible in my wrinkled uniform.

I asked one of the women to take me to the outskirts of the west side of town. I stuck out my thumb and stood there, wearing my sunglasses, nursing a bad headache, and waiting for some Good Samaritan to give me a ride. I felt horrible, but the worst of it was that my soul was sick with remorse at what I had done. I apologized to Jesus, and whispered a humble prayer to God, standing there, hung over, in that brilliant Sunday morning sun. I hated myself, knowing that I had just wasted two days and a night with these people when I could have spent it with Mom and Dad. What a loser I was! I knew it was my fault that Mom would be worrying needlessly when I didn't get home when I was expected to.

A man and his wife with two small kids picked me up. They were all dressed up nicely and were on their way to church. I thought, *How ironic. These fine folks, going to church to worship God, picked me up; me the person who had just been involved in two days and nights participating in the worse kind of debauchery.* I crawled into the back seat with the kids. They were very excited about the badges on my uniform and asked me all kinds of questions about them. I told the folks I was on my way to Kansas to visit my parents. They invited me to go to church with them, but I kindly declined, explaining I need to keep on the road, because Kansas was a long way away yet. They only took me three or four miles until they had to turn off to go to the church. I thanked them for the ride, and I asked them to pray for me. I got out on the road again and stuck out my thumb.

I finally made it to Kansas with the help of God and the good will of some very nice people giving me rides. One driver dropped me off at a service station at the intersection of Highway 69 and 31, in the small town of Fulton. My sister Margaret and her husband, Lawrence, owned and operated the station. Margaret was very surprised and happy to see me. It was so good to see her, too! We hugged, laughed, and talked for a little while. I drank a coke and ate a snack to refresh myself.

I was really tired, and I was anxious to get on out to the farm to see Mom and Dad. Margaret was running the station by herself that afternoon, so she couldn't leave it to take me on out to the farm. She did, however, ask one of her customers who had stopped in for gas if they could give me a ride, since they were going that way.

These nice folks dropped me off at an intersection on Highway 31 west of Fulton at a gravel road, just a quarter of a mile from my house. Though I was very tired, I really enjoyed the walk up this shady gravel road, the last leg of my journey home. On either side of the road were giant elm, walnut, maple, hickory, and many other trees, shrubs, and undergrowth, which provided cool shade on up to the house. As a boy, I had grown up playing in this timbered area, chasing rabbits and squirrels, and looking for tadpoles and crawfish in the little stream that ran through it and emptied into Lost Creek. Many fond old memories flooded my mind as I walked on up toward the house.

As I topped a small hill and followed a slight turn in the road, I could see the old farm place where I grew up. There was the old clapboard house, a huge, old rickety barn, leaning to the east, as if at sometime in the past, a fierce windstorm had almost blown it over. Dad had it propped up with some long poles on the east side. There was the chicken house, and I could see chickens roaming around the yard. This was home, sweet home, for sure!

As I got closer to the house, I saw Momma come out the back door and throw some water out of a pan. My heart just leapt, and tears filled my eyes, just at the sight of her. I fondly remember the moment that she looked up and saw me walking up the road. She instantly stopped in her tracks, put her hand over her mouth, and exclaimed, "Oh my! Oh my!" She stepped off the porch and took a couple of steps into the front yard to meet me. We met and hugged and hugged. There is no hug more wonderful than a hug from one's mother. We both shed tears together. She said, "Oh, I'm so glad to see you! Are you okay?" I assured her that I was just fine. So many things had happened in my life since I had last seen her. It was so wonderful to be home!

The days at home visiting with family and friends was wonderful and passed quickly. All too soon, it was time to head back to Camp Lejeune and resume with my duties as a Marine. My Uncle Raymond Newcomb and Aunt Melinda were leaving to go on vacation and were kind enough to give me a ride all the way across Missouri. They let me off at an intersection outside of Poplar Bluff, Missouri. They were driving a brand new Mercury Turnpike Cruiser, a huge, luxury car. It was a wonderful ride, and I enjoyed so much visiting with them.

Uncle Raymond and Aunt Melinda were among my most favorite people in the entire world. They had always been like second parents to us kids for as far back as I can remember. We always referred to them as "Auntie and Raymond." We were always so excited when we'd look up and see them coming up the road or pulling into the driveway. We'd shout, "Auntie and Raymond are coming! Auntie and Raymond are coming!" and run out to greet them.

When my leave was up and I departed from home, for most of the way I took the same route back to North Carolina as I had come. I caught rides rather quickly. In the late afternoon of the next day, I recall walking on a two-lane highway in Eastern North Carolina, getting closer to Camp Lejeune. A ride didn't seem to be forthcoming, so I kept walking. I was in the heart of tobacco country. The sun was going down behind me, sending golden streaks of fading light that radiated across the tobacco fields and the hot, sultry world around me. I walked past some farm houses, and some little children playing in the gathering dusk ran out to the road waving at me, while barking dogs also added their greetings. Seeing these kids playing made me so heartsick to see my little boy, Bobbie. How long it would be before I saw him again, I didn't know.

It was past midnight when I finally reached my barracks at Courthouse Bay. I was famished. There was no place open to buy some food. The chow hall was closed and wouldn't open until early morning. I took a short walk over to the Interior Guard House, because I knew the chow hall often provided them with sandwiches, doughnuts—some kind of food for the watch standers. Maybe I could bum some food there.

At this late hour there were only some pieces of stale fried fish and some old bread. I wasn't particular, so I asked the Sergeant of the Guard if I could have some, explaining my circumstances. Grudgingly, he said okay. He acted like the fish were his personal property. I thanked the arrogant Sergeant for the food anyway. I remember after midnight sitting on the steps of the guardhouse eating that stale fish and bread and washing it down with stale, bitter coffee. It tasted good. I knew that I'd be the first one in that chow line when it opened the next morning, that's for sure! I *loved* being a Marine!

That trip to Kansas, and back to my base, had proved to be a memorable odyssey, filled with much happiness along with some deep regrets.

CHAPTER 20

REUNION WITH CONNIE

About once a week I would get a handful of quarters for the pay phone and call Mrs. Smith to see how she and Bobbie were doing. Then, on a late summer evening while I was at the barracks, I received an emergency Red Cross message that my wife was in a hospital in St. Augustine, Florida. She had had a miscarriage and was requesting my presence. I didn't even know she was in St. Augustine. I knew that if she was having a miscarriage, it wasn't my child.

I called Mrs. Smith. She hadn't heard about the miscarriage and didn't know where Connie was. She went on to say that Connie and her boyfriend had come by a week or so ago and had taken Bobbie with them. This news really bothered me. Was Bobbie with her in St. Augustine? Was he okay? Was he being cared for? With these unanswered questions, and due to some strange sense of loyalty to Connie (after all, she was still technically my wife), I quickly made arrangements to take emergency leave and depart for St. Augustine that evening.

I couldn't afford a bus or train ticket, so I decided to hitchhike. I packed a small tote bag with a couple pairs of underwear, socks, a summer civilian shirt, and trousers. Almost as an afterthought, I tossed in a six-inch bone-handled hunting knife in a leather sheaf. I dressed in my summer class-A uniform.

It was twilight, with darkness quickly slipping in, by the time I left the barracks. I walked the mile to the intersection to catch a ride. I was already tired from a hard day's work, and I put my bag down beside me, stuck out my thumb, hoping to catch my first ride to begin my overnight trek to St. Augustine, Florida.

It was mid-morning the next day when I reached St. Augustine. My ride let me off at the exit to St. Augustine from the interstate highway. I had no idea how far it was from this exit to the downtown area. I soon found out, as I walked the mile or so down San Marco Avenue to the downtown area under a blistering hot summer sun. I stopped at the Trailways bus station to freshen up. I changed from my uniform into some summer slacks and a shirt. There I inquired as to where the hospital was located. Luckily, it was close by in the downtown area. As I walked the few blocks to the hospital, I wondered how my meeting with Connie would go, considering the unusual circumstances.

I soon found the hospital, went inside, and asked to see my wife. The clerk looked in some files, made a quick phone call and told me that Connie was no longer a patient there. It seemed that at some point after she'd had the miscarriage last evening, she had left the hospital without being properly dismissed—and hadn't paid her bill. It was then that it dawned on me that perhaps that's the reason why she requested my presence: to pay her bill. If that was the case, it didn't surprise me.

Well, I certainly wasn't going to pay her hospital bill! The hospital had neither an address nor a phone number for Connie. They must not have had time to get that information before she left.

I left the hospital to try to find my wife and my little boy. I had no idea how to go about finding a person in a city this size, with no information to go on—I had no contact number, no records of any kind, no car, and limited funds. I thought that maybe Connie had some kind of address, or perhaps a Post Office box. I managed to find the main Post Office in the downtown area. I inquired at the counter, and, sure enough, she had a box number but no address.

The very helpful gentleman at the window told me that the owner of this box matched my description of her, and she usually came in around noon every day to pick up her mail. She always had a little boy with her, he said. The gentleman checked her box, and found that she hadn't yet picked up her mail for that day. I decided to just wait there in the lobby, since it was nearly noon. I was very grateful to this gentleman and I thanked him sincerely. I will *never* forget his kindness and compassion!

Either good luck or a guardian angel was with me that day, because within the hour, Connie came walking into the lobby, leading little Bobbie by the hand.

She didn't see me when she walked up to the window and asked for her mail. She was pale and sickly looking, her hair uncombed, her clothing wrinkled. My little boy also looked like he was sick. He had a runny nose, a bad cough, and his clothes were also all wrinkled.

She turned to leave—and then she saw me. At first she looked startled but showed no sign of being happy to see me. There was no real greeting—not even a quick hug or any sign of gladness that I was there.

But there was my little boy! I picked him up and gave him a big hug. It seemed like he didn't recognize me, and he seemed a little confused and unresponsive in general. But as for me, it felt so *good* to hold and hug my little boy! My heart just broke to see him in this condition. There was no way to know just how badly he had suffered during all this turmoil between Connie and me. We decided to go the city park, and we found a picnic table where we could sit down and talk.

In Miami, with my son Bobbie.

After talking for a little while, we headed over to a small cafe to get something to eat. During our conversation, I began to piece together what was going on. I don't now recall in detail what she said. Her boyfriend had been called away by his job, so he rented an apartment there in St. Augustine for her. She wouldn't tell me much about him—who or where he was. She still had the apartment, which was nearby.

We mainly talked about what we should do now. We discussed a little about her coming back to Camp Lejeune with me. She really didn't want to do that, plus I didn't have a place for her there. I didn't have a car, and I certainly didn't have enough money to set her up properly. I kind of sensed that she was struggling with competing affections between him and me. I never learned if the two of them had had a dispute and he'd left her, or what might have happened.

She finally decided that she should go back to Miami to stay for a while. She made a phone call to her father and stepmother to ask if she could stay with them temporarily. They lived in North Miami. They agreed that she could. We pooled our money and caught a Trailways bus to Miami. It was a long, six-hour, overnight trip, and we arrived in North Miami by midmorning the next day.

Her father, also named Connie (she was his namesake), and her stepmother, Hazel, were Christians and very accommodating folks. They had an extra bedroom set up for us. It felt so good to have a place where I could shower and lie down and stretch out. I'd been on the go without sleep for two days and two nights. Hazel and Connie's father just showered affection on little Bobbie! He really needed some love and attention, and they were just the kind of folks to give it to him. The little guy warmed up to them right away.

I stayed there for a couple days, trying to recover from my journey and all of my mixed emotions. I was in the back yard pushing Bobbie on the new swing set they'd purchased for him. Hazel came out to speak to me, and I could tell by the worried look on her face that something was wrong. She told me that Connie was out front talking with her boyfriend, who had pulled up in his car. I was *instantly* angry—way too angry!

I looked over there and saw the car parked along the curb. Connie was leaning through the window on the driver's side talking with him. I didn't have a plan; I was just pushed by adrenaline and anger. I ran around the side of the house and was upon them before they knew it. I jerked open the door on the passenger side and slid into the front seat with him. He was startled and looked scared. Connie started to cry and jumped into the back seat. The guy immediately pressed himself as far as he could against the driver's door and almost started crying, trying to explain that he didn't know she was married when he'd first met her. He said he would just leave, and that there would be no more trouble.

I told him how awful it had been for me, not knowing where my wife was most of the time, and not knowing whether our son was being taken care of or not. I told him, "You are staying right *here* while Connie goes in the house and packs all of her clothes!" I told him that I wasn't going to support her any more while he was still screwing her. I said to him, "You are going to take her with you, since you love her so much!"

I told Connie to go inside and pack her suitcase and come back out, because she was going with him. And I added that she was *not* taking Bobbie with her! She was still sobbing, but she went into the house. I told her to hurry, while I remained in the car with him. He appeared very scared of me and wasn't about to challenge me. It took a lot of will power for me not to just start punching him! He looked like a whimpering, scared rat.

Connie soon came back out with her suitcase. She put it into the backseat and climbed inside. She was still crying. I told him to get out of there, and take her with him and that I never wanted to see either of them again.

He started the car, and, as an after thought, I took out my wallet, and took out a twenty-dollar bill. As I got out of the car, I threw the bill into the front seat. I said something like, "Here's some money.

That's because you're doing me a favor by taking her—and she's not even worth that much!" Then I repeated what I'd said before, that I wasn't going to continue to pay for her support while she was sleeping with him.

Connie quickly got out of the back seat and into the front seat and they drove away. I don't believe I ever saw her again. I seem to recall that I stayed several more days, just resting and playing with Bobbie. Her father and stepmother and I had some long talks about Connie and me, and what options we had. I told them about the arrangements I'd made with Mrs. Smith for his care. They were fine with that and said that they would take Bobbie over to her house after a few days.

I don't know that we came to any real conclusions, but they did say that Bobbie could stay with them for as long as was needed. I know I came to the conclusion that Connie and I needed to get a divorce, and I was going to work on that. I didn't think we could ever have a happy marriage again after all of this.

After a few days, I began to get ready to head back to Camp Lejeune. It was so hard to part with these fine folks and my little boy. I really didn't know when I would ever see him again.

One of Hazel's relatives, who happened to be visiting, took me to the main highway, where I stuck out my thumb and began my journey back to the base. It had been a very long and stressful adventure so far. Now, I had a long and uncertain journey back to North Carolina. Maybe things would settle down a little when I got back to the barracks and resumed my daily routine again. I thanked God for the many blessings.

CHAPTER 21

TIME MARCHES ON

In the fall of '58 I bought an old car, a 1949 Studebaker. I made one trip to Miami, where I stayed with Mrs. Smith and slept on her sofa. I had a good visit with Bobbie. Of course, the Studebaker broke down on the way back while I was in the Everglades. The engine began to run hot, and steam was coming from under the hood. I pulled over and checked it out. One of the heater hoses had developed a leak, and I was losing all of the coolant.

I took stock of my situation. There wasn't a service station or repair facility for several miles in either direction. There were alligators and snakes in that swamp on either side of the road, which made me nervous. As far as I could see in every direction was swampland. I began to pace up and down the road pondering my situation. Several cars went by, but nobody stopped. I didn't have a screwdriver or any other kind of tool. (I made a note to myself that when I got back to the base, the first thing I was going to do would be to put together a toolkit for the car.)

Then I happened to notice a piece of an old hacksaw blade lying along the side of the road. Where did that come from? I was glad to see it. It hit me then that I was going have to bail myself out of this situation. I used the blade from my razor to cut off the busted part of the heater hose, and then I used the end of the hacksaw blade as a screwdriver to reattach the clamp on the hose. Perfect!

Next, I needed some coolant to fill the radiator. I took one of the hubcaps off the wheel and used it to dip water out of the swamp to fill the radiator. I must have made ten trips back and forth from the edge of the swamp to the car to fill that thing! Each time I reached into the swamp to dip the water, I was sure that a snake or an alligator was going to attack me. I got my feet and legs wet one time when I slipped into the swamp up past my ankles. When I was done, I started the car and proceeded on my way back to Camp Lejeune, North Carolina. I didn't have any trouble after that.

During my trips to Florida to see Bobbie, I stayed at Mrs. Smith's house. Connie and I never talked about Bobbie's long-term future. I think it was too painful for either of us to discuss it. Maybe more time had to pass before we'd be able to make those decisions.

Well, time marches on, as they say. Connie eventually filed a petition for divorce in the Circuit County of Dade County. I didn't contest the petition, so in March of 1959, the divorce was granted, giving custody of Bobbie to Connie. I agreed to the arrangement, since there wasn't any way that I could care for him. I was still living in the barracks, but I promised myself, that if at some time in the future I happened to remarry and was able to make a home for him, I'd make every possible legal effort to gain custody of him.

On one of my trips down there, Mrs. Smith (without consulting me), fixed me up with a date with a woman she worked with. Her name was Dixie. She was quite attractive, with dark eyes, and dark curly, fluffy hair. I learned that she was of Cuban ancestry. We went to a dance club, had a couple of drinks (the first I'd had in eons), danced some, and then we went to Miami Beach.

It was a beautiful warm summer evening. We took a blanket that I had in the car, found an isolated spot, and spread it on the sand. We spent a couple of hours there, talking, listening to the surf, and necking. (I believe that's what it was still called at the time.) I loved Miami Beach at night! I remember that at 10 PM every night a Miami radio station used to play the popular tune, "Moon over Miami."

We went back to her apartment, where we had more to drink. Pretty soon, she was quite intoxicated and I remember her jumping up and down on her bed like it was a trampoline, laughing and clapping her hands.

We had only this one night. We made no plans for the future, though we both knew that we had really hit it off. She was the first person who ever told me that I was handsome.

I remember saying, "Really?"

She said, "Yes, very, very handsome!" (I put that in my mental footlocker to cherish later.) She asked me to contact her the next time I was in Miami, and she gave me her phone number. I said I would, but I never did. I just wasn't ready to feel obligated to a woman at this time. I still had too much pain over Connie in my heart. Regrettably, I never saw Dixie again. It was probably for the best.

CHAPTER 22

MEETING MY TRUE LOVE

In March 1960, I reenlisted in the Marine Corps for six years. Because of my critical job skill I received a nice reenlistment bonus. I had more money in my pocket than I'd ever had before. It felt good! I traded in my Studebaker at the Ford dealership and purchased a new Ford Falcon. It was the introductory year for the Falcon and the first time that Ford had produced an economy car. I thought, *Now, I'm really living "high on the hog"*! I had a great job. I had respect. Plus I had a new car and cash in my pocket!

In June of 1960, I took leave and went to Miami to talk with my lawyer about the possibility of getting custody of Bobbie. This trip to Miami was much more enjoyable. I wasn't hitchhiking. I had a new car, some new clothes, and money in my pocket. *Maybe*, I thought, *I can meet a nice woman or contact Dixie.*

I enjoyed the trip to Miami and pulled into Miami Beach about 10 AM. I had decided not to stay with Mrs. Smith but to stay on at Miami Beach and make this time a few days of a real vacation. Driving south on Collins Avenue, I was looking for an affordable hotel. I stopped at a red light, and I remember that the car radio was playing, "Yellow Polka-dot Bikini," one of the top hits of the day. While I was waiting for a green light, I looked to my left and saw a large hotel, the Sea Gull. It looked impressive. I hesitated for few seconds, then decided at the last minute—before the light turned green—to turn left into the driveway, when I saw a large banner advertising that a convention was being held there. I thought that this might mean that there'd be a party atmosphere going on. I pulled into the driveway to the entrance and got out of the car. A bellboy was instantly there to help me with my baggage, which included a suitcase, a couple of shirts, and a couple pair of trousers on hangers, and a shaving kit.

It was a beautiful hotel. I was somewhat embarrassed by my lack of luggage. Nevertheless, I checked in at the main desk and the bellboy took me up to the room. It was very nice and had a view of the ocean. The bellboy, seeing that I was alone and assuming that I was there to meet some women, called my attention to three young ladies sitting on lounge chairs down at poolside. He told me that they had just come down from Pittsburgh the night before. He even suggested that they might be here to "meet someone." I thanked him, gave him a tip, and went to the bathroom to freshen up. Little did I know that within the next couple of hours, I would meet and eventually fall in love with the woman I would marry, raise five children with, and with whom I have lived with for nearly sixty years.

I put on my swim trunks, grabbed a towel and my camera, and went down to the pool. I took a lounge chair within talking distance of these three pretty women and struggled with loading my camera as a ruse to perhaps gain their attention. None of them responded with an offer to help me, but they were friendly and responded to my casual "hello."

All of a sudden, a brief rainstorm came right over us. We all took cover under a sheltered area and exchanged small talk. When the rainstorm subsided as quickly as it had begun, we all returned to our lounge chairs. The hot Miami sun suddenly popped out. It felt good—warm against my skin. I introduced myself to the three young women, and they told me their names. One girl, the one closest to me, said her name was Delores. She was by far the best looking of the three, and I immediately set my sights on her. The girl sitting in the middle was Marge, a brunette, and, on the far chair, was Jo Ann. I found out later that Delores was also instantly attracted to me as I was attracted to her.

I thought that maybe I could lure her to the pool, so I said I was going to take a swim and jumped in. Well, my plan worked perfectly, as Delores quickly joined me. Much later, she told me that she knew that neither of her two friends knew how to swim, but she did. As I recall, she was a very good swimmer. The water and the hot sun felt so good. We spent some quality time together, frolicking in pool. As we talked, we began to really hit it off. I don't remember too much, but Delores told me many years later that I had put my arm around her for the first time in the pool—and she was thrilled. At some point, we left the pool and went down to the beach, leaving the other girls behind. Of course, playing in the water and the surf, lying on a blanket, only brought us closer together. I was so glad that I had met her!

Miami Beach, Florida, Seagull Hotel. June 1960.

I learned that her full name was Delores Mae Gregorovich, and that she was from North Braddock, Pennsylvania, a suburb of Pittsburgh and an old steel mill town. She was of Slovakian ancestry, a Catholic, 26 years old, single, never married, and had a good job at U.S. Steel in North Braddock. Her mother and father were from the old country in Eastern Europe. She was the youngest of ten siblings.

Delores had a beautiful slender figure. She was fair skinned, with green eyes, blonde hair, and really nice legs. She was also very shy and soft spoken. I loved that quality about her! But I found that she was not shy about laughing. She had a wonderful laugh! It was full and sincere. I'd certainly had my fill of a mean, loud-mouthed screaming woman.

Delores and I were together for most of the afternoon. At some point, I invited her to go out that evening, and to my great delight, she accepted! We went to a nice restaurant in Miami that I knew about, and we had a very nice dinner. I learned that Delores had an easy, comfortable manner, and she laughed easily and appropriately. Looking back, I remember that I loved her sense of humor right away, which seemed to fit with mine.

After supper we went to a popular dance club, had some drinks, and danced to some of the most popular songs of the time. The song, *Since I Met You, Baby*, became "our" song—our dance song, and we must have danced several times to it that night. The song, *Walking to New Orleans*, by Fats Domino, was at the top of the charts. We later played it over and over. These songs became "our" songs, and from then on, every time we heard one of these songs, we would experience all over again those warm, sweet memories of that long-ago magical night when we danced, held each other close, and, yes, fell in love. We hadn't yet spoken the words, "I love you." That would come later. But, we felt it then.

Later that night, on our way back to Miami Beach on the MacArthur Causeway, I pulled off the road and parked. From this point, we could see the skyline and the lights of Miami Beach basking in the warm glow of a silver moon. It was a soft, warm, summer evening, and this combination of lights, drinks, music, the passion of youth, and a tender kiss, made it easy to fall in love.

When we returned to the hotel, I had some ideas in my mind that, I was soon to learn, were not shared by Delores. I had thought (and hoped), like most red-blooded males my age, that she would come up to my room and we could have sex, and that she might even stay with me overnight. Well, I soon learned that Delores, while she was seriously attracted to me—and probably in love with me, as I was with her—had no intention of being that intimate. I learned that it was one of her fundamental values to save herself for her husband. When it came to being intimate, she drew a line that she would never cross.

It played out like this: I invited her up to my room, telling her that it had a wonderful view of the ocean. After looking at that view, Delores said, "Thanks for a wonderful evening," and she gave me a quick hug and kiss. Then she turned and left the room. I must say, I was a bit shocked—and disappointed. This was not the perfect ending to the wonderful evening that I had in mind, and I wasn't happy. But one thing I learned was that Delores was a strong-willed person who would never violate her personal honor and sense of what was right or wrong. Well, so be it!

Over the next two or three days, we were together a lot. Time had passed too quickly, but now I had to go back to Camp Lejeune. Delores and her friends were scheduled to leave the next day for Pittsburgh. She and I had a sweet but sad goodbye, especially since we hadn't set up a specific time or place when would see each again.

I believe, however, that we both understood that we would definitely see one another again, and that we were very serious about this relationship.

During the next couple of months, Delores and I talked by phone several times and exchanged quite a few letters. While we were in Miami, we hadn't actually made any commitments to one another, but I think it was clear to both of us that we considered our relationship to be at least, a very serious boyfriend/girlfriend relationship and possibly the beginning of something big.

In August, Delores surprised me when she called and told me she was coming to see me and would be staying several days. She was planning on flying in, and would I meet her at the airport at New Bern, North Carolina (a town not far from Camp Lejeune)? Since she was on vacation, we had decided that she would stay in Surf City in a motel right on the beach.

Surf City is a small beachfront community on Topsail Island in Onslow and Pender Counties on the Atlantic coast. It's mostly supported by tourism and has several souvenir shops, a couple of bars, and a nice little cafe. The magnificent beachfront was within easy walking distance of the motel. There's not a lot to do on this stretch of coastline—no dance halls, nightclubs, or carnival rides for kids, etc. In fact, the area is rather isolated, making it a perfect place for lovers, where they can frolic in the surf, lie on a blanket under the sun, or play in the sand. There always seemed to be a gentle breeze wafting in from the ocean, which was fairly warm at that time of year. This was the perfect place for lovers to be alone together. For Dolores and me, it was perfect.

The next several days were magical. It was crazy how fast the time passed! We spent a lot of time walking on the beach and eating snacks and burgers at the small cafe, where we played our favorite songs on the jukebox, "Since I Met You Baby," and "Walking to New Orleans," over and over again.

I told Delores that I wanted her to meet one of my best friends in the Marine Corps, Sgt. John Mac Laughlin, and his wife, Dorine, a dear lady whom we came to love. Delores said she'd be happy to meet Mac (as we all called him) and Dorine. Mac, worked with me at the Refrigeration and Air Conditioning School. He was an outstanding Marine and instructor, and I valued his opinion about things.

The couple lived in a mobile home near the base. They had one child at the time, a son named John. I had told Mac that I was very serious about this girl I had met in Miami. However, having made such a terrible mistake in the past in marrying Connie after such a brief, torrid, relationship, and, against all the advice of family and friends, I was very afraid of making the same mistake twice. I encouraged Mac to invite us for dinner with him and Dorine. Afterward, I wanted them to tell me what they thought of her and to compare her with another girl, Gerry, whom I had been dating before I met Delores. I had previously brought Gerry to dinner at their house. (I know this may sound rather crude to some, and perhaps even unfair to Delores, since we were comparing her to another woman without her knowledge.) I was able to justify it without a guilty conscious, however, and later on, thankfully, Delores wasn't angry when I told her the entire story. In fact, she thought it was pretty funny, and was, of course, very happy that she had won "the contest" hands down.

Mac and Dorine really liked Delores, and I was so proud of her. Likewise, Delores really liked them. Mac is a great storyteller, and Delores laughed delightedly at his stories. As we were leaving their place, Mac and I went outside first and had a few minutes to chat while Dorine and Delores were inside saying their goodbyes. I asked Mac what he thought about Delores. I don't recall his exact words, but I do recall that he was very impressed with her and said that she had certainly won his vote. All in all, he thought she was great.

It was at some point around this time, seeing Delores again, feeling her nearness, her warmth, and seeing more and more how she reacted and related to other people, I knew that I wanted to marry her. But now I had to find the perfect time to ask her if she would marry me. It takes a lot of courage to ask this question, as every guy knows, because . . . *what if she says no*? Sometimes, for me, gathering up that much courage takes alcohol—maybe some good whiskey.

Back at the motel that evening, Delores and I were feeling especially close. I was nursing a bad cold and had brought a bottle of Jack Daniels, which I preferred to any other cold medicine. After a couple of drinks of Jack, my cold seemed to be better and I had a slight buzz on. Delores didn't like whiskey, so she politely abstained. Feeling rather amorous (with Jack's help), I sprung the question. I asked Delores if she would marry me. She accepted! *Wow*!

We were both so happy! As it turns out, we had both been secretly thinking of this since the time we met at Miami Beach, but we hadn't revealed our true feelings to each other or to anyone else. Now that our future with one another was to become a reality, suddenly a lot of pressure was relieved, and we were finally free to tell everyone about it and openly show our joy. Well, rejoice we did, and we couldn't wait to tell anyone and everyone!

The next few days passed very quickly, and all too soon it was time for Delores to go home. I took her to the airport. We were feeling a bit melancholy, because we knew that being separated was going to be tough, and we both had a lot to think about. We had to consider things like, when would we get married? Where? I had to find a decent place for us to live near the base. We would also have to come up with a plan for me to come to North Braddock and meet her family. So many things to think about . . . but we so were excited about our future!

CHAPTER 23

TOGETHER AT LAST!

My job was going well, and I was heading into my third year as an Instructor. I knew that the Marine Corps didn't keep a person on a specific base indefinitely. The Marine Corps has an established rotation system that monitors each MOS, so that overseas assignments are fairly assigned. I hadn't served overseas except for two temporary training exercises in Puerto Rico in 1955 and 1956.

I had known that the time would soon come when I would receive orders overseas. I certainly didn't want to go overseas, with Delores and I planning to get married. I put in some serious time thinking and praying about what action I could take to better my career, and, at the same time, avoid overseas assignments as long as possible. Then, as if in answer to my prayers, a bulletin came in announcing that the Parris Island, South Carolina, Marine Corp Recruit Depot was seeking qualified Marines to become Drill Instructors.

Marine boot camp at Parris Island is legendary, as are its Drill Instructors. Parris Island was one of two bases where the Marine Corps conducts its basic training. The other base is Marine Corps Recruit Depot (MCRD) in San Diego, California. These are the two locations where recruits are subjected to the most rigorous military training possible. Marine Corps training had always been known as the toughest training of any of our military services.

A Drill Instructor selection team would be at Camp Lejeune in the near future. The senior staff where I worked encouraged me to apply for this position, because they knew that having a successful tour of duty as a Drill Instructor was the best thing I could do to enhance my career. Also, if I was accepted and became a Drill Instructor, I wouldn't be ordered overseas for at least two or three years.

I knew from the beginning that I had very little chance of being selected, as Corporals are seldom assigned that duty. There was another consideration: Drill Instructor's school was arguably the most difficult school in the Marine Corps, with a high dropout rate. If I was accepted but failed the course, I would likely be sent overseas immediately.

As I weighed my options, I made the decision to bet on myself that I could make it through the school. I submitted my application. My friend, Mac, also submitted an application. Within a couple of weeks, we were notified that we had been selected for an interview by the selection team. The selection team was notoriously tough, and we couldn't determine whether we had made a good impression or not. All we could do was to wait.

Delores and I kept in touch through phone calls and letters. We were very excited and impatient to be together, but there were a lot of decisions to be made. I was eager to meet her family, and she was excited to meet mine. In mid-October, I went to Pittsburg for the weekend. I was looking at about twelve hours of intense driving, but I mainly went so that I could meet Delores's family—and she had a lot of family! She was excited to show me off.

I left Camp Lejeune at about five p.m. on Friday and rolled into North Braddock at about six a.m. on Saturday. I had driven all night. It's funny how when you're young and in love you can do things like that! Delores was waiting for me with open arms. It was so good to see her!

My True Love, Delores Gregorovich

Pittsburgh was in the throes of a celebration, as the Pittsburgh Pirates had just won the World Series. What a glorious time to be in Pittsburg! You could almost feel the excitement and magic in the air. We didn't have much time for celebration, however, because we had a lot of things to do.

I was excited but nervous to meet Delores's family. That Saturday night, she took me to her family gathering. They all were eager to meet the man who had won Delores's heart. She was the baby of the family and 26 years old. Other men had tried to woo her and had failed. All of her relatives wanted Delores to meet a good, stable man who had a future. I knew that they would be tough but fair evaluators. Just who was this man from Kansas—this career Marine—who was a teacher of some sort, had been married before, and had a small child? And, to add to the mix, he wasn't Catholic. How does that figure in?

I had looked forward to meeting Delores's father, Charles Gregorovich. I wanted to make a good impression. Delores's mother, Anna, had passed away before I met Delores. Anna (Fiyalko) Gregorovich had ten children, with Delores being the youngest. Delores was twenty-two years old in 1956 when her mother died. Her siblings, by name, oldest to youngest, were: Margaret (known as Peg) Ann, Helen, Elsie (deceased at that time), Wilma, Paul, Albert (known as Abe), Charles (known as Chuck), and Emily.

Most of these siblings had spouses and children. In addition, there were several longtime friends of the family to include. Counting the entire extended family and friends, there were perhaps thirty people.

Being there for one of Delores's family gatherings was a unique experience. I learned that an event of this kind usually takes place in the kitchen of her father's house. It was a combined kitchen and dining room that held a large old table and chairs, along with some appliances. Hers is an ethnic family, and some of the older folks spoke in their native Slovak language, though most of the conversation was in English, with a few native words and phrases thrown in from time to time.

First meeting Delores, Miami Beach. 1960

There was a wonderfully free flow of language, jokes, stories, with a lot of it being spoken at the same time. I told Delores much later on that it was kind of like having ten TV sets placed in a circle facing each other, each turned way up, and all on different channels. I wasn't sure if that made Delores a little mad at me, but if it did, she didn't show it. But, in truth, I had observed the same behavior with my own family. The only difference was there were a lot less of us.

At the gathering, there were a lot of dishes with snacks and treats, with plenty of beer around the table. (The whisky drinking was more discrete.) There were a number of children running around, and some teenagers that floated in and out doing whatever it is that teenagers do. It was a memorable occasion for me.

Delores's family often got together to celebrate a holiday or someone's birthday, or whatever; or maybe they just wanted to get together for the fun of it. My first time as a part of the family turned out to be fun, though I admit, it was a bit stressful. Delores's brother, Albert, known by all who knew him as Abe, quickly became one of my best friends and was like a brother to me over the many years I would know him. By contrast, my own extended family rarely got together because we lived so far apart. And even when we did, there was only a fraction of the number of people that were part of Delores's family.

When the weekend was over and I returned to work, I had to focus on my teaching, because a new refrigeration class was due to start the next week. I worked hard and enjoyed teaching.

Much to my surprise, I did receive orders to be transferred to Parris Island, South Carolina, to attend Drill Instructor's school. Mac also was selected and received the same orders. I had almost forgotten that I had made application to go to the school. Wow! I had been selected for Drill Instructor's school, an honor in itself! I'd been interviewed and screened, but I didn't think that I would be selected. During the screening process, the screening team from Drill Instructor's school had told me that very few Corporals are selected for the school. Because of that, I had thought my chances were quite remote. So you can imagine that I was thrilled to get the orders! This now became another factor that Delores and I had to work into our marriage plans.

It was important for me to focus on preparing myself to go to D.I. School. I had to get my uniforms in top shape, make sure that my shoes and boots were highly shined, and begin a daily exercise routine.

When I began my exercise program, I focused primarily on jogging to get my cardiovascular system good shape. I also went through the process of checking out of my unit. This entailed using a so-called "Checkout Sheet" that listed all the various departments to finish up, like clearing up any business with them, etc. For example, I had to turn in all my field gear, packs, and cartridge belts, and the supply department had to sign the sheet. There were numerous other departments, including medical, dental and pay records. It was always a happy time when all the necessary signatures had been collected and I could turn the sheet in to the company office. Then, on the effective date of your orders, you could pick up the official orders and depart from the base.

Finally the time arrived when I was all checked out and ready to depart for Parris Island. I had arranged to take four or five days leave, in conjunction with the travel time required to get from Camp Lejeune, North Carolina, to Parris Island, South Carolina. My plan was to go to North Braddock to see Delores for a few days before reporting in to Parris Island. On the afternoon of the day before I was to depart, I was notified that my orders had been cancelled! The reason given was that my MOS as a Refrigeration Instructor was considered a critical skill at the Engineering Schools. Someone decided that my services as a Refrigeration Instructor were more important than those of a Drill Instructor at Parris Island.

What was I going to do? Go on leave as planned, or check back in with each department and go to work tomorrow morning? I decided to go ahead and take the leave and go to Pennsylvania to see

Delores. Then, when my leave was finished, I'd return, check back in, and report back to my job and continue to teach.

I called Delores and told her what happened and that I was taking the leave, and was heading out that evening for North Braddock. The company office had informed me that it was likely at some point that I would again receive orders to D.I. school when a new class of Drill Instructors was convening—and if my Refrigeration MOS came off the critical list.

I left Courthouse Bay that evening heading north to Pittsburgh. Once again, the drive took all night. Delores was waiting to greet me. I checked into a motel, where I could have some privacy to rest and be more comfortable than at Delores's relative's house. The next few days, she and I sort of just hung out together, enjoying one another's company, and then on Saturday and Sunday, she took me to see various famous sites in and around Pittsburgh. We had a great time together, and we began making plans about when and where we would get married. It was all very exciting.

Because Delores was a Catholic and I a Protestant, and I having been married before, we had to rule out being married in the Catholic Church, which was fine with me. (I wasn't in favor of getting married there.) Most of her immediate family were devout practicing Catholics, as was Delores, and we knew that if we told anyone in her family of our plans, they would want to discuss and argue about it to no end.

Not wanting to hurt anyone's feelings, we decided that we would sort of "run away" and get married and not tell anyone until it was done. Delores knew that her family really liked me, and ultimately they would approve of our marriage once it was done. We also decided that I would come back to North Braddock in the days between Christmas and New Years, and we'd get married during that time.

Pennsylvania had a three-day waiting period to obtain a marriage license, but since the state of Maryland didn't have a waiting period, we'd just drive there. It wasn't very far away, so we'd just get married, come back to North Braddock, and surprise everyone! (Delores did tell several of her very close girl friends of our plans.)

I returned to North Braddock two days after Christmas. Delores and I happily planned for our wedding. Then our plan to "run away" to Maryland had to be cancelled thanks to a huge snowstorm! However, we learned that because I was an active duty service member, the three-day waiting period was waived! We were able to finalize everything and make arrangements to be married by a local Justice of the Peace on the evening of December 30, 1960. Delores had asked two of her very special friends, Joan and Bernie, to stand with us as witnesses for the wedding ceremony.

Most of Delores's family were planning to go to her brother Paul's place to get a head start on celebrating New Year's Eve, which, I learned, was a custom in her family. Because it could be dangerous, they didn't want to be out and about on New Year's Eve. Therefore, it was easy for us to get dressed up and leave the house with them having no clue that we were going to go get married instead of going to the party.

Delores wore a stunningly beautiful white dress. She looked so pretty and just glowed with happiness. We met Joan and Bernie at the home of the Justice of the Peace. The Justice and his wife were very accommodating and invited us into the living room of their very nice home. When we were all ready, we took our places in the living room. We said our vows sincerely and with emotion, and within a few minutes, the Justice pronounced us man and wife. We were married! Wow, how excited we were! I could hardly believe it! This beautiful woman, and all she stood for, was my wife! Yes, we were going to have a great life together.

Married, December 30, 1960. Pittsburgh, Pennsylvania.

After the wedding, we went to her brother Paul's house. When we arrived, the party was in full swing. It took them all only a few minutes to realize that we had just gotten married. Someone had either known or suspected that that was what we were up to. Once they knew the truth, everyone cheered, and they right away began drinking toasts to our happiness, and whatever else they could think of to drink to. It was such a happy time! I felt like they had accepted me whole-heartedly into the family.

Before the party ended, Delores and I slipped away. We had made reservations for our wedding night at the Hilton Hotel in downtown Pittsburgh, on the Point, where the Monongahela and Allegheny Rivers meet to form the Ohio River. It was a beautiful hotel, and we had a luxurious room. The view of downtown Pittsburgh and nearly the entire metro area were visible from our room. It was stunning, especially with all the holiday lights everywhere and with the ground covered by a soft blanket of white snow.

I remember thinking, "Well, you old Marine, you are doing pretty good for yourself! Here you are, in this beautiful hotel, with a pretty, sexy woman who you just married, driving a new car—compared to not long ago when you were about to croak in wet, cold infantry training, dragging yourself around at Camp Geiger!"

We stayed up most of the night, slept in late, and in the morning went down to the fancy dining room for a breakfast brunch. We still could hardly believe we were married. It took both of us quite a while to get used to that feeling.

We checked out of the Hilton and into a motel closer to North Braddock. There wasn't a refrigerator in the room, so I stowed my beer in a deep snowdrift right outside the door of our room. I stayed around for several more days, mostly visiting her family members and spent the New Year there before having to head back to Camp

Lejeune. We had fun planning how we were going to begin setting up our household together. Delores still had to decide when to give notice to her employer, U.S. Steel, and I had to find a place for us to live outside of Camp Lejeune.

With all the sweet sadness of newlyweds parting, I left my new bride in North Braddock and returned to Camp Lejeune. Finding a suitable place for us to live was difficult. Courthouse Bay is not close to the town of Jacksonville and regular base housing. We wanted to find a place as near as possible to Courthouse Bay. The closest community where we might be able to find a home was in a little old fishing and farming community named Snead's Ferry. It was out the back gate and on the other side, and directly across the Bay from the barracks and work areas of the Marines who were stationed at Courthouse Bay. There were no new apartments there, and it appeared that no new construction was in progress.

After a lot of inquiries, I was feeling discouraged. Then, one of my Marine friends gave me a lead. There was a small private trailer park right across the water from the barracks where I lived and worked! If we owned a little boat, the trip would take only about five minutes. The owner had a small trailer home available for rent. I looked at it and found that it was very nice inside, but small. It also had a covered porch.

I was in a quandary. The trailer was situated in the last space in the park, and therefore, the one side of the trailer was next to a wooded area. It was easy to hear the hooting of owls at night. And, the short road off the blacktop was dirt. Would it get muddy when it rained? Also, just across this dirt road was a large field that was fenced in by a single strand of electric wire to keep the pigs in the field. The farmer who owned this field had just harvested a crop of peanuts, and the pigs were put out there to graze on the old peanut vines and peanuts that had been missed by the harvesting machine. If the pigs were grazing nearby, it was easy to hear their grunts. It might even be scary at night if a person didn't know anything about pigs and the noises they made.

Considering all options, it still seemed like this would be okay, at least in the short term. I paid for one month's rent, and our hunt for housing was over—for the present. I really didn't know how Delores would react to living in this very rural area in a tiny trailer house across the road from a pig and peanut farm! This poor, old community and little trailer on a dirt road was far removed from the modern city life to which Delores was accustomed. Would she like it? Could she adapt to it? Only time would tell.

We communicated almost every day by phone or letter during this time. We were both excited and anxious to be together. I told her about the difficulty I'd had in finding a place for us to live. When I told her about the trailer house that I had rented, she said she was excited to see it!

During this time period apart, Delores' family and friends had a wedding shower for her. It was a great success, and I wished that I could have been there. We received a lot of wonderful gifts—just the things we needed to set up a home. We were very thankful and humbled by the generosity of everyone.

CHAPTER 24

BEGINNING OUR LIFE TOGETHER

On February 14, 1961, I traveled to North Braddock, Pennsylvania, to move my bride to Camp Lejeune, North Carolina. I left my car at the base and shared a ride with another Marine who was traveling to Pittsburgh that day. Our plan was to pack all of Delores's clothing and personal items into her car and drive to Camp Lejeune. She had a really nice car—a 1956 four-door Chevy Bel Air.

We spent a whole day just getting her things packed and into the car. We planned to leave in the late afternoon of the 15th. Most of her family was there to say their goodbyes. This was a big deal for them! They were saying goodbye to their baby! She was leaving the nest and going off with her husband, a U.S. Marine, and there was no telling what adventures and hardships might lie ahead.

It was obvious that they were all very sad at her leaving, and tears flowed freely. I promised them that I would take care of her, and I felt a deep obligation to do just that. We had planned to get on the road in the late afternoon. However, with everyone gathered together, the time just flew bye, and pretty soon, we had a party atmosphere going. There was singing and dancing, while I played guitar. By the time we were winding down, it was almost 9 o'clock p.m. An unexpected heavy snowstorm had settled in for the night! We decided that we were not going to let that spoil our plans.

We headed out about nine or ten, planning to take the Pennsylvania Turnpike to the Breezewood exit, which was over a hundred miles east from Pittsburg. When we got out on the Turnpike, not many cars were traveling at that time. We were making new tracks in about three to four inches of snow as we headed east, with more snow still falling. It was actually pretty exciting for us! This was our first big adventure together, and we weren't afraid of anything.

In fact, if we had only known, this would be just the beginning of a great many dangerous and risky adventures by which we'd be challenged in our future together. We figured that if we could just make it to the Breezewood exit, we'd be able to get a motel there, where we could spend the night. In looking back, it seems like a crazy thing to do—heading out late at night in a storm like that. But we were young then and afraid of nothing. Delores's car was a heavy solid car that did really well in the snow.

It was after midnight when we got to Breezewood. We took the exit and immediately found a nice motel. We were tired but excited. It was almost like having another honeymoon—a nice warm room, a clean bed, and soft snow falling: a perfect time for snuggling with the one you love.

The n ext morning, we headed south through Virginia toward North Carolina. The snowing had stopped, but there were about four inches on the ground to drive through. The hills and the narrow two-lane road on which we were driving presented quite a challenge.

Not long after starting out, we had a flat tire along the narrow, snow-covered highway. I pulled over as far as possible off the road to change it. I had to remove everything from the trunk to get to the spare tire and jack. Large trucks traveling through were able to slip by with only inches to spare. In spite of the difficulties, we got the tire changed and continued on south. The further we went, the less snow we encountered, until we finally had a clear road to travel on.

It was getting late as we approached Camp Lejeune. By the time we arrived at Snead's Ferry and our first home, the little trailer, it was dark. It was *really* dark! Here we were, out in the country, with no streetlights. I was kind of anxious to see how Delores reacted to her new surroundings. When we pulled in, parked beside the trailer, and got out of the car, it was a bit spooky, especially with the grazing hogs nearby, grunting. My wonderful bride was excited and didn't seem a bit intimidated by the situation! I was so proud of her!

We unloaded some items from the car, went in, and began to set up our first home. We were both looking forward to our new challenges. Over the next few days we went grocery shopping, and I drove her around to get her acquainted with the area. We went to the base so that I could show her where I worked, and we also picked up my car, which was parked at the barracks parking lot.

CHAPTER 25

A HOME FOR BOBBIE

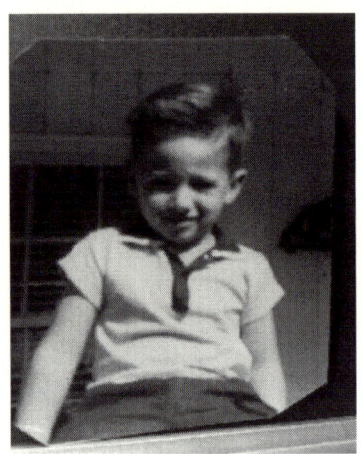

From the time we had first met, I'd told Delores that I'd been married before and had one child, a little boy named, Bobbie, Jr., and that in the final divorce, I had agreed to give custody of Bobbie to my first wife, Connie. I had done this this because I was single and lived in the barracks and knew that I couldn't possibly care for him while in this situation. Delores knew that Connie's mother, Mrs. Smith, had been caring for Bobbie because Connie had recently pretty much abandoned him. I had also told Delores that when we married, I was going to file a lawsuit to obtain custody of Bobbie.

Delores was fine with this and said that she looked forward to caring for him. Delores, being the youngest of her siblings, had a lot of experience taking care of their children while they were growing up. She genuinely loved children and was, in my opinion, a natural mother.

We wanted Bobbie to finally have a place that he could call home, with parents to care for him. I had learned that he hadn't had the best of care in recent months, as Mrs. Smith had been ill and Bobbie had been taken to first one baby sitter and then another, as she tried to work and manage her illness *and* care for Bobbie! Please know that this is no criticism of Mrs. Smith. I always cared for her and looked upon her as a very dear woman who did her absolute best to care for her only grandchild at the time.

In March 1959, the Dade County court had granted a divorce to Connie and me, which assigned custody of Bobbie to Connie. Not long after Delores and I were married, I filed a lawsuit requesting that the Court modify the final decree of divorce and grant custody of Bobbie to me. Shortly after getting settled in our trailer home, I was notified that I would have to appear in court in Miami on March 2, 1961, to attend a hearing on the custody of Bobbie. Mrs. Smith had signed an agreement to give custody over to me, as Connie had disappeared, leaving Bobbie in her care.

Delores and I made plans to drive to Miami to make that appearance, and if Connie didn't show up to contest the change of custody, I would likely be given custody and be able to bring Bobbie home with us. Delores and I chose to look upon this as a short holiday trip instead of as a chore. And we both loved Miami! I thought that I could drive it straight through overnight, but I soon became too tired. Somewhere around West Palm Beach we pulled over in a rest stop and slept in the car for a couple of hours. The sun, shining through the car windows, woke us up.

That same afternoon, I appeared in court as scheduled. Connie did not appear to contest the matter, so the judge granted custody to me. Delores and I went to Mrs. Smith's house to pick up Bobbie. Mrs. Smith was kind and magnanimous about the whole matter, giving up her grandson that she loved, knowing that she might never see him again.

After a short visit, we loaded up all Bobbie's clothing and some personal items and started back on the long trip to North Carolina. We made the trip with frequent rest stops, but we didn't stop to get a motel. This whole thing had been a lot to ask of a new bride. But Delores held up like a real trooper, as we both faced being parents so shortly after getting married. I think we both felt optimistic about our future. I was so happy to finally have my little boy to raise! I wanted to be a good father to him.

We were glad to get back to our little trailer and finally begin our day-to-day life together. It was fun, and we delighted in learning more about each other. We explored Snead's Ferry, which was more of a small community than a town. There was only a post office and one very old general store, which carried a large variety of items certainly not found in the stores of Pittsburgh, Los Angeles, or Miami. It was fun! There was a dock area where the fishermen docked everyday with their catch. Most of them were willing to sell part of their catch of the day, which included flounder, sea bass, trout, shrimp, and oysters, and clams. Several times, Delores went down to this area and bought some of this fresh seafood and tried her hand at preparing and cooking it. She did a great job! There also was a gas station, and, just a few miles up the road, a popular seafood restaurant. After we discovered this restaurant, we were regular customers, because their menu included the very best fresh seafood. I remember that our favorite items were the broiled flounder, the fried oysters, and the hushpuppies. We also visited Mac and Dorine frequently, as they lived nearby.

CHAPTER 26

DRILL INSTRUCTOR DUTY, PARRIS ISLAND, BEAUFORT, SOUTH CAROLINA

Just as we began to feel like we were getting settled in together, I received orders to Parris Island, South Carolina, to attend Drill Instructor's School. This time, I was told there would be no cancellation of orders like before—I was really going this time. My friend Mac was on the same orders, so we'd be in the same class. The orders required that we report in for duty no later than June 29, 1961. Mac (Sgt. John McLaughlin, U.S. Marine Corps) was one of my best Marine Corps friends. He was one tough ol' Marine. Strong-built, with square shoulders and hips, he was sort of like a cement block, and I sure wouldn't want to fight him.

We met when he was a student at the Refrigeration School and I was an Instructor. When he, too, was chosen to stay on as an Instructor, our friendship was sealed. In our off-duty hours, we had hung out together a lot, hunting rabbits, squirrels, and quail together in North Carolina and out on the little islands surrounding Parris Island.

I knew that Mac would make a very good Drill Instructor. Delores and I were very happy about the prospect of moving to South Carolina and glad that our Marine friends were going, too! We knew that the old historical town of Beaufort was right outside the gate of Parris Island, and we were eager to see it. Nevertheless, although we were excited about our orders and the move, in the back of my mind, I knew that I was facing what would likely be the most difficult school in the Marine Corps. Failure was not an option.

We immediately began to plan our trip to Beaufort with Mac and Dorine. Mac and I picked up our orders from Engineer Schools Battalion on June 8th, and we began our journey together the following day, each of us pulling a small U-Haul trailer heading South on old Highway 17, the same road that I'd hitchhiked on so many times before. I was excited but a bit awed by the idea: I was going to be a Drill Instructor! Did I have what it takes?

We really enjoyed our trip, stopping several times to take a break and eat. It was twilight when we all pulled into Beaufort. We found a motel on the outskirts of town and checked in for the night. The next day, working with a realtor, we both found places to live, although we weren't too impressed with the quality of housing that appeared to be available. But, as "old Marines," it would be okay—at least we had a place to drop our packs and live while going to school.

The apartment that Delores and I found, named Beaufort Gardens, was close to town. It was probably the best we could do with the time we had, so we paid the first month's rent and moved our things in. It wasn't very fancy, that's for sure—definitely not the kind of place where you'd have a wedding reception. The structure was made with cinder blocks and was in need of a paint job. There was no air conditioning, and we soon found out that the screens on the windows had holes large enough for hordes of mosquitos to enter. It was summertime and very hot. Welcome to South Carolina!

We were anxious to get settled in a bit, because we wanted to go to Kansas to visit my mom and dad and introduce them to Delores. They were really looking forward to meeting her, as she was to meeting them. After we felt like we'd gotten things somewhat organized, we told Mac and Dorine, "So long for now!" and we headed for Kansas. We had to return with enough time to finish getting settled and also check in to D.I. School.

The day passed swiftly as we rolled along toward Kansas, and soon darkness overtook us. Delores and Bobbie leaned back to take a nap. As I drove along in the quiet darkness, I tried to piece together in my mind everything I had read and heard about Parris Island and boot camp. It was, indeed, a legendary place, and long before the first rays of the South Carolina sun beamed across the tidal marshlands surrounding Beaufort and Parris Island, the Drill Instructors have begun their long days work of transforming young recruits into that special breed of soldier, the Marine.

Meanwhile, the blue herons, marsh hens, and hundreds of the other species of wildlife in those marshes, as they have for eons, go about their daily cycle of life, which amounts to searching for their daily sustenance and mating, oblivious to Drill Instructors, recruits, and their pain, toil and suffering.

For recruits, reveille comes early, 5:00 a.m. For the Drill Instructor, however, it begins much earlier. The D.I. must rise, shave, shower, and square away his uniform, shine his shoes and be ready to awaken the recruits at 5:00. It's important that he be immaculate, both in his appearance and manner, regardless of the hour.

Probably more has been written, both fact and fiction, and more stories told about Drill Instructors than any other group of

Marines, including in popular movies like, *The D.I.,* starring Jack Webb, and, more recently, *Full Metal Jacket,* starring Gunnery Sergeant. R. Lee Ermey. And, every Marine remembers, for the rest of his life, whether fondly or in angst, their Drill Instructors. In many ways, the title "Marine Drill Instructor" has become synonymous in the public eye with the idea of harshness, perfection, and military professionalism. Well, very soon, now, I was going to get my chance to enter into the lofty realm, the subject of legend: the Marine Drill Instructor. Would I measure up?

But that would have to wait just a bit longer. For the present, Delores and I were feeling happy and carefree. Delores, Bobbie, and I were headed to Kansas to see my family. We actually felt like we were on a big new adventure, and it was exciting! The drive was long, but we had an almost new car, and we stopped to sleep one night at a motel. I couldn't help but wonder, as I was driving, how Delores was going to react to life on the farm, where, in this case there was no indoor plumbing, no hot water, and a stinky outhouse instead of a bathroom, and, of course, no air conditioning.

Mom and Dad and my sisters, Betty, Margaret, Dorothy, and Judy, welcomed us with open arms and warm hugs. It was summertime in Kansas, hot, but a new adventure every minute for Delores and Bobbie! I had a great time showing them around the farm and taking them for a walk down on Lost Creek. I showed them how to milk the cows, feed the chickens and pigs, and care for the horses. I could tell that Mom and Dad had already fallen in love with Delores. And she fell for them, too. It was really great for me to see how well they all got along, compared to the short, tragic, and painful relationship with Connie four years earlier. That awful time still rests in the deep recesses of my mind like a horrible nightmare. In some ways, I felt like I had redeemed myself by bringing this wonderful woman, Delores, home to my folks as their new daughter-in-law. I was so proud of her!

In June 1961 I received orders to report to Drill Instructors School, Parris Island, South Carolina. Delores and I found a place to live in Beaufort, a town just outside of the base. Prior to the commencement of school I and Delores drove to Kansas to visit folks. My parents got to meet Delores for the first time, and I was so proud to introduce Delores my folks.

Kansas is at its best in June. Life is blooming everywhere: fresh garden vegetables for the table, sunflowers in full, bright yellow bloom, daisies, daffodils, dandelions, and the ubiquitous grasshoppers, butterflies, bees, horse flies, house flies, and even an indolent moth, resting on a window pane. We even found time to go bass fishing in an old farm pond where I had fished as a boy. I was lucky and pulled out several large bass. Cleaned and fried in cornmeal and flour, fresh bass has a unique sweet, delicate taste all its own. It's simply delicious, especially with warm cornbread, and a fresh garden salad.

But, as they say, all good things must come to an end, and too soon we had to say goodbye to the wonders of Kansas in June and head back to South Carolina.

On June 29th, I checked in at Drill Instructor's School, and classes began a few days later. D.I. School was everything it was alleged to be, and even tougher in many ways. It took everything I could muster in terms of physical and mental energy, every single day, just to get through the day's classes.

It also took Delores helping me a lot! On many nights, while I sat soaking my aching feet in cool Epsom salt water, trying to memorize the drill manual, Delores was ironing my uniforms or shining my shoes. And, on many of those hot, sultry nights, we slapped mosquitos most of the night, trying to sleep, and we sweat until the sheets were wet.

It seemed like we never got enough sleep, as reveille came early at our house. Since I had to be at the base and in the barracks at 05:00, we had to get up at 03:30. But, we worked together to help me make it through that torturous school.

Well, it was finally over, and I graduated on August 18, 1961— and proudly, near the top of the class. At the graduation ceremony we were issued our long, sought-after, and revered Campaign Hat, the badge of distinction for the Drill Instructor. I was honored to wear that hat, and while I had it on, I always carried myself tall and proud, with a professional demeanor. After graduation, I was issued my orders to the 2nd Recruit Training Battalion for duty. I was ready—thrilled to begin my job as a Drill Instructor!

Cpl. B. G. Lay

JDI

Junior Drill Instructor (JDI).

In the meantime, Delores had found us a better place to live. It was really a huge step up from Beaufort Gardens. Since I needed the car most days, she walked with Bobbie, in the sultry heat of Beaufort, looking at apartments. What a tough lady! Our new home was in one half of a duplex. Another Marine and his wife lived in the other side. The house was located on Hermitage Road, one of the prettiest old streets in Beaufort. Hermitage road was a wide, one-way street with a wide, grassy median, and plenty trees and flowers. We could hardly believe our good fortune! Our place had two big old mossy oak trees in the front yard, and we had a large back yard, too! The front porch was nice and shady. Most all the other residences on Hermitage road were private homes, owned by some of Beaufort's upper middle class. We were so happy to move into our new place!

One drawback, though, was that this new place wasn't furnished, and we had no furniture of our own. So, one weekend we drove to Savannah and bought enough furniture to furnish the living room, kitchen, and two bedrooms. The furniture was delivered one day before we moved in. We even had a telephone installed. We thought we were really living high, and were very happy. Things were really beginning to look good.

I soon learned that being a Drill Instructor requires a huge amount of energy. The D.I. must, every minute he is with the Platoon, be energetic, alert, and forceful in his demeanor, often for as many as 14 to 16 hours a day. And, since regulations require at least one Drill Instructor be with the platoon twenty-four hours a day (one DI sleeps in the barracks at night), it's difficult to have any time off while working a platoon.

I found that there was little time for family life—hardly any time to spend with Delores and Bobbie. Much of the Drill Instructor's schedule is determined by the Senior Drill Instructor. It's common, and was required by all the Senior Drill Instructors I worked with, that *all D.I.s* be with the platoon during *all* scheduled training, and the overnight stay was rotated between Drill Instructors. Although I already knew this, I again learned, first hand, that if you're the leader of a group of men, whether it be recruits or any group of men subject to your orders, they will soon ferret out any small weakness you may have, and they'll capitalize on that weakness at some time in the future, diminishing their respect for you.

On the other hand, if you demonstrate some strength of character and persona, these men will also pick up on that and will not only respect you for these strengths but will even add them to their own image.

There's nothing quite like the graduation of a recruit platoon, both for the Drill Instructor and for the recruits and their families. For everyone, it means the final result of many hours, days, and weeks of toil and anxiety, all building up to this one moment. This is the day when they are essentially introduced to their families—and to the world—as fully trained and certified United States Marines. It's the first time they can truly claim to be Marines, something they'll remember for the rest of their lives, and a title they will always be proud of. It is, for all who have seen or participated in a graduation ceremony at Parris Island, or at Marine Recruit Depot, San Diego, a day they will always remember with pride. And at the ceremony, when the new Marines pass in front of the reviewing stand, with the Marine Band playing "The Marine's Hymn," there aren't many dry eyes in the crowd. It was also a proud moment for me to pass in review with these new Marines that I had trained—Marines that I may have to serve with at some time in the future, and I ask myself, *Can I trust these new Marines in any situation, including combat, not to let me, their unit, or other Marines down*? My answer must always be "yes!"

After we were settled in our new home and I had gotten settled in at my work routine, we began to explore the sights, sounds, and activities of Beaufort. Foremost, we enjoyed the laidback pace of this old, historical, Southern town. The city of Beaufort had been featured in the New York Times and named the Best Southern Small Town by *Southern Living* magazine. There were a number of old mansions and homes, beautifully preserved, on streets lined with old mossy oak trees and endless shrubs and flowers. Beaufort is renowned for its scenic location and for the historic preservation of its antebellum architecture. Most of the businesses on the only main street had remained much as they had been a half-century ago. Walking down the main street was, in itself, a great adventure. We visited some of the businesses, and sometimes we just window shopped. We ate fresh seafood at a very reasonable price in one of the fine restaurants in Beaufort. The local people were friendly and laid back in their speech and demeanor. We found our way to Lady's Island and Hunting Island State Park, where there was a magnificent beach, and the white sand and warm blue water made a great place to swim and enjoy the sun and surf.

I also found out that there were endless places to cast a line and fish, whether you wanted to try your luck casting in the surf or on the tidal streams that ebb and flow with the tide. After while I found a couple of places where I could catch the tide coming in, and using live shrimp for bait, I would reel in more than enough nice sized sea trout, which are speckled like fresh water trout, and just as delicious fried in flour and cornmeal, or baked.

We also made some good friends. In addition to Mac and Dorine, we found that one of my long-time Marine buddies, Chris, and his wife, Elaine, were stationed at the nearby Marine Air Station, just on the outskirts of Beaufort. We got together frequently, and we had them over at our house to play card games, have refreshments, and compare sea stories.

We also found that Beaufort is a well-known art center, and there were many artists who painted both in oil and watercolors, practicing their skills. There were several art shows scheduled every year, and some of the schools offered painting classes using oil, water, and other mediums. Many of the products from these schools and from well-known artists in the area were frequently displayed in various venues around the Beaufort area. It wasn't unusual to see a lone artist sitting at his easel around the Bay Street area, painting the ever-charming sight of the Beaufort River and the Bay Area surrounding Beaufort.

I was happy to see the way that the art community was so much a part of Beaufort, going back many years. I had always been interested in oil painting, but hadn't ever attempted to learn, nor did I think I had any particular skill at painting. But when I saw an advertisement inviting people to enroll in painting classes, I thought, *What do I have to lose?* I enrolled in a class that met once a week in the evening, bought some paints, brushes, several canvases, and went to class. This was a beginner's class, and I soon found out that I had no skill whatsoever to draw a picture and paint it! However, it was great fun, and I looked forward to the classes. I enjoyed the smell of the paint, the bright colors, and mixing and spreading the medium on the canvas. During the course of this class, I produced several paintings that I eventually gave away to family members. (I found that if you give your paintings to family members as gifts, they feel obligated to hang them on the wall! Otherwise, they may never be seen and end up stored in the closet with other so-called junk.)

When my tour of duty as a Drill Instructor was drawing to a close, I began to worry about receiving orders for overseas duty and having to leave Delores and Bobbie for thirteen months or more. When I finally did receive orders, however, I was surprised and pleased. I was ordered to report to Guard Company, Headquarters Bn. at Parris Island. This meant that I was assigned to work in the base Military Police Department, serving as a Sergeant of the Guard of the Military Police.

The Military Police, known as M.P.s, were responsible for providing security and public safety on the base, much like a city police department would do. I was issued all the accessories worn by the military police, such as the white web belt to attach a holster for the .45 cal. service pistol that I carried, a white helmet with Military Police identification markings, and a red arm band identifying me as a Military Police Officer. The unit contained approximately thirty men who served as roving patrols, sentries who manned the Main Gate to the base, and other miscellaneous guard duties. I learned that there were two other sergeants like me who served as Sergeant of the Guard. With a total of three sergeants, each of us would work every third day, serving a 24-hour shift. This means I would assume the duty at 08:00 AM one day and serve till 08:00 AM the following day. I would then have the rest of that day off, plus two more. It was a great system, and it worked well for me.

On the 24-hour shift when I was on duty, my responsibilities were similar to those of a Chief of Police of a medium-sized city. There were always three to five Military Police, roving patrolmen on the base, who continually drove around in vehicles marked Military Police and equipped with red lights and sirens. They were there to enforce the traffic laws, traffic control, public safety, and respond to emergency calls, like fire alarms, breaches of security, and frequently had to respond to reports of recruits who had gotten fed up with the training and couldn't take it any longer, and went AWOL (Absent

Without Leave). AWOL recruits often try to get off the base and go home. They soon learn it's nearly impossible to get off Parris Island, as it is, indeed, an island. Anyone trying to leave must either swim and wade through a mile or so of tidal marsh lands and swamp, or try to go out the Main Gate by hiding away in one of the many vehicles going off the base.

There has been the rare escape of a recruit hiding in a car to get through the Main Gate, but to the best of my knowledge, no recruit ever made an escape successfully through these swamp, although many tried. During my duty of patrolling to locate AWOL recruits I became very familiar with the routes they'd take and also their hiding places. Untold numbers of recruits over the years had used the exact same hiding places. Often I would be able to track the route of the AWOL recruit by the trail he would leave along the edge of swamp, which often included discarded items, candy and gum wrappers, banana peels, apple cores, etc.

The one-and-only land route and road in and out of Parris Island was one narrow causeway, on which was a Guard Station that was always manned by two Marines. It wasn't unusual to find a recruit hiding under the only bridge on the causeway crossing. When I discovered one crouching down in the only available space under the bridge, just to frighten him from going AWOL again, and to impress upon him the severity of his offense, I would treat him like a dangerous criminal. I'd draw my .45 caliber service pistol from my holster and pull back the receiver, letting it slam shut, as if I were loading a round into the chamber. In reality, the pistol wasn't loaded. I would order him to lie face down on the ground, with his hands behind his back. Then I would handcuff him and place him in the secure cab on the back of my vehicle and transport him to the Provost Marshall's office.

AWOL recruits were usually not able to evade capture for very long. One morning, I was on patrol duty at approximately 05:00. I had exited my vehicle to ascertain that some buildings were secure when I heard someone running across the pavement. I climbed into my vehicle and turned on the headlights. The lights illuminated a recruit running at top speed across the road and then off into a grassy area. I started the engine of my vehicle and quickly drove across the road, jumped the curb, chasing the AWOL recruit through the grassy area. The chase only lasted about fifty yards, when he turned around and threw up his arms in surrender, yelling, "I give up! I give up!" I quickly took him into custody and returned him to his platoon in 1st Battalion. His "freedom" while AWOL only lasted about ninety seconds.

It wasn't unusual when I assumed duty for my 24-hour shift that we would have a report pending about a recruit or two being AWOL. Usually, one of the M.P.s would find the recruit, or recruits, quickly and return them to their unit. It was the desire of their unit and our unit to find these people as quickly as possible before they hurt themselves or committed a serious crime in their attempt to get off the base. In nearly all cases, these recruits would be counseled by their unit, given special attention, and end up graduating with their platoon.

One morning, when I assumed duties as Sergeant of the Guard, the unit had received a report that there was a recruit AWOL. The report indicated a recruit who was a patient at the psych ward had escaped by breaking a window and jumping out of the second floor. Before he left, he set fire to one of the office desks. About 10:00 we received a fire alarm. Our M.P. unit receives all the fire alarms that go through the fire department. As usual, I quickly left the unit and responded to the call, driving the vehicle assigned to me, a pickup truck equipped with red lights and siren and with an enclosed secured cab in the back to transport persons who were under arrest.

I noticed a large wooden structure in the 2nd Battalion area was fully engulfed in flames. I arrived at the scene just ahead of the fire department vehicle, and noted that it was a serious fire. The old wooden structure had once served as a mess hall but was now being used as a Chapel. I saw several Drill Instructors and other Marines who were trying to put out the flames with water hoses and a large fire extinguisher. The Fire Department arrived and quickly set up their hoses. I pointed out to one of the firemen that a large propane tank was sitting very close to the building and was probably in danger of exploding. They quickly began hosing down the tank to keep it cool.

At about that time, I felt someone tap me on the shoulder. I turned around and almost went into a mild shock, as I was looking up into the face of none other than the Commanding General of the base, General Raymond Murray. Of course, I had to look up at him, as he was 6'3". I think I recovered quickly and saluted.

The General said, "Sergeant, get all those Marines and others away from the building—let the firemen fight the fire. I don't want any of my Marines hurt!"

I stood stiffly, said, "Aye, Aye Sir," and spun around, ran toward the burning building, grabbing and ordering any person not a fireman to get away from the building. Everyone complied.

General Murray then approached me and pointed out that some of the insulation around the overhead steam pipes was burning. He told me to post a sentry on the sidewalk to keep people from walking under those burning pipes. Again, I saluted smartly, said, "Aye, Aye, Sir." I complied by quickly enlisting the help of recruit who just happened to be walking by carrying his rifle. I went up to him and told him that I needed him for a very important duty. He looked like he'd seen a ghost. I stationed him at that dangerous spot on the sidewalk and gave him an order to not let *anyone* walk under the burning pipes. He said, "Aye, Aye, Sir," and quickly assumed his place at the pipes.

I collected my thoughts and realized, "Did I just take two direct orders from a *General*?" It was highly unusual for a General to be giving a direct order to an enlisted man. Even more unbelievable was that the General was Major General Raymond Murray, a much-admired hero in the Marine Corps, and the only person I've ever considered as my own hero. Over the years I have read a lot about his life and career. General Murray had just assumed command of Parris Island the past summer, and I had only caught glimpses of him in passing on the base.

The General was a hero of the battles in the South Pacific during World War II, having led a Battalion of Marines in several of the Island campaigns and being seriously wounded on Saipan. He was also considered a hero of the Korean War. He commanded the 5th Marine Regiment in the battle at the Chosin Reservoir. When the First Marine Division, which included the 5th Regiment, was completely surrounded by thousands of Chinese troops in late November and early December of 1950 in sub-zero temperatures, General Murray provided the knowledge, strength, leadership, and inspiration for his men to break out of the trap, fight their way through the hordes of Chinese, and escape, bringing out most of their dead and wounded—and even the equipment—and made their way to the sea for evacuation. There is no other man of whom I was in awe but General Raymond Murray. *And I just had just taken two direct orders from this man!* That is pretty special to me.

[Much later in my life I had the occasion to speak by phone with none other than General Murray's wife and widow, Zona Gayle Murray. The General passed away in 2004. After he passed, Zona wrote a book of his life titled, *Highpockets: The Man. The Marine. The Legend*. Most of the book was taken from General Murray's personal journal, and is very inspirational. The book has been advertised for sale in *Leatherneck* magazine, a popular magazine for and about Marines, dating back many years. I purchased a copy of *Highpockets*, and along with the payment to Mrs. Murray for the magazine, I wrote a brief note telling her of my respect for the General and the unusual circumstances of my brief encounters with him. She wrote me a note in return, and, to my surprise and pleasure, she also gave me a phone call to personally thank me for my kind words about him. I find it hard to adequately explain the humble joy I felt receiving this phone call from Zona Murray herself.]

Returning to the burning building narrative: no one was injured, but the building was a total loss. However, while the building was still burning, one of the M.P. patrolmen discovered and arrested the recruit who was AWOL from the psych ward. He was discovered hiding in some shrubs near the fire, masturbating and watching the building burn. He later confessed to setting the chapel on fire because he was angry with God for placing him in the psychic ward. We treated him gently, recognizing that he was a very sick young man, and we took him to the psych ward for treatment.

One other incident that occurred during this time that I think is interesting enough to share. As it worked out with the rotation of Sergeant of the Guard duty every third day, unfortunately, I was scheduled for duty on Christmas Day. The base was quiet that day, because the recruits were on holiday routine, so there weren't many people moving about the base. I was in the Guard office about midnight when we received a phone call. The dispatcher answered the phone. The caller was none other than General Murray! He asked to speak to the Sergeant of the Guard. I picked up the phone and answered. The General, calling me by name, explained that there was a Marine on his front porch banging on the front door, and the General asked me to come over to his quarters and get him, because the man was intoxicated and wouldn't go away.

I told him that I'd be right over. The General's quarters were actually in a large, old, historical mansion that had been restored to be the residence of the base's Commanding General. It was only a few blocks from the guard building. I drove over to the General's house. Sure enough, an intoxicated Marine was on the porch, banging on the door with his fist. I parked and walked into the yard, when I met General Murray coming from around the back of the house on the sidewalk. He was wearing a long robe and house shoes. Again, I noticed how tall he was. I saluted and spoke, "Good evening, General." The General nodded, acknowledging my salute. He told me to just get the man and take him back to his barracks. He went on to say that since it was Christmas, he didn't want any charges filed against the man, but just take him back to his barracks.

I saluted, responding with, "Aye, Aye, Sir." Once again, I had taken a direct order from a General. I went up on the porch, took the man by the arm, and firmly told him to come with me. Surprisingly, and happily, the man, a lower-ranking Marine from the Guard Company, recognized me, and my authority, and came along without any resistance. I took him to his barracks and his rack area. By that time, he was sleepy and just wanted to go to bed. It seems that he had been drinking at the service club, and had become unruly, loudly singing Christmas carols. He was subsequently kicked out of the club. That made him angry, and he wanted to tell the General personally. I did as the General had asked, and didn't report the incident to his superiors.

That was just one of many interesting incidents that I responded to during my assignment as the Sergeant of the Guard of the Military Police. None, however, were as interesting and destructive as the day of the Chapel fire. I enjoyed my assignment to the base Military Police and was a little sad when it was over.

It came to an end one day when I was called to the Company office, where I was told that I was being assigned to a special duty. It seemed that the relevant Marine authorities and the Beaufort County Sheriff's Department had decided it would be equally beneficial to the county and to the Marine Corps to have a Marine Sergeant ride with the Deputy Sheriff on duty every night. Since there were two large Marine bases, Parris Island and the Marine Corps Air Station in Beaufort County, a large number of Marines were on a liberty status every night, looking for recreation, and they often got in trouble with the local police authorities.

Also, the night deputy often needed a backup when he was dealing with civilians breaking the law or disturbing the peace. It was decided to assign me to this special duty, working with the deputy sheriff who rode patrol around Beaufort County at night. I was also told that I would have two nights a week off duty. They asked me how I felt about this assignment, and I told them that I was pleased and excited about it and was ready to go to work. They told me to report to the Beaufort County Sheriff's office the following day for a briefing and to be introduced to the deputy with whom I would soon be riding.

CHAPTER 27

MOONSHINE, CIVIL RIGHTS, AND A NEW BABY

The next day, about mid-morning, I dressed in my uniform with Military Police accessories and went downtown to the Sheriff's office, where I was greeted warmly. I was introduced to the Sheriff, some of the staff, and to the deputy to whom I would be assigned, Deputy Sheriff Bo Parker, who gave me a brief tour of the offices and the jail. It wasn't a large place, and the offices appeared old but well kept. Deputy Parker and I chatted a few minutes, and he said he would pick me up at my place that evening at 7:00 p.m.

Deputy Bo Parker was a large man, 6' 2" and weighing about 230 lbs. He wore a holster that carried a large frame .38 caliber revolver and had a pair of handcuffs attached to the back of his belt. He had broad shoulders and appeared a few pounds overweight. He walked with a bit of a swagger and emanated confidence—not the kind of man I'd want to pick a fight with. He was my age, twenty-seven, and had been a deputy since he was twenty-one. He liked his job, and he was good-natured, with a relaxed, easygoing disposition.

When he pulled into my driveway to pick me up, I must admit I was pretty thrilled. Just climbing into the deputy's car was exciting. The vehicle itself was beautiful—everything was highly polished, and it had the markings of the Beaufort County Sheriff's Department on the doors and a flashing light mounted on top. We sat in the driveway for a few minutes while he explained all the accessories inside that are common to most police cars. There was a shotgun, the police radio, two large flashlights, a traffic ticket pad on a clipboard, and other items. The vehicle was equipped with a spotlight mounted on the driver's side and controlled from the inside.

It was a 1962 four-door Dodge sedan with a 383 cubic inch engine. Bo later told me that the county mechanics kept this car finely tuned, and it had some "souped up" features. He said he didn't want any long chases—he liked to catch his "prey" quickly. I knew from personal knowledge that this model Dodge with the 383 engine was an excellent car. It was equipped with oversized fog lights and was powerful and fast even if it hadn't being souped up.

We started out on our patrol and were just a mile or so from my house when we received a call on the radio. There was a two-car accident with a number of injured out on Lady's Island. Bo flipped on the red light and siren, kicked the Dodge in the ass, and away we went! We crossed the Beaufort River to Lady's Island, and were soon traveling in excess of 90 miles per hour on a narrow two-lane blacktop road.

We came up behind the State Highway Patrol and Bo passed him, going dangerously fast for this road. It seems that Bo and this highway patrolman knew each other quite well and had this friendly competitive game going on about who could get to the scene of an accident or an incident first.

We soon arrived at the accident site, and the Highway Patrolman pulled up right behind us. It seems that one car had been attempting to pass another when he lost control, sideswiped the other, and both cars rolled over and over. Both vehicles had been filled with people.

There were injured people lying along the roadside and in a nearby field. I saw one woman sitting in the grass, moaning and crying, with her eye hanging out of its socket down on her left cheek.

We had scarcely gotten out of the car to start helping some of the injured when we received a call reporting a domestic fight, with one person threatening the other with a gun down in the Hilton Head area, way on the other side of the county. Deputy Parker said, "Let's go, Bob. I hear ambulances coming to help these people."

We got back into the patrol car, did a quick turnaround, and away we went to respond to the domestic disturbance. This time we were heading to Hilton Head at a very high speed. On the way, the radio kept us updated on the accident and any new developments on the domestic problem. Bo briefed me on the way about how he would handle this situation, and what he wanted me to do. He said to just follow his lead and "don't take out your firearm unless our life is clearly threatened."

Thankfully, by the time we got to the site of the disturbance, the two who were involved had cooled down. The man had put away the gun, and some other family members were there, talking to the man and woman. I learned that frequently, on these kinds of calls, when someone calls the police, the individuals involved settle down, at least temporarily, because no one wants to go to jail and maybe have to pay a fine.

However, a few of these occasions can, and do, lead to a very dangerous stand off, where someone could get shot. And you never know what kind of situation you'll find until you get there.

Bo spoke with the people involved and told them they'd better work out their differences before someone gets hurt or goes to jail. It happened to be a black family, and Deputy Parker told them, "You two had better work this out. I don't want to have to come here again because you two can't get along." He spoke in a chastising tone of voice. Both parties said, "Yes, sir. Yes, sir. We sure will work things out, boss; we sure will," or words to that effect. I learned that these kind of domestic disturbance reports are commonly received and responded to by the Sheriff's office.

Another type of call we received were reports of a disturbance or fighting in one of the bars in and around Beaufort. I was with Deputy Parker several times when we responded to these kinds of calls. A lot of them were caused by Marines fighting in one of the numerous beer joints in the Charles Street area. Usually these disturbances ended upon the arrival of Bo and me. But, if not, we had to get physically involved, separate the parties, wrestle down and arrest one or more people. When Marines were involved, my mere presence as a Marine Sergeant, and with a Military Police officer, would be enough to resolve the problem peacefully without someone going to jail. And that was the main reason that I was on this assignment— to keep these Marines from getting into serious trouble and becoming a threat to others in the community. It seems that this is true equation: Marines + Alcohol + Women = Fights.

Another kind of call that the deputy and I responded to several times was an eye-opening experience for me. Out in the rural areas of Beaufort County, in several heavily wooded areas, there were drinking and partying establishments referred to as "Juke Joints." There were at least three Juke Joints in Beaufort County, which Bo and I would visit from time to time. The ones we went to were in old, run-down, unpainted buildings that were frequented only by Blacks. Inside these joints were tables and chairs, a bar on one side, and a clear place for dancing to the music that came from a blaring jukebox. Most of the time, we weren't called to quell a disturbance, but we'd just make an appearance so the patrons could see that "the law" was always near, or so it seemed to me.

When the deputy and I visited, we always parked right in front of the entry door, where we were clearly visible, and went inside. It was usually loud, with people talking, music, and laugher all in one large, crowded room. As soon as we walked in the door, the noise, laughter, and talking immediately ceased. The deputy and I stood there a couple of minutes just looking around the room, then he slowly walked straight across the room, looking from side to side, turned, hesitated a couple moments, just looking around at the people, then we slowly walked out, got in the car and drove away. No one spoke a word.

As soon as we exited the room, you could hear the talking and noise began again. There were some very tough-looking people in those Juke Joints. It seemed to me that the Sheriff's office was conveying a message to the Black community, that, in my opinion, said something like, "The sheriff wants you to know that we're watching you. We know that you're making and drinking illegal whiskey, but as long as you behave yourselves, and stay out of trouble, we'll leave you alone." It was clear to me that it was blatant intimidation, and these people did fear the Sheriff's Department. These tactics may be criticized by some, but they kept the peace, and that's what counted, I guess.

Illegal whiskey, i.e., moonshine, was a problem in Beaufort County. Several times Bo told me about raids the Sheriff's office had made, busting up a still and confiscating large amounts of whiskey. They would send samples of the whiskey away for testing, and if the test results came back negative for impurities, the whiskey was distributed among fellow members of the police community and close friends. Good, pure, corn whiskey is delicious and a highly desirable drinking whiskey. Bo gave me some one time. It was good, but I had to drink it sparingly because it was potent, and I didn't drink it to become intoxicated. It was more like a sipping whiskey.

A number of times, when we made traffic stops for drunken driving, it was standard practice to search the vehicle. Bo would search the car and at times find moonshine. He would confiscate it, and the person would receive a citation for possession of illegal whiskey and given a summons to go to court. One night, Bo and I passed by a side road and saw two cars backed up, trunk to trunk. Bo came to quick stop and turned around. The parties had been transferring gallons of whiskey from one car to another. By the time we got turned around, both cars had sped away. We gave chase to the car we thought had the whiskey. We caught the party in less than a two-mile chase. He did indeed have a lot of whiskey in the back of the car. Bo arrested the guy and had his car towed to the police compound for storage. I never found out the results of this case, but I do know that possession of large amounts of illegal whiskey, selling illegal whiskey, and evading the law was a pretty serious crime, and the party probably went to jail for quite a while.

It's important to remember that the time period when I was in Beaufort was 1961-1963. This was still very much the "old south" in Beaufort County, South Carolina, as it was in most southern states at that time. And, this was before the federal Civil Rights Act of 1964 came into effect. In fact, the 1964 Civil Rights Act did not end discrimination. Blacks and other minorities still had to continue to fight for their rights then, and even up until the present. Some of the vestiges of slavery were still clearly apparent when we lived in Beaufort. In fact, racial tensions were at an all-time high across the country. After much violence and many protests, confrontations with police, and with the support of President Kennedy, James Meredith became the first Black to enroll in the University of Mississippi, sparking violence and riots, especially across the southern states. Martin Luther King, Jr., was arrested and jailed in Georgia. It was just the beginning of a time of great racial turmoil across the country.

In Beaufort, there wasn't any rioting or demonstrations. Everyday life was calm and peaceful and moved along at the same slow pace as it had for decades. Every morning, about seven o'clock, you could still see dozens of Black women wearing work clothes walking down the streets, going to their jobs as housekeepers, nannies, and other menial jobs, as they and their mothers before them had always done. It seemed there was an unspoken understanding between Blacks and White people of Beaufort. The understanding was this: Blacks knew "their place," and as long as they stayed in "their place" everything was just fine. Of course, to do this, meant that Blacks had to endure the most blatant forms of discrimination and separation of the races. The schools were segregated, as were public places, separate water fountains, waiting rooms in bus stations and train depots, and all the other hideous forms of racism.

In the Spring of 1962, Delores broke the news that she was pregnant! The baby was due around the first week of October. We were overjoyed and quickly spread the word to our families and friends. We also continued to worry about me getting overseas orders. But, if I did, we resolved to just deal with it the best we could. We had both known from the beginning that as a Marine family, separations would be a part of our future.

My assignment to the Sheriff's office continued, providing me with experiences I had never foreseen as a Marine. I wasn't required to report to any Marine authorities, and as far as I could see, no one was monitoring me. As long as I continued to do my job and not get into trouble, the Marine Corps left me alone. What a great assignment!

On October 2, 1962, Delores went to the Beaufort Naval Hospital and delivered a handsome baby boy. He was a big baby with a lot of black hair. What a cute little guy! We were both so excited. We had already picked out a name. After having lived with the name Bobbie all my life, I wanted our children, if boys, to have strong male names, preferably after strong military figures. Delores agreed. So, we chose the name Mark Douglas Lay—the first name after the famous Army General, Mark Clark, and the second name, Douglas, after General Douglas MacArthur. Delores liked the name because of Saint Mark. It was a good strong name.

Mark grew up to become a very tough and talented young man. He wasn't a tall man if one only considered feet and inches, but he was a very tall man in spirit, demeanor, and achievements. Shortly after graduating from high school, he joined the Marine Corps. He thrived, and quickly rose to the rank of Sergeant. He applied for and was chosen to attend probably the most prestigious school in the Marine Corps, Embassy School (Marine Security Guard School), at Quantico, Virginia. It's difficult to be accepted into this school and even tougher to make it to graduation. Some of the training for Embassy Guard students is conducted by the FBI and the State Department. Graduates are assigned to guard the US Embassies around the world. The United States wants only the very best people guarding its Embassies. After his enlistment was completed, he attended law school in Oregon. As an attorney, Mark worked as a criminal defense lawyer and served as an Assistant Attorney General for the Oregon Department of Justice.

October 1962 also saw our nation becoming involved in a dangerous standoff with the Soviet Union about their secretly placing nuclear weapons and missile sites in Cuba. President Kennedy demanded that the Soviets remove the nuclear missiles and missile sites. The President instituted a naval blockade of Cuba, preventing any Soviet ships from reaching Cuba. We were on the brink of a nuclear war if the Soviets did not remove the missiles. For seven days, the world was gripped in mortal fear as President Kennedy and Soviet Premier Khrushchev negotiated the removal of the sites. The missiles could reach most American cities, causing nuclear devastation never before seen. All military bases and units were placed on high alert, and all leaves were cancelled. Delores and I, like millions of other Americans, watched the television in fearful attention as the deadly standoff played itself out.

Thankfully, on October 28th, Khrushchev blinked and agreed to dismantle the missile sites and weapons and move them back to the Soviet Union. This incident left the world with a constant fear lingering in the background of their daily lives. The Soviet Union, the United States, and several other NATO countries, had enough nuclear weapons to destroy the world many times over, and perhaps all it took was a simple misunderstanding or a miscalculation of one's intent. For the first time, a "hot line," a private, secure phone line from President Kennedy to Premier Khrushchev was established to help prevent any future misunderstandings. I think for the first time all Americans realized that we were living in a dangerous world.

In June 1963 we received our long-anticipated transfer orders. Again, the Marine Corps surprised us. Instead of overseas orders, we received orders to Camp Lejeune where I would attend Utilities Chief School. This school was approximately six months long and covered all Utilities subjects; like, Electrician, Water Supply, Refrigeration, Air Conditioning, and Construction. The school was located at my old Alma Mater, Marine Corps Engineer Schools, Courthouse Bay. In my previous assignments, I had taught the Refrigeration and Air Conditioning part of the Utilities Chiefs course. In addition, I had attended the Water Supply part in my first assignment after Boot Camp. It appeared to me that the school would be relatively easy.

CHAPTER 28

SAYING GOODBYE

In late June, we left Beaufort and headed for Camp Lejeune. It was hard to leave Beaufort, and we were sad as we drove away, leaving our nice home on Hermitage Rd. It was our first real home and our first baby was born there. In my duties with the Deputy Sheriff, I had become very familiar with and fond of Beaufort and Beaufort County. It will always remain a wonderful memory for us.

After arriving at Camp Lejeune, we found an apartment in Jacksonville, the town right outside the main gate of the base. We knew that we'd only be there for six months, so we didn't spend a lot of time looking for an apartment. We did, however, find a nice, comfortable two-bedroom place in Jacksonville and were able to move right in.

I started Utilities Chief School in early July, and the class would graduate in early December. It was almost certain that I would receive overseas orders upon graduation from the school. We began to plan where Delores and the kids would live while I was away.

Meanwhile, we settled into a nice comfortable routine at Jacksonville. I had every weekend off, and the subject matter of the classes was very easy for me.

Happily, I discovered that a longtime Marine buddy—going all the way back to my first enlistment while stationed at Miami—and his wife, lived nearby. He and I were both Privates First Class back then, both newly married, and both serving on mess duty. We were very poor in those days, and we used to take home food from the mess hall. He and I remembered that we took home a lot of pies and accumulated quite a collection of metal pie pans.

Over the years, he had become a Warrant Officer. He and his wife visited us, and I had to first tell him that I had a different wife now. They invited us to Thanksgiving dinner. They also had another officer and his wife as guests. We had a great time, although it was just a bit uncomfortable with he and his guest both being officers, and I only a sergeant. But I was happy for him, and I think he was no doubt a good officer. They quickly warmed up to Delores, as she did with them.

Other friends, Chris and Elaine from Beaufort, came to visit us. It was great to see them! Time passed quickly at the school, and, almost before we knew it, it was time to plan on moving again.

Then, on November 23, 1963, our nation was shattered with sorrow and shock at the assassination of our beloved President, John F. Kennedy. The hideous act was carried out by a former Marine and rifle sharpshooter, Lee Harvey Oswald. It angered me that the news media played up the fact that Oswald was a Marine, as if somehow this was part of the reason that he murdered the President. I first heard the news at about 1:30 in the afternoon at the school when one of the guys from class had his car radio on. We all gathered around the car to listen to the news. Everyone was stunned and tears were in many eyes. I had a lump in my throat and could hardly speak.

The school cancelled classes for the rest of the day and sent everyone home. I went home, and as soon as I walked through the door, Delores and I embraced without speaking. Both of us were crying. Like millions of others in our country and around the world, we were deeply grieved and shocked. The unanswered question was on everyone's lips, "Why? Why would anyone do such a thing?"

We watched the news all that weekend and witnessed Jack Ruby shoot Oswald. What a tragic time for our country! However, we all should be proud that in spite of the assassination of our President and the turmoil that followed, our government functioned as it was designed to. The mantle of power was smoothly transferred to our Vice-President, Lyndon Johnston, a very capable and qualified man.

My Utilities Chiefs class graduated on December 6th, and I received my orders. We were correct in our anticipation of being sent overseas. My orders indicated that I was to be assigned to the 1st Marine Air Wing in Iwakuni Japan, for further assignment to a sub unit, MASS-2, a unit on the island of Okinawa. Although I was happy to be assigned to the Air Wing rather than the Infantry, it was still sad to have to leave Delores and the boys for such a long time.

Utilities Chief school in 1963.

We had decided while I was gone that Delores and the boys would try to find a suitable place in North Braddock, Pennsylvania, near all her family. In other news, Delores found out that she was pregnant again, and living close to her family would be very helpful. Wow! Another baby on the way, and I wouldn't be there for the birth. I regretted this very much, but there wasn't anything I could do about it. I would be leaving Delores in the middle of the winter, pregnant, and with two children to take care of. In truth, I wasn't really worried that much about it, because by now I knew that Delores was a very tough and capable lady, and if anyone could handle something like this, it was she.

In conjunction with my orders, I took 30 days leave. That, with travel time, meant I would have to leave Delores and the family in mid-January to report to Camp Pendleton, California, for processing prior to leaving overseas. We left Jacksonville, North Carolina, and drove to North Braddock, staying with her family for a few days while we looked for an apartment.

We soon found that there was a critical shortage of apartments in North Braddock. There were absolutely no new, modern apartments whatsoever! All the existing apartments were in the old, turn-of-the-century buildings. It was very disappointing to us. But, it was what it was; and we resigned ourselves to renting one of the older apartments. We found a downstairs, one-bedroom apartment only a few blocks from where Delores had grown up, and where some of her family still lived. We rented the place and moved in, and were soon settled.

By the time we moved in, Christmas was upon us. We planned to have a wonderful Christmas together, in spite of my orders, which would take me away for about fourteen months. Although we could have had Christmas dinner with her family, we decided to cook our own turkey and have our Christmas dinner together as a family.

By Christmas, Delores was comfortably settled in. I helped her to prepare a traditional turkey dinner, and it was fun. Of course, we will always remember when I was moving the cooked turkey from the oven to the table; the turkey slid off the tray, landed on its back on the floor, and slid under the table. We had quite a laugh, and there was no harm done. I just crawled under the table, slid the turkey back onto the tray, got up, and put it on the table. In fact, perhaps the fall was useful, as it sort of loosened the turkey parts, making it easy to pull apart and serve. I wouldn't, however, recommend this technique to anyone as a rule with turkey dinners. That incident goes into our mental footlockers as a fond memory. We had a great Christmas dinner, one that we will always remember.

We also, on December 30th, celebrated our third wedding anniversary. My, how time flies! And neither of us had any regrets, only happiness and looking forward to many more years together.

We rolled into the New Year, and the time was drawing close to when I'd have to depart. I had my choice of what kind of transportation I would use to get to Camp Pendleton on the Southern California coast. It was too expensive to fly, and a bus would be a very long, tiring trip. It was at this time that I discovered that there were times when some people, for whatever reason, wanted their car delivered to California instead of driving it themselves. Therefore, I contracted with a guy to drive his car and deliver it to Los Angeles, and he would pay the cost of the gas. This worked out great, and it even allowed me some time to stop in Kansas for a few days to visit my folks.

Sadly, mid-January arrived, and it was time for me to say good-bye to my little family, knowing that I was leaving them for more than a year. That seemed like an eternity to us. The morning I got up to leave, there had been an eight-inch snowstorm, with more coming down. I had picked up the car I was to deliver the day before. I gathered up my things, took my bags out, and cleaned the snow from the car. I came back into the house, lingering as long as I could.

Finally, I had to get on the road. I gave little Bobbie a huge hug. I told him that I loved him and explained to him that daddy would be gone for a long, long time, but I would come back home someday. I told him to be a good boy and help his mom around the house. I held little Mark on my knee and gave him some good hugs. Of course, he was too young to understand what was going on, so the hugs were mostly for my benefit. I could hardly quit hugging the little fellow. I wanted to remember how he felt in my arms and I wanted him to maybe have some memory of me if I never came home.

Singing with Mark. On this day, January 10, 1964 in North Braddock, Pennsylvania

And then came the hard part—saying goodbye to Delores, my beloved wife. I was leaving her here in this shabby old apartment, pregnant, with two children to take care of, in the middle of the winter—and a very cold winter at that. What could I say to diminish the pain of parting? There was nothing that could be done about it; we'd just have to bear the pain. I hugged her, and I must have kissed her a dozen times, as our tears mingled together. Finally, I just grabbed my last bag and went out the door, not turning around to look back.

I got into the car and drove away, tears flooding my eyes and running down my cheeks. I drove carefully, as the snow was deep. Soon I was on the Interstate heading West. The snow continued on into West Virginia before it began to taper off. I believe I cried all the way to Ohio, or at least until there were no more tears left to cry. I kept telling myself, *This is what you agreed to when you decided to become a career Marine. This was what a Marine must do; leave his family and go wherever the Marine Corps needs them. The Marine Corps comes first. That's the price you pay to be a Marine.* Happily, the further west I got, the more I left the snow behind me. But, the further I went, mile after mile, the sadder I became. I was leaving the place where I wanted to be with my loved ones. It was truly an awful, emotional experience.

By late evening, I was in Terre Haute, Indiana. It was still very cold, with snow and ice still on the ground. I got a room at a motel and checked in. I knew our friend, Dorine, was living in Terre Haute while Mac was overseas. I called her to say hello and see how she and Mac were doing.

When Dorine answered the phone, I could tell by the tone of her voice that something was wrong. She was happy that I had called, but she said that something really awful had happened. She said their baby boy, Michael, had fallen out of his crib, landed on his head and was in critical condition in the hospital. She began crying while on the phone. There wasn't anything that I could say to comfort her. She told me that Mac was on his way home from overseas and would be home tomorrow. I just tried to talk to her as a friend and told her my prayers were with her. And, I meant it. At that time in my life, I felt very close to God and often prayed quietly to myself for strength.

When I got to Camp Pendleton a few days later I called Mac and Dorine again. I found out that little Michael had died. He had passed away due to the injuries to his head. What a sad, sad thing for them to bear. As people usually feel in these circumstances, I wanted to do something for them. But there's nothing to do but let them know that you share their grief. I picked out the most touching sympathy card I could find and sent it to them and included a personal note from me. There wasn't anything else that I could do.

For the rest of my trip, as I drove along, all by myself, I was profoundly sad for Mac and Dorine. This grief, plus my own sadness over leaving my own family, sometimes felt too great to bear. I am glad I was close to God at that time in my life, as I was comforted, thanking Him for His many blessings, and I prayed humbly for strength.

As I drew nearer to Kansas, I took a detour so that I could stop by to see my mom and dad and family, who still lived on the old home place. My grief and sadness were somewhat relieved as I looked forward to seeing them. It always seemed like going back to my roots from time to time charged my battery, giving me renewed strength.

As I had expected, it was really cold out on the old farm. There was still some snow and ice on the ground, but at least it wasn't snowing at the time. It was so good to get a long hug from Mom. I have learned over the years that it's really a special thing to hug your mother. And it's something I missed and remembered fondly long after Mom had passed away. Dad looked the same in his denim shirt and old overalls: tough and in good cheer. He still had to work hard everyday just to make enough money to support them and save a little every month. He still had to get up early every morning, feed and milk the cows, feed all the other animals, then go to his day job as a laborer on the county road crew. Then, in the evening, after he got home from working all day, he had to feed and milk the cows and do it all over again. He did this for many years, and there was never a break or day off from those chores. It didn't matter if he was sick—he still had to do it. Again, I've observed, time and time again, that Dad was the best man I ever knew or would ever know.

I had a lot of fun for the three or four days I was home, teasing my sisters and talking with Mom and Dad, and getting some of Mom's good old home cooking. I also got up early with Dad and helped him with milking and other morning and evening chores, hoping to give him some relief. But, it was enough to reaffirm my decision that I would never be a farmer!

The time soon arrived when I had to leave Mom and Dad and get back on the road and continue my journey to Camp Pendleton, California, and my further trip to the far side of the planet in the South Pacific. From Kansas I took the southern route—down through the panhandle of Oklahoma and Texas and into New Mexico, Arizona, and into Los Angles, where I was to deliver the car I was driving. I stopped and stayed one night in a shabby motel in Tucumcari, New Mexico. That motel was a cold, lonely place, but I needed the rest. It had been a long, lonely drive, and again I was aware that every mile I traveled took me further and further away from the ones I love.

I delivered the car in Los Angeles and took a bus to Camp Pendleton, where I turned in my orders. Soon I was assigned to a replacement draft, a unit that was forming for further transfer to various bases in Japan and Okinawa. My orders indicated that I was to report to the Headquarters of the 1st Marine Air Wing at Iwakuni, Japan. I also found out that this unit was to travel by ship, and the trip would take about two weeks. I wasn't happy about that as it would mean an extra two weeks away from my family, and I also wasn't looking forward to being on a ship.

CHAPTER 29

SHIPBOARD LIFE

On February 14, 1964, like thousands of Marines before me going way back beyond World War II, I boarded a U.S. Navy ship at the pier in San Diego, in this instance, the USNS Hugh J. Gaffey, bound for Japan. It was a large ship carrying several thousand troops and some civilian military dependents. After we had a chance to get ourselves settled on the ship, liberty call was sounded. We were warned that liberty expired at midnight, and we were due to sail at 08:00 the next morning. A couple of buddies and I decided to go out on the town for a few hours and see San Diego.

There were several streets that led right down to the pier and were the regular haunts for Marines and sailors who were attached to one of the ships docked at the pier. We went bar hopping on a couple of these streets—nothing serious, just goofing around. The bars teemed with expensive whiskey and cheap women, as they had for decades. San Diego had always been considered a good liberty town.

We were in one of these bars that had a standing offer—the bartender would pour various kinds and colors of liquor, layered in a glass, and then light it on fire. If anyone could chug-a-lug this drink while it was burning and still be on his feet ten minutes after drinking it, the drink was free. We watched with interest as a sailor took the challenge. He managed to chug-a-lug the concoction while being cheered on by everybody at the bar. Then we all watched intently as the sailor went from being a composed, behaved person to a bumbling, human mass , whose legs seemed like rubber bands and he couldn't even stand up. His buddies paid for the drink and carried the sailor out. I hope the fellow made it to the ship and recovered.

At 08:00 the next day, the ship blew its whistle and began to back away from the pier. It was a sad moment as I and other departing men gathered at the rail to witness the time of leaving. There were perhaps a couple dozen people, girlfriends, wives, family members, and others on the pier, all waving goodbye to the departing men, who were beginning a long journey, leaving their loved ones behind. Tears were shed, both by the departing as well as by those left behind. I swallowed a big lump in my throat, and tears flooded my eyes, as I couldn't help but think of my little family, Delores and the boys, in that shabby old apartment, and I was going even further away from them. But that's the life of a Marine.

As the big ship slowly backed away from the pier and turned around, it was quite a new experience for me, as I watched the California coastline slowly fading from our vision. Again, I felt sad, knowing that I was getting farther and farther away from the ones I loved.

Not long after we were underway, a call came over the speaker system for me to report to a specific place. I went up from below deck, deep in the bowels of the ship, where the Marines live, to an office, topside, where I was met by a pretty female Navy Officer. Then I remembered that before the journey had begun, back at Camp Pendleton, a memo had hung on the bulletin board at the barracks, listing jobs for which people could volunteer during the journey. The truth was that some people want something useful to do on the long journey to make the time pass quickly and contribute something that the Navy needed done anyway.

One of the jobs listed was editor of the ship's newspaper. I had entered my name for that job, even though I had never had any experience as a newspaper editor. I thought that it couldn't be too difficult, and I knew that I was a fast learner. The female officer introduced herself and said she had picked me to be the editor and told me what was expected. A daily newspaper would be published, and she showed me a current copy. It was nothing more than a half-dozen or so mimeographed pages.

Back when I was in high school, I had worked with the school newspaper staff, so I did have some experience. She gave me a nametag to wear that identified me as the editor of the ship's news-paper. This nametag enabled me to go almost anywhere on the ship except the dependent's quarters. All other Marines and ship's passengers were much more restricted.

Next, she took me to the newspaper office. I was pretty impressed. There were several desks with typewriters, a mimeograph machine, and a teletype machine, where daily, the national and international news of the day, including sports news, was always arriving. The officer told me that I could use the intercom on the ship to ask for volunteers to help me with positions such as typists and anyone who had any newspaper experience. This officer also told me that every day she would read the mimeographed pages and give her approval before we could print and distribute the paper. It sounded pretty easy to me.

So, I began my reign as editor of the ship's newspaper. I got a great response. I was able to get two good typists, and a corporal who had actually been an editor at a newspaper before he joined the Corps. I could tell that he knew what he was doing, so I hired him and titled him Assistant Editor. I also accepted a young Chinese American Marine who was a cartoonist. We were pretty much up and running to print the first paper the next day!

To do our job, basically, we just collected all the news that had come in on the teletype, arranged the articles the way we wanted, and retyped the information onto the mimeographed sheets. Also, every day I would go to the ship's Captain's office and speak with one of the Navy personnel who worked there to see if there was anything the Captain wanted to put in the paper. I also would ask the senior Marine officer if there was anything he wanted to be printed.

All in all it, was a pretty easy job. Then, with the permission of the female officer, I started a column titled, "Our Man on Deck." It would be my own column. I would think of an item of interest or a controversial subject and formulate a question. Then I would go all over the ship and ask the question to different people and print their answers in the daily paper. I thought it was fun, and, as it came to pass, people looked forward every day to this column! At deadline time, every day, when I would take the completed pages up to the officer for her to read and approve, I'd sit in her office while she read the pages. There was rarely anything she wanted to add or change.

Often we engaged in general conversation. She told me how she had come to be an officer in the Navy. I also told her some stories about some of my inglorious paths to becoming a Sergeant. I know I was the only Marine on the ship who had the pleasure of visiting with a pretty lady every day.

After the paper was printed, I had a young Marine who handled distribution, who would come and get the papers, distributing them all over the ship. He thought that was a cool job. All went well and we settled into a routine. After a few issues were printed, I put the corporal I had named as Assistant Editor in charge of the daily activities, while I did other things of interest. I would go up to the coffee shop, have a coffee, and maybe a breakfast roll, and visit with people. None of the other Marines on the ship had this privilege. My nametag identifying me as Editor of the newspaper—that was all I needed to go pretty much wherever I wanted. I always wore my best-pressed clean uniform with highly polished combat boots. I wanted to look sharp every day.

I even made friends with a couple of the military dependents that I visited with. One might say, compared with all the other Marines aboard the ship, that I had it made. When I would go down to my rack area where I slept and kept my clothes, I took a lot of ribbing from my buddies. But it was obvious that they envied me. They sat around all day, playing cards, smoking, telling sea stories, bitching about everything, while I went up to the top decks and enjoyed myself. I was pleased that I had taken on this job, because it did make the time pass quickly and I didn't have to sit around feeling sad.

The fourteen-day journey went quickly, and on February 29, 1964, we arrived and docked at Yokohama, Japan. Two days later, we flew by government aircraft from 1st Marine Air Wing Headquarters at Iwakuni, Japan, to Kadena AFB in Okinawa. I then boarded a military bus, which took me to the Marine Air Base at Futenma, more toward the south end of the island. Well, my long journey was over and I needed to find my job duties and get settled in.

CHAPTER 30

DUTY AT FUTENMA, OKINAWA, 1964

The Futenma Marine Corps Air Station was established in WWII after the defeat of the Japanese Imperial Army in the battle of Okinawa. The building where I was stationed was one of the newest on the base. The buildings were designed to withstand typhoons and were made from reinforced concrete, with long overhanging eves and shatterproof glass windows.

In my barracks, I shared a cubicle with another sergeant. For a reasonable fee, I had the services of an Okinawan housemaid, who did my laundry and cleaning. I checked in at my worksite and took over my job duties. As I was a Utilities Chief, I learned that I was in charge of the unit's Utilities section. Even at full strength, the Utilities Section consisted of less than ten people. These Marines would fill the positions of Water Supply, Refrigeration Mechanics, and Electricians. Our shop was only one-half of a

Quonset hut, and half of that was my office. In essence, this squadron had very little use for a Utilities Section when it wasn't needed for operations or combat situations.

The unit to which I was assigned was the Marine Air Support Squadron (MASS-2). The purpose of this unit was involved with highly specialized radar support. This Squadron had several rather small metal and fiberglass self-contained radar units, about the size of a large living room. These "boxes" are mobile and could be picked up and moved about with a helicopter. Inside these units were highly specialized radar electronics that have the capabilities of directing and controlling an aircraft, such as a bomber or other aircraft making air strikes at night or in inclement weather. The controls inside are manned by one person, who must be a specially trained pilot. Usually, on top of this box is a rotating radar screen. The purpose of this entire unit is to give our pilots the capabilities of accurately bombing an enemy target at night or in inclement weather conditions.

When a pilot is carrying out a bombing mission and cannot see the target, he can, essentially, hand over the operation of his aircraft to the pilot in the radar unit. The pilot in the radar box can actually fly the aircraft and release the bombs, and then turn the operation of the aircraft back to the pilot.

Due to the nature of the duties of this squadron, a large number of its personnel are pilots. The formations of the squadron every morning look significantly different from that of an infantry unit. The formation would have nearly a platoon of pilots, and perhaps only a dozen motor transport, clerical, and utilities personnel combined. It always seemed that during our daily operations there would be a number of pilots wandering around, trying to find somewhere to hide or attempting to look busy. Their only duty was to operate inside one of these radar units when in training operations or in combat. I felt kind of sorry for them, as I, who was only a sergeant, at least had an office, and a large office at that! Sometimes they would come to my office just to hang out and drink coffee. It was an unusual squadron, but in combat situations, they made up a critical unit.

After about a week of getting settled in with my living situation and job duties, I took stock of my situation. I liked where I was living, and it seemed like my job was going to be pretty easy, unless we went on a training operation or into combat situations. It would seem to some people I should be very happy. However, I wasn't happy. I was more homesick than I ever had been in my life. I found myself wishing there was some prescription for homesickness, but there wasn't such a thing. I missed Delores and the boys so much. It was almost unbearable to face the fact I would be separated from them for more than a year. I found myself wondering if other men felt like I did, or was I really just a wimp? I tried to hide my emotional discomfort the best I could. I found that the best thing to do was to get really busy doing whatever needed to be done, or create something to do.

I wrote Delores a letter almost every day, and I looked forward every day for mail call, hoping for a letter from her. I vowed to myself that no matter how homesick I was, outwardly I would remain a hard charging Marine, and I would throw myself into my daily job of being such a Marine.

After about a month on the job, I was called to the squadron office. The Commanding Officer wanted to see me. What could this be? I went in to the Major's office and reported. He was a pilot and a squared-away looking Marine. He invited me into his office and told me that I was being transferred to another unit, and eventually headed to a unit in Da Nang, Vietnam, for six months.

He asked me if I knew where Da Nang was located. I said, "No sir, I don't believe I do."

He turned to a huge map on the wall behind his desk and motioned to me to come around his desk to see the map. It was a large map of the South Pacific area South China Sea. He pointed to Okinawa and said this is where we are now, and this is where you are going—and he pointed to South Vietnam and to the coastal city of Da Nang. He explained that I was being temporally transferred to another Air Wing Squadron for six months, and they had a sub unit in Da Nang. Simply put, the Marine Corps had a Helicopter Squadron operating in South Vietnam with some support troops. Their overall purpose was to support South Vietnamese troops in carrying out their operations against enemy forces.

This Marine Corp helicopter task force, code named SHUFLY, consisted of a helicopter squadron and support elements. The helicopters were being used to ferry the South Vietnamese troops into and out of battle. The Sub Unit was the support unit for the Helicopter

Squadron. It consisted of personnel such as supply, motor transport, utilities, and other personnel. It seems they were badly in need of Utilities people, especially a Refrigeration Mechanic. Well, in that subject I was highly trained.

He asked if I had any questions. I said, "Yes, could a person get killed there?" The Major said, "Yes, they could." He invited me to sit down for a moment. I sat, and he briefed me on the operation in South Vietnam and what I could expect. He went on to say that this helicopter unit and the MABS sub unit were the only combat operational units in the entire Marine Corps operating in a combat zone, and he said, for that reason, some people looked forward to serving there. The Major said this operation wasn't exactly secret, however, it wasn't widely known by the public, and that was the way our government wanted it to remain. In closing, he said they would cut my orders immediately and get me on my way, as the word was that they were pretty desperate for a refrigeration mechanic right now, and I was the guy. So, he told me to pack my bags, shook my hand, and wished me good luck.

Wow! This was some news! It was something that I hadn't counted on. Well, the good side was, it would most surely help the time pass quickly. But, for sure, Delores and my family would not be happy that I was going to be operating in a combat zone, even further away from the ones I love. But this is what Marines do; this is what I was trained for; and now the Marine Corps needed me.

I went back to my barracks and told some of my buddies. A couple of them said I was a "lucky dog" to get to go do something exciting. But others said they would prefer to just stay out of Vietnam. Well, no matter their reactions I was going, and I had better get packed up. I would write a letter that evening to Delores about where I was going, but I would play down any fear of danger.

It would be better if I just waited until I got to Vietnam and assessed the situation there before I told her much.

The next several days passed quickly as I packed my gear, picked up my orders, and checked out of my unit and into the MABS unit. I soon found myself at Kadena Air Force base boarding a large C-130 aircraft that was packed full of operational gear of all kinds, including .50 caliber machine gun ammunition.

Soon we were airborne and heading to South Vietnam, a trip they said would take a little over three hours. I settled into one of the canvas seats lining each side of the aircraft, which were facing inboard, and I snapped my seat belt. All the cargo was stacked in the middle and secured down with cargo nets. I couldn't help but notice that there were only two or three other passengers—not many people going to Da Nang! The big plane shook violently and loudly as it revved its four big engines at the end of the runway, warming up for the takeoff. Said takeoff went smoothly, and soon the big aircraft made a long swooping turn and headed southwest toward what used to be French Indo-China.

As I settled down for the flight, I got as comfortable as possible in the canvas seat, closed my eyes, listened to the powerful drone of the big engines, and let my mind wander back to Delores and the boys in the small apartment in North Braddock. I tried to picture what they were doing now. How I longed to hold them close again and feel their warmth! So, here I was again on another leg of my long journey away from them, now on an aircraft that was taking me even further and further away. But, I told myself, I must not focus of them. I must focus on being a Marine and doing whatever job I had to do. I must focus on keeping myself alive so I can return to them.

Well, so I was going to be the only refrigeration mechanic in the Marine Corps operating in a combat zone. How did that come to be—I asked myself—that this poor country boy from Kansas, now had a technical skill that was greatly needed in the only combat zone our country was operating in? I didn't know whether to be scared or proud. But fate had set my future, and there was nothing I could do about it. I suddenly felt very tired and drifted off to sleep.

CHAPTER 31

DA NANG, VIETNAM: OPERATION SHUFLY, 1964

The flight went without incident, and almost too soon, so it seemed, we were approaching Da Nang. Everyone became alert when it was announced that we would soon be landing at Da Nang, South Vietnam, and we were told to fasten our seat belts. The local time was about 17:00. Winds buffeted the plane on the landing approach, and it was a relief when the tires finally screeched onto the runway. Over the intercom, the pilot welcomed us to Da Nang. He also announced that there was transportation waiting for any passengers checking in for Sub Unit 2. That was me, and, as it turned out, only me.

I grabbed my sea bag and clothing bag and debarked out the back ramp. I set down my bags, stood up, and looked around. The first thing I noticed were the smells of Vietnam, something that all new arrivals discover immediately. It's not just one smell but many smells, mingled together. There was an overriding pungent musty odor that I was to later learn was from the rice paddies—the ever-present rice paddies—which, in some areas, are fertilized with human waste. On top of that was a light smoky odor of burnt grass or wood, which I later learned was from the small cooking fires the natives used to cook their meals—and, in some instances, included dog, roasted over an open fire.

It was overcast with lead-gray clouds hanging over a low mountain range in the distance. There was one very prominent hill, which I later learned was Hill 327, so named because it was 327 feet above sea level—a landmark seen for many miles around. A Marine with a jeep drove up and asked if I was Sergeant Lay, going to Sub Unit 2. He helped me put my bags in the jeep and away we went. Welcome to Vietnam, Marine!

I still vividly recall my trip from the old, dilapidated air terminal, around the south end of the airstrip, and to the Marine living area on the other side of the runway. Just off the south end were some rice paddies. A lone figure—a bent over, Vietnamese farmer, wearing one of those conical hats—was working in the paddy field. With the sun just beginning to set, it was a memorable moment.

We turned off the perimeter road onto a dusty, red dirt road and into the compound where the Marines lived. The driver again helped me with my bags. The Squadron Office was inside a stucco-like building with a screen door that hung loose on its hinges. I turned my orders in to a sergeant who stamped them and returned a copy to me. He explained that I would be sleeping in a temporary place tonight and would get my permanent barracks assignment tomorrow. The sergeant motioned to the PFC jeep driver, who apparently also doubled as runner, and told him to help me take my bags to a nearby building, where I would sleep. He also showed me where the mess hall was located. I was glad, because I was definitely hungry.

I dropped my bags beside the empty rack that had a folded up mattress and a pillow on it. There was no mattress cover, sheets, or pillowcase. None were offered, and I didn't ask. I was thinking that maybe asking for sheets and a pillowcase might be too much to expect here in Vietnam. Then I noticed that neither was there a blanket. None was offered, and, I realized, none was needed. Even at that late evening hour, it was sultry hot, and I was sweating.

This building was a single-story plywood structure with a tin roof, and the top three feet of the walls was screen wire. On one side of the building, and separated by a reinforced security fence, was a very busy roadway that led through a Vietnamese village. I later learned that the Marines had named the village Dog Patch. It appeared that the roadway was lined with many small businesses, people, and bicycles, scurrying to and fro. On that side of the building, sand bags were stacked six-feet high.

It was getting dark, so I went into the large old stucco building with loose-hanging shutters that had been designated as the mess hall, hoping to get some evening chow. It was nearly empty because it was almost closing time. The mess hall was nearly empty because it was almost closing time. I ate heartily and returned to the building where I was to sleep.

It was dark by now. There was certainly no green grass here, only sand and dust everywhere. Although this building had a couple dozen racks, it appeared that I was the only one sleeping there tonight. That was fine with me! I unrolled the mattress on my rack and unpacked a few things. I was tired so I lay down early, hoping to fall right to sleep, but some healthy mosquitos had other plans for me.

I finally fell asleep, but not for long. I was awakened by what sounded like gunfire. It didn't sound like it was very close, but I knew it was definitely gunfire. I sat up on my rack and listened carefully. Yes, sure enough, there it was again. I could hear it in the distance, including a few automatic fire bursts, and I heard the "thump" "thump" of probably mortar fire or hand grenades. Was there an attack in progress? I pulled on my trousers and boots and went outside. A Marine was walking by going to the head, so I asked him what was going on. He looked at me, then asked me if I was new here. When I answered in the affirmative, he said, "Don't worry about it!" He said it was, indeed, action that went on "out in the valley" nearly every night, but he assured me that it wouldn't come close to us. I remember thinking, *I sure hope it won't!,* and I wished that I'd been issued a weapon of some kind along with some ammo. I believed what the guy had told me, but nevertheless, I didn't sleep much that first night in Vietnam. Several more times during the night I was awakened by gunfire and muffled explosions in the distance. I again wished that I had a weapon. What was I suppose to fight with, my bare hands? Find a club? Why didn't they issue every man a weapon as soon as he checked into this area?

I was up early the next morning and began my first day in Vietnam. I found the head, shaved and showered, and went to chow. After that, I reported to the squadron office and met with the first sergeant. I was told that although I was a Utilities Chief, there was a Staff Sergeant, a Construction Chief, in the Utilities Section, and he was senior and would officially be the Utilities Chief. He went on to say that I would be working as the refrigeration mechanic.

I thought, *That's fine with me*! I was given a check-in sheet, and a clerk took me to the building where I would be living. The building was a single story stucco rectangular building that was designated as the Sergeants' quarters. It was filled with single racks, most of them equipped with mosquito nets, and a couple of rifle racks. I picked a rack in the middle of the building and dropped my gear. I met two or three other sergeants who lived there. Right away, I took my check-in sheet and found the armory, where I was issued an M-14 rifle and a dozen fully loaded magazines. This was more like it! I felt much more comfortable. I liked the M-14 and was much at ease with it. I actually preferred it over the M-1 Grand, because of its greatly increased firepower. By mid-day, I was finally fully checked in, had made my rack, and was ready to go to work.

I soon learned that the area we lived in was called a compound. It was completely surrounded by reinforced barbed wire. It had been a French fort when Vietnam was a colony of France. French foreign legion troops had once occupied these barracks. It was no wonder they were dilapidated, with a lot of pockmarks on the outside walls of the buildings from snipers shooting into the compound. Some of these pockmarks were recent.

Most of the old buildings were made of stucco and were in pretty bad shape. I was told that an infantry company was also stationed here to provide security for the compound. My immediate thought was, "Only a company? How long would they last under a full-scale attack?"

That question was finally addressed when, exactly a year later, in March of 1965, elements of the 9th Marine Expeditionary Brigade were landed at Da Nang to provide security for the airstrip. Throughout 1964, and before, the Viet Cong had been secretly building up their forces all around this area, especially the airstrip. The United States was forced by circumstances to increase their forces. This landing marked the first official introduction of ground forces into the Vietnam War.

I found the utilities section, which was located in a southeastern Asian hut. It was a plywood building on stilts, with screening on the top three feet to allow air circulation, and a tin roof. The building and its contents were in a shambles. As far as a refrigeration section was concerned, in one small corner of the building I discovered a toolbox with a few assorted tools, a couple cylinders of freon-12, and various spare parts for refrigeration units. That was it. So, it seemed that the refrigeration section consisted of just me and these tools in an eight-foot square corner of an old plywood building. Hmmm. I quickly cleaned out and inventoried what I had. It wasn't much.

When I realized that I was pretty much by myself with not much to work with, I did a walking survey of what kind of units I was responsible for and where they were located. What I found was pretty distressing. There were about thirty various refrigeration and air-conditioning units, most of them badly in need of maintenance or replacement. I also met another sergeant, Roger, who was the electrician for the unit. He was a really likable guy whom I would work with for the rest of my tour in Vietnam. I learned that he was a outstanding Marine, who really knew his job.

Roger and I worked together to keep electricity and refrigeration systems in good repair for the unit. We worked hard every day, and by the day's end, we were wet with sweat and could hardly wait until 17:00 when the club opened.

The club consisted of no more than one-half of one of the stucco buildings, hardly more than a forty by twenty-foot space, with a small bar across one end. There were six or seven tables and chairs, some bar stools, and two very attractive Vietnamese waitresses. We were almost always in that club as soon as it opened and could hardly wait to get a bottle of that ice-cold beer. To this day, I will never forget how good that beer tasted after working hard all day in the tropical sun. After a few beers, we went next door to the Mess Hall for some of the best chow I've ever eaten in the Marine Corps.

I soon found out why that chow was so good. The Chief Mess Sergeant was an old Marine buddy of mine, Sergeant Hunter, going all the way back to my days in Miami in 1954 and 1955, when he was a cook in the mess hall and I was a mess man. We struck up a friendship there that has lasted all these years. Later I saw him again at a mess hall in Camp Lejeune, where we both were stationed after leaving Miami. I remember the chow in that mess hall was always the best. It became a firm conviction in my mind that if Sergeant

Hunter were the chief Mess Sergeant in a chow hall, you would be treated to very best food.

I have found, as I'm sure many others would agree, one of the things that makes the Marine Corps great, is the longevity of its friendships. Since the Marine Corps is very small compared to the other branches of the services, it's more and more likely that you will run into people whom you know over and over again. And renewing old friendships is always an enjoyable thing.

I fondly recall how, not long after I arrived in Okinawa in 1964, I walked into a large Marine Corps service club, and as soon as I entered the doorway, I heard a loud voice call out, "Bob Lay, you old son-of-a-bitch! Come over here." Most of the other patrons stopped what they were doing and looked up. It was an old Marine buddy I hadn't seen in years. What a great reunion!

Here in Vietnam, I started by first ordering a number of specialty tools for refrigeration work. I found out that since we were the only Marine Corps unit operating in a combat zone, everything we needed was considered "Combat Essential." If these items were anywhere in Japan, Okinawa, or elsewhere, they were to be located and sent down to Da Nang the next day. I learned the C-130 that I had flown on was a daily flight sometimes called the "milk run." It began at Iwakuni, Japan, everyday, and first went to Okinawa, then to Da Nang, Vietnam. It returned the next day to Okinawa then on to Iwakuni, a very useful operation.

While this helicopter unit and its support personnel were the only Marine Corps units operating in a combat zone, my day to day work was pretty much routine. Only rarely would snipers from the village across the road fire into our compound. When security officials indicated that it was safe enough, we were granted liberty to go into the city of Da Nang for shopping, sightseeing, visiting, and eating and drinking in the bars, restaurants, and clubs. Only certain areas of Da Nang were approved, while much of the city was off-limit.

Looking back on these times, I realize that it was a rare opportunity to be in this very old Asian city and see what it had been like when it was a French colony before 1954 and before more American military units moved in to support the growing war against the communist insurgency. One of the more popular and prominent places to visit was the Grand Tourane hotel on the waterfront in the city. The Grand Tourane hotel, in its heyday, was considered by many as another French Riviera and was a favorite vacation place of rich French and other world travelers. By the time of operation SHUFLY, when I and other American military began to visit Da Nang, it was sadly run down, and only a shadow of its former self remained, due to many years of war.

There were some occasions when liberty off our compound was not granted due to security reasons that were never fully explained to us. After I had been there about a week, I decided to visit the city of Da Nang. On the days when liberty was granted, the Marine Corps provided transportation from our compound to downtown Da Nang. The transportation was usually just a truck, sometimes with its canvas cover, and sometimes a larger vehicle that we referred to as a "Cattle Car." On the weekends and evenings the transportation would travel back and forth about every hour. The drop-off place in Da Nang was in front of the Grand Tourane Hotel. It was very convenient place and a center of activity in Da Nang.

In addition to just visiting this exciting old city, I was eager to again participate in a favorite pastime of Marines everywhere, that of bar hopping, having a few drinks, telling sea stories with other Marines, and teasing the bar girls. I was also hoping to buy a cheap guitar to play in my off-duty time. Ever since I was a kid and my

Uncle Elmer had taught me to play a few chords on his guitar, I've been a guitar lover. I didn't feel complete unless I had a guitar to play.

I owned a very nice Gibson guitar that I had left back in North Braddock, which was much too expensive and too nice to travel with around the world. Most often, when I was sent to a new duty station, one of the first things I had to do was to find an affordable guitar. Well, Vietnam was no exception. I needed a guitar, and I was told that I could buy a fairly good guitar in Da Nang for a good price. So, I went guitar shopping.

Shopping in Da Nang was indeed a unique experience. The streets were filled with hordes of people, bicycles, dogs, Vietnamese Army troops, American military, pretty young Vietnamese women, dressed in their traditional Ao dai, a tight-fitting silk tunic with black silk trousers. Sometimes they wore conical hats, and there were usually two women together. These women, with their long black hair and dark eyes, are perhaps some of the most beautiful women in the world. It's not surprising that a number of men fell in love with these women and sought permission from the military and from the girl's family to marry. Arranging a marriage between an American serviceman and a Vietnamese woman was a paper nightmare. But some men persisted and got married.

Included in the mix of pedestrians on the street were stooped, wrinkled old men with goatees, old wrinkled women, and flocks of impoverished young children, all looking malnourished and begging for money, candy, gum, and cigarettes. If you gave them anything, they would remember you, and the next time they saw you they would beg you for more, bringing fifteen or twenty more of their friends.

One time I made the mistake of buying bubble gum for them. I believe I bought $10 worth of bubble gum in the PX on base and took it to town. I had a large paper bag filled with it. I handed gum out to a crowd of twenty or more kids. In a short time, it seemed like every kid in Da Nang was chewing bubble gum. The next time I came to town, they recognized me and swamped me with twice as many kids. When I didn't have anything for them, they gave me the "thumbs down" sign and called me bad names in Vietnamese. They called me a "number ten G.I.," which is as bad as it gets. If they called you number one, that was the best. We all learned, I know I did. I never bought them anything again.

There were very few cars, so the center of the streets were used for people traffic. There were dozens of small businesses of all kinds packed into every block; small noodle bars, pawn shops, jewelry stores, clothing stores, tattoo shops, etc., all actively seeking our business. And, yes, there were plenty of prostitutes and their pimps plying their trade. There were even young boys pimping their sisters or mothers. One of them would pull on your sleeve or shirt, pat their hands together, and say something like, "You boom-boom my sister/ mother," and sometimes would add, "she is a virgin." When I first heard this, even this old Marine in me was shocked.

It seemed like there was a huge national effort to separate the American service men from their money. And they were very good at it. The Americans, however, were restricted from using American money in country. We were required to use Military Payment Certificates, (MPC). The Vietnamese currency at the time was Piasters. And, we were advised that it was unlawful to convert your American cash to the Vietnamese currency, Piasters, off the military base. It didn't take most servicemen long to learn that if you had American cash, and you exchanged it off base, there was a lot better exchange rate, as the Vietnamese really wanted that American dollar. I do remember the exchange rate in 1964 in Da Nang at one time was 325 Piasters per one American dollar. I must emphasize that, like nearly everything else in Vietnam, this exchange rate was always negotiable and changed constantly. With this exchange rate, American service personnel were considered wealthy. A serviceman could go into Da Nang, have a nice dinner at the Grand Hotel and several beers or cocktails for less than $10. And, according to rumor and unofficial sources, a prostitute would be available for about the same price.

One of the main commodities was jewelry. There were a lot of jewelry stores in Da Nang. And, surprisingly, there were very good prices on nearly all kinds of jewels. Most servicemen that I knew made some good jewelry buys, as did I. One item I bought was a very nice gold bracelet for Delores, set with green emeralds, which is her birthstone.

On that first visit to Da Nang, I was in a jewelry store when I heard the sounds of an electric guitar being played upstairs. I inquired about it, and the owner said it was his son playing. When I told him I was a guitar player, he insisted on taking me upstairs to meet his son. The kid was a teenager and had a pretty nice electric guitar and amplifier. He invited me to play it. I sat down and played some of the tunes I knew, including the Guitar Boogie, which I could play quite well then. He was very impressed and kept me there playing for about an hour.

After I left I continued my shopping and did find a cheap guitar, which I bought for probably less than $20. I was very happy with my purchase, and rode around town for a while in a cyclo, which is a three-wheeled bicycle taxi that appeared in Vietnam during the French colonial period. A cyclo had two wheels on the front and one wheel on the back. The driver would sit behind the front passenger seat pedaling. I sat up there in the seat, playing my new guitar while the driver pedaled me around town sightseeing.

When it was about suppertime, I went to the restaurant in the Grand Hotel, and ordered a large plate of fried frog legs, one of the delicacies in Vietnam, and a beer. I was sitting there eating, with my guitar propped up in the seat beside me, when three guys came rushing up to me, and introduced themselves. They were all in the Air Force. One of them asked me if I was the guy who happened to be playing the guitar upstairs over a jewelry store that afternoon. I said that indeed, that was me. They had heard me from out in the street and said they had been looking all afternoon for me. By the time they had got to the jewelry store, I had left.

They asked permission to sit down, which, of course I granted. They explained that they were Air Force, and musicians, and had a country music band. But, they explained, their lead guitar player had been transferred back to the states, and they were looking for a lead guitar player. They wanted to hire me to play lead guitar in their band. I told them that I was flattered, and, yes I could play a little guitar, but I wasn't good enough to play lead guitar with a band.

The older of the three, a guy named Chuck, said, "If you were the guy playing that guitar boogie, and other country stuff, upstairs above the jewelry store, you are definitely good enough. We want to hire you."

So, again, I said, "Well, that was me." So, then we began to talk seriously about their band and exactly what they wanted me to do. I told them that I didn't have an electric guitar that I could play lead on, or an amplifier. Chuck said, "No problem!" It seems that the guy who had left the band had left his Fender Jaguar guitar, and he would sell it to me for $50, and I could play it through his amp.

Well, I couldn't turn that down. So, I bought the guitar and we made arrangements about when we could get together for a practice session before they played in a gig the next weekend. It seems that the only place they were playing right then was at a private club in Da Nang named the "Take Ten" club. It was a popular club, where members of all the U.S. military services frequented, along with services members from allied nations, including Australians, British, and Koreans. It was operated by the military through a board of governors from each branch of the service. The place was secured by heavy screen wire on the windows, and was guarded by Vietnamese Army personnel.

When I joined the band they were only playing on Saturday nights, but were soon going to be playing Friday nights as well. So, just like that, I was going to be playing in a country band on the weekends. I didn't know whether to consider myself lucky or perhaps a bit crazy. After all, this was Vietnam, and a war was going on! Perhaps I should have waited and ask the command if it was okay. But the deal had been made, and I decided to go for it. I thought that it would sure be better than sitting in the hot barracks Friday and Saturday nights, sweating and being bored, homesick for Delores and the boys. Maybe the time would pass more quickly until I could return home to them.

One evening, the Air Force guys came over to our compound, picked me up, and we went to the Air Force area where we got together with our instruments and worked out a repertoire of songs and tunes we could play at the club engagements. I knew about ten instrumental tunes, plus at least eight or ten songs I could sing. I was also able to do some background guitar work on most of the songs that the other members sang. I surprised myself that when it came right down to it, I knew a lot more songs and guitar pieces than I thought!

Our first night playing at the "Take Ten" club went very well. After all, we were the only country music band playing in the entire northern area of Vietnam. One of the tunes the patrons liked was my version of the Guitar Boogie Shuffle. It was one tune that I had learned early in my guitar learning days, and I could play it quite well. I got a lot of requests for that tune. I had also learned the lyrics and instrumental of a popular song of the day, "The Ballad of Jed Clampett," the theme song of the TV program, "The Beverly Hillbillies." The audience really came alive when I played that tune. I had also learned some of the lyrics of several "Johnny Cash" tunes that were popular at the time. I had a deep voice, which served me well in singing Johnny Cash's songs. In a way, this experience playing in Vietnam at the "Take Ten" club gave me my start in playing and singing with a real band. Yes, I had played some programs at local functions with the Shroyer family when I was a teenager, but that wasn't the same as I was doing in Vietnam.

Playing music in nightclub, Da Nang, Vietnam. "Take Ten" club.

From the time I began to play in this band, until I returned to Okinawa in October, I believe that I played every weekend. Also, on one or more occasions, we played in the grand ballroom at the Grand Hotel, and at two of the larger Vietnamese clubs in Da Nang. At these Vietnamese clubs we were paid in Piasters for our work. It was amusing to see what a large roll of cash that amounted to, even thought it didn't amount to much in America money. In fact, it was so big that we could hardly get it into our pockets.

CHAPTER 32

BACK TO OKINAWA, 1965

Once I had settled into my daily routine, I realized that it was one of hard toil. I was constantly repairing and servicing various refrigeration units. The most important ones were located in the mess hall. These were large, refrigerated storage boxes for frozen foods, as well as units designed to keep vegetables fresh. These units couldn't be without power for more than a few hours in these very hot weather conditions or the contents would begin to spoil, resulting in the loss of thousands of dollars worth of food. There were also some refrigeration units at the medical department, where certain medications and other supplies had to be refrigerated. These were old units and required constant attention to keep them operating. In addition to all of these, there were various other refrigeration and cooling units that needed repairs and maintenance. Although most of my work was somewhat routine, perhaps it will help you to grasp the whole picture if I describe some of the more unusual events that occurred while I was there.

On one occasion, I was called upon to go to the flight line and check out a specially design air conditioning unit that was used to keep the electronics in the center at a specific temperature. These computers and other electronic equipment wouldn't function properly if the temperature was not kept constant. I grabbed my toolbox and hitched a ride around the airstrip to the old airplane hangar where the unit was located. When I got there, I discovered that the unit was located up on the roof. I couldn't find a ladder to use to get on top of the building, but there was a large tree very close to the hangar with some of its limbs protruding over the roof. Sometimes in life a person just has to improvise. Carrying my toolbox, I climbed the tree and stepped off onto the roof. I checked the unit, found the problem, and repaired it. However, in the process of checking it out I had to reach inside of it to make an adjustment. On doing so, I accidentally laid my arm across a high-voltage relay and received a severe electrical shock! The jolt of electricity knocked me backward several feet and I was stunned for a few seconds. I also received a painful burn on my right forearm. I sat there on the roof, stunned, for a few minutes, wondering what had just happened. I did figure out the problem, and it was another good reminder of adhering to the safety rules when working around high-voltage electricity. I knew better, but I just got careless, and it could have cost me my life.

When I returned back to the Marine Compound, I went to sickbay and told them what had happened. They checked me out and bandaged the burn, which was minor. Still, I felt rather sick and nauseated for the remainder of the day. The medical people at sickbay said that receiving a strong electric shock like I had could make a person feel that way, along with a slight headache. They gave me a couple of aspirins. I took the rest of the afternoon off, lying in my rack under the mosquito netting and with my fan on. After awhile I felt good enough to resume my duties.

I remember another time after I had just arrived there and was still checking in and getting settled, an announcement came over the speaker system that broadcast all over the compound. They wanted anyone who had Type A blood to report to sick bay. I immediately answered the call. By the time I arrived, several other donors were already there. We were told to just stand by. We learned that one of our helicopter pilots had received a severe wound in his leg while on a strike mission. He required a lot of blood. From where we were waiting, we could see into the room where the pilot was being treated. His flight suit had been cut away, and I could see the doctor and corpsmen working on him. His leg was bleeding very badly from a large wound on his leg below the knee. They finally got him stabilized and told us we could go on back to our jobs. This scene certainly convinced me that there was a very real life-and-death war going on every day here for our pilots and flight crews. It was a sobering experience.

On another occasion a gentleman drove into our compound in a construction vehicle, introduced himself, and said that he worked for the worldwide construction company, RMK Construction, which had built the new runway and various other large construction projects. He said they needed a refrigeration mechanic, as one of their refrigeration units in the dining hall wasn't working and the food was going to spoil pretty quickly if it wasn't repaired. They weren't able to fly someone in on time to save the food, so they asked if they could borrow me.

The Staff Sergeant in charge of the Utilities section said that he was okay with my assisting this civilian company if I wanted to do so. The construction company representative said that, although it wasn't necessary, I could bring my weapon with me if I wanted. Trust me, I wasn't going *anywhere* in this area without my weapon!

I took my toolbox, a cylinder of Freon-12, my M-14 rifle, and several clips of ammunition, and away we went. Their living compound was on the Tien Sha peninsula across the bay from Da Nang at the foot of "Monkey Mountain." This was an area I had never been before. They had quite a large living compound that was guarded by the Army of the Republic of Vietnam, ARVN. It was somewhat like the fox guarding the henhouse. However, these construction workers, for the most part, were pretty safe, as the Viet Cong had no animosity toward them as they did with members of the American military. Still, I kept my rifle and ammo close by, just in case.

I was surprised at how much luxury these workers lived in. Their dining hall was very modern, and there appeared to be a substantial supply of quality food. After touring the dining facility, I turned my attention to the refrigeration unit that wasn't working as it should. The problem was something I was able to correct in less than an hour.

Needless to say, they were very happy with me. They insisted that I sit down and order anything I wanted from their menu. I gladly accepted and was very pleased with my meal. The gentleman whom I was with at the time took me to his quarters, where he gave me a bottle of scotch whisky for my work, and even suggested that if I wanted to have sex with one of the pretty young housemaids, he could make it happen right then. Well, of course, I declined. When the gentleman took me back to my area, we parted on a very positive note. He said he was certain that with my skills, when I got out of the Marine Corps, I could get a very good job with RMK, who had construction projects all around the world. It was a great experience, and I enjoyed the whiskey.

One day, when I reported to work, I learned that one of our Marines had gone missing the past weekend. I didn't know the man personally, but he did work in the Utilities section in construction, and I would see him frequently. From what we could learn, on Sunday, he and a buddy illegally slipped out the back gate on the side of the compound, where the village was located, on the main roadway going south of our area. This was a very serious violation of orders. They reportedly had rented two motorbikes and followed the roadway to a stream or river. They parked their bikes, took off their clothing, and went for a swim in the stream. Well, it turns out that they were captured by the Viet Cong. I never learned what finally happened to them. The last report I can remember is that they were seen being carried through villages in bamboo cages, where they were mocked, spit upon, and tortured. It was a sad ending for these unfortunate young men—a very hard lesson for them as well as for the rest of us, not to mention the grief they caused their families. An unauthorized Sunday afternoon motorbike ride in this beautiful country may not have seemed like such a big deal, but it was a violation of orders and apparently cost them their lives.

In July, I finally received the news I had been expecting; I was the proud father of a beautiful baby girl! The baby was born on July 22, 1964. Delores and the baby were fine. We named this little girl Valerie Judith Lay. Valerie has grown into a beautiful, tall, slim, and charming lady. Before she married she joined the Marines, and became a Combat Correspondent. She thrived in this tough Marine Corps environment and became a Sergeant before her enlistment ended. Later in life, she became a nurse, and is employed at a large, tough state penitentiary. She and her husband, Ron Martin, founded a successful real estate business and raised two tall, handsome, successful sons. We all think God worked a little overtime when he made Valerie.

I was so thrilled at the news of her birth, but there was also a sadness that accompanied it. It would be a long time before I would get to see my new baby girl. I likely would not get home until March of 1965, approximately eight long months away. Delores would really have her hands full now. But she was a tough, competent lady, and I was confident that she could handle it. Besides, she was close to all her family who were happy to help her.

In August, tensions between North Vietnam and the United States reached a new high when American ships operating in the Gulf of Tonkin, just off the shore of Vietnam, reported being fired upon by North Vietnamese torpedo boats. In retaliation, the United States Joint Chiefs of Staff authorized air strikes against North Vietnamese patrol boats, bases, and fuel storage areas. Also, President Johnson authorized strikes against selected targets in North Vietnam. On August 7, 1964, Congress passed the Gulf of Tonkin Resolution, giving the President the authorization to take all necessary measures to repel any armed attack against forces of the United States in order to prevent further aggression. The resolution gave the President broad authority to use American forces without a formal declaration of war by Congress. As time went by, due to additional information that was revealed, considerable doubt was placed on whether there were ever any attacks on the American ships named.

The Gulf of Tonkin incident occurred without any knowledge to most of us at the Marine compound. There was no change in my daily duties. At some point later on we learned, just from rumor, what was going on. I recall that liberty into Da Nang was curtailed for a few days at about that time. I believe this level of information wasn't normally shared with operational troops unless it affected their mission.

My time in Vietnam was soon coming to an end. According to administrative regulations, a Marine could only be assigned Temporary Assignment Duty (TAD) away from his parent unit for six months. In early October I was due to return to my unit in Okinawa.

One night, near the end of my tour in Da Nang, when I returned to the compound from liberty in Da Nang I noticed a lot of the perimeter lights were out, as were most all the lights in the compound. When I got off the "liberty" truck, I noticed a lot of activity at the generator shed.

The generator shed was a covered structure housing the generators that provided about half of the electric power to the compound. The remainder of the power was provided by the Vietnamese power company located in Da Nang. Someone at the generator shed recognized me as I walked across the compound and called me over.

I went over to assess the situation. I was very familiar with the power arrangement, as it directly affected the refrigeration units at the mess hall. When I got to the shed, I saw a small group of people, including the Commanding Officer, Colonel Hay, and several of the Utilities Section electricians. The problem was that the generator that was supposed to be providing the power wasn't operating properly. The fact that we had no power at the perimeter presented a clear danger to the compound, because it made an attack by the Viet Cong or other enemy units much easier to accomplish. An attack could be imminent and perhaps this outage was caused by sabotage.

Already that evening, there had been several sniper shots close together, which may have been due to the lights being out. At least two of those shots hit the sandbag wall surrounding the generator shed. The Colonel and others who knew me welcomed me anxiously, hoping that I could help. The two electricians and others there hadn't been able to determine why the generator was not able to provide the power needed.

It was hot, and some of us were stripped down to our waists and wet with sweat. I was a Utilities Chief, and with my training, I was clearly expected to be able to diagnose this problem and repair it, even though it turned out to be a rare problem. It seemed that the generator was operating okay and would start and run as it was designed to do. The problem was that the electrical switch, which engaged the power to the grid system, would "pop out" and disengage instead of remaining closed. The important question was why?

I was familiar with these types of switches, as they are used on several large refrigeration units, with which I was familiar. It took me about fifteen minutes to diagnose the problem and repair it. I will always recall that dark, hot night, working in a pair of civilian trousers and old tennis shoes, and soaked with sweat. While I worked, the Colonel and several utilities men watched over my shoulder, holding flashlights to light my work, all very anxious to have the lights come on again.

I finished my repair and told everyone to just stand by as I started the generator and prepared to engage the main switch. Everyone there was praying and crossing their fingers that the lights would come on, including me. I engaged the switch, and the big generator groaned as all the lights in the compound came on. The switch stayed engaged! A big cheer rang out from all of us! I cannot find adequate words to describe how happy I felt, as it was one of those moments in my life when I was called upon to prove to the command that I was a Marine who could be trusted to do his job. Years later, in another command, I came across Colonel Hay! He remembered me, and we exchanged a bit of reminiscing. It is still a fond memory.

As expected, in early October I received orders to return to MASS-2, my parent unit in Okinawa. I was to take the C-130 on its return "leg" of the "milk run" back to Okinawa. However, when I went to the Squadron office to pick up my written orders, I noticed what appeared to be an error. The orders read that I would "proceed to Iwakuni, Japan, and report to the Commanding Office of MASS-2 for duty." I pointed out that MASS-2 was at the base in Futenma, Okinawa, and not at Iwakuni, Japan. The administrative chief was either was too lazy to listen to me or too arrogant, even though I pointed it out the second time. So, I just shrugged my shoulders, accepted the orders, and walked out to catch my ride to the airstrip.

I wasn't sad to leave Da Nang. I admit, I had a lot of fun playing music, shopping, and seeing the sights of old Da Nang town, but I was happy to leave the hot and hard work of keeping all the refrigeration units going besides always living with the threat that at any time you could be shot by a sniper, step on a booby trap, or be injured by any one of the dozens of ways a person can lose their life in Vietnam.

I boarded the big plane and settled into one of the canvas seats, and got as comfortable as one can get in these airplane seats. I enjoyed the roar of the big engines and speeding down the runway, especially as it meant that I was, at last, leaving Vietnam and getting closer to home. When the plane cleared the runway, it made a huge, sweeping turn, headed northeast to Okinawa. I settled in for the trip. I can remember the moment that when the tires cleared the runway on takeoff, and I and the several other passengers cheered. I also recall holding my middle finger up to one of the windows and saying, "Fuck you, Vietnam. I'll never see this place again," as the plane lifted off.

When we landed in Okinawa at Kadena AFB, I was able to leave the aircraft for a short break and to get some food at the cafeteria. It also gave me the opportunity to call the Administration Chief at my unit at Futenma. He was a friend of mine and was glad to hear from me. I told him about my orders and the error in ordering me to Iwakuni, Japan, instead of Okinawa. He laughed about it but agreed that I should follow what the orders read. So, I got back aboard the plane to proceed on to Iwakuni, where the headquarters of the 1st Marine Air Wing was located. It was about a three-hour flight from Okinawa.

It was dark when we arrived at Iwakuni. When I disembarked from the plane, I had my orders stamped to verify my arrival. Transportation was provided to a barracks, where troops in transit are billeted. Wow, I was in Japan again! I stepped outside the barracks to get some fresh air and smiled at not having to breathe the smells of Vietnam. Japan had its own smell, which I noticed was much better than my previous location.

The next morning, I got up early, showered and shaved, and found the mess hall. The food was excellent, and I enjoyed a good breakfast. While I ate, I took an assessment of my situation. I was in Iwakuni just as my orders had directed. My orders did not specify what else I was supposed to do. I was beginning to formulate a plan—a plan to give me three or four days in Japan before I reported to the headquarters of the 1st Marine Air Wing. Perhaps I could just stay there in the Casual Company barracks and no one would notice! I had been in the Marine Corps long enough to know how these matters are handled. I thought I could do it without getting into trouble. I would just stay there and see some of the sights of Japan. Being a Sergeant, I didn't need any further permission, except for my I.D. card, to go off and on the base.

Before I left the base, however, I recalled that my old Marine buddy Chris was perhaps stationed there. I contacted the base locator service and easily located him. He was very happy to see me and was able to take some days off and join me. It was great fun when Chris and I left the base and went to see some of the sights of Japan. He had been there for a while, so he sort of knew his way around.

For the next four days, Chris and I hung out together and ate some fine Japanese food, which I discovered I loved. One day, he and I took a train to Hiroshima to visit the site of the explosion of the first atomic bomb dropped on Japan in August of 1945. We visited Peace

Park, which is located at ground zero where the bomb actually fell. It is a somber and sad place, with a lot of Japanese people visiting the park and shrine there.

While in Hiroshima, we visited one of Japan's largest bath and massage parlors. It was one of the most relaxing and rejuvenating experience I have ever had. That visit, followed by a fine traditional Japanese meal, capped off a memorable day for Chris and me, and with that we wound up our short vacation together.

The next morning at 07:30 I reported to the offices of the 1st Marine Air Wing. When I checked in, the person who accepted my orders took a quick look at them and excused himself for a moment. I watched as he took the orders to a superior and showed him the orders. A brief discussion took place, and some pointing was going on at me.

Then the fellow came back to me and told me that I was supposed to be in Okinawa. He said it bluntly: "Your unit is in Okinawa. You're at the wrong place."

I pointed out to him that I had followed my orders and reported here, where I had been directed. He told me that "Tomorrow we will make arrangements for you to fly to Okinawa and join your unit at Futenma." I continued to play dumb, shrugged my shoulders, and said, "Okay." He went on to say, "Come back in here at 08:00 tomorrow, and we'll amend your orders and take you to the airstrip to catch a plane, okay?"

I said, "Okay," and left the office. There were no questions about where I had been for the past four days. In essence, I had gotten away with four days free leave in Japan!

The next day, I flew to Okinawa and landed at Kadena Air Force Base. I took the military bus to Futenma and reclaimed my cubicle in the same barracks I had left six months ago. Several of my buddies were still there, and I even hired the same housemaid. It was fun getting settled again. After our greetings, it seemed like no time until my maid had my rack all made and was unpacking my bags, putting things away, and gathering up my dirty clothing. Wow! It was good to be back in Okinawa! I felt like I had it made. Thank you, Jesus, for watching over me.

The next day I checked back into my old unit and reclaimed my job as Utilities Chief along with my former office. Our mission, and my job responsibilities, had not changed. I spent the remaining six months of my overseas tour with no unusual occurrences—just keeping the equipment we had in good condition, making sure that everything was ready to be able to mount out and go anywhere in the world that we were needed.

Over the next six months, I made some efforts to get hired by one of the country music bands operating in Okinawa. I didn't have time to put a lot of effort into it, and I needed a break from playing music. However, twice I was invited to play at gigs with what was considered by most as the best country band in Okinawa. The gig that I thought was the most fun was a Sunday afternoon at the large Air Force club at Naha, Okinawa. The club was packed with a good-natured crowd, who seemed to really appreciate the music. The band was pretty big, with perhaps seven musicians, and they all were very good. I wasn't hired to play lead, but to just play rhythm and sing several Johnny Cash songs, and "The Ballad of Jed Clampett."

It was a terrific crowd, and they seemed to love my songs. I was beginning to become convinced that I was doing quite well and maybe had a future as a country singer. It's a thrilling feeling to sing before a large crowd and have an enthusiastic response.

On one other occasion, this same band invited me to play a gig at our Staff NCO club at Futenma. Again, the response was excellent, but the club and crowd was not nearly as large as the one at the Air Force Base. This was all taking place not long before I was due to leave Okinawa. The leader of the band, an Air Force fellow, told me that if I was just beginning my tour of duty he was sure he could work me in as a regular member and pay me well. But, there was no way I was going to stay in Okinawa for any reason! I wanted to go home and see Delores, the boys, and my new baby daughter, Valerie. Most of my thoughts were now occupied with leaving Okinawa, how I would get back to the states, and where my new duty station would be.

CHAPTER 33

DUTY IN THE PHILIPPINES

One of the good things about serving in MASS-2 was that they had a radar team stationed at U.S. Naval Air Station at Subic Bay in the Philippines. These troops would rotate frequently with our personnel at Futenma. As a result, there were almost daily flights between Futenma and the Philippines. Our command was lenient enough to allow other unit personnel to travel on these flights and take a few days leave in the Philippines.

In mid-December, I was able to get temporary assignment orders to our unit in the Philippines to administer a General Military Subjects test to our people there. Giving a General Military Subjects test was technically just a legal excuse to go to the Philippines. Yes, this test was required periodically, but it wasn't necessary at the time, but it was okay if I wanted to go and administer it now. It was really just a cover to conceal the real reason—I wanted to go to the Philippines!

I caught a flight to Subic Bay, checked in with the Radar Team commander, and claimed a rack and locker in the very nice barracks The staff there helped me to establish a date in which to administer the test, and I was able to do whatever I wanted until then! After I administered the test and checked back in at the command, I was told that I wouldn't be able to catch a return flight to Okinawa until about ten days before Christmas. In the meantime, I was able to take a free vacation!

I visited the local and notorious town of Olongapo, right outside the main gate of the base. To get to Olongapo required crossing the Olongapo River, a small, stinking, filthy stream, called "Shit River" by American servicemen. There's a reason for this name. When you get close enough to smell it, you will know it. The bridge was like an omen of what was to be expected in the town. Everything—the street, the bars, the restaurants, all seemed dirty. But, over the years, many servicemen—including me—have eaten the food and not died from it.

Olongapo was a wild, rip-roaring town where almost anything goes and is primarily supported by American servicemen out having a good time. Dozens of bars, from tiny little places squeezed in, somehow, between larger bars, to very great places, with dance floors and live bands. The bars are filled mostly with very pretty Filipino women competing for the American dollar. Sex is available, in about any form desired. But, sex isn't free. It was considered an insult to ask a girl for free sex. It was like saying to the girl that she wasn't worth anything.

Most newly arriving servicemen are briefed about the Filipino culture and what is acceptable and what not to do before their first liberty. One of those things was that one should not tell a Filipino girl casually that you love her unless you are truly in love. Due to something in their culture, they take the word "love" very seriously. In fact, if you tell them that you love them, they more than likely will believe you and try to become pregnant. Then when you leave, they will try to find and follow you.

Of course, this doesn't mean that some truly serious relationships never develop. In fact, many relationships have blossomed into marriages thanks to encounters with Filipino women there. But a serviceman arriving in the Philippines needs to know about certain customs and dangers before they have to learn from their own bad experiences.

One truly shocking incident that I was personally aware of involved a young Marine Sergeant who shared a cubicle with me at Okinawa. He had spent some time in the Philippines, then he returned to Okinawa. After his tour "down south," as we sometimes called serving in the Philippines, he told me he had met a Filipino girl, and they had fallen in love. He showed me pictures of a beautiful young woman. But he had no choice but to follow his orders and leave her and return to Okinawa.

They were exchanging serious love letters, even though he was scheduled to rotate back to the States, where he had a wife! Then, one day at mail call, he received a package from this Filipino girl. He opened it and discovered a small glass bottle containing some kind of clear liquid, and floating in the liquid was a dead, partially developed human embryo about the size of the first joint of your thumb.

When I first saw it, I recoiled and was truly shocked. There was a letter enclosed telling him that if she couldn't have him, she was sending him his child to keep as a memory of her. The young sergeant was very shocked, and it affected him deeply. The question for him was, *What do I do with this? Do I just bury it, or turn it in to the command and ask for guidance?* Well, I was happy it wasn't my problem, and, thankfully, I was getting ready to come back to the States in a few days. I never knew what he did with the embryo, or with the girl in the Philippines, but I will never forget that awful situation.

A few days before Christmas, I terminated my orders in the Philippines and went to the flight line office to catch a flight back to Okinawa. I had run out of money, and my mail was not being forwarded. I couldn't get paid there because my pay records were in Okinawa. At the flight office, I was told that all the flights were filled with persons traveling who had a higher priority than I. They told me to come back the next day. When I returned the next day, the situation hadn't changed. I was on the lowest priority for space available.

Well, this actually continued until Christmas. The last time I went to the flight line, I was told not to expect any flights until a day or so after Christmas. This was a very disappointing development. It appeared that I would be spending Christmas in the Philippines, flat broke, homesick, and unable to receive mail. I really dreaded spending Christmas alone in the barracks. I really wanted to go into town and at least have a good meal. But I had no more than a couple dollars. I did, however, have a couple of cartons of Winston cigarettes, and Winston cigarettes were valuable on the black market in Olongapo. The problem was, a serviceman going out of the main gate of the base could carry only two packs of cigarettes. Well, I taped a carton of Winston cigarettes to my leg under my trousers and went out the main gate without incident. Perhaps the sentries at the main gate were feeling generous and knew what I was doing and let me pass. As soon as I got in the edge of town I found the opportunity to sell the carton for about ten times its original value at the Post Exchange. This was strictly a violation of law, but who was watching? Finally, I had enough money to get a good meal and drinks and be around people and not all by myself in the barracks on Christmas Eve.

The next day being Christmas, and being totally without funds, I spent the day on the base. The barracks were nearly empty as a number of the men who lived there were either on duty, or on leave, or on liberty. Christmas was a brilliantly hot day. I slept late and ate a late breakfast at the mess hall, which was mostly staffed with Filipinos—and the food was excellent. I spent a couple of hours at the swimming pool, lying in the sun around the pool, and listening to the sounds of the native birds in the trees and flowers surrounding the pool. It's difficult to accurately describe how lonesome and hollow I felt, and I hoped the day would pass quickly. I wanted Christmas to be over.

On the day after Christmas, I again packed my bags and went down to the flight line, because they had told me by phone that my chances for catching a space available on the flight back to Okinawa were looking pretty good. Sure enough, I managed to score a flight and left the Philippines. What a truly beautiful scene it was looking down from 30,000 feet at the magnificent Philippine Islands, surrounded by deep blue waters and the neatly terraced rice paddies, with the mountains basking in the brilliant sun light! It's a picture I will never forget.

The flight lasted about three hours, and then we landed at Kadena Air Force Base. After I gathered up my gear and got inside the terminal I called my unit. I spoke with my friend, the Administrative Chief. I asked if he could send some transportation to pick me up. He said sure! It was so good to get back into my barracks and cubicle—almost like coming home. The housemaid gathered up all my dirty clothes for the wash. I went to the pay office and was paid the money I was owed. Finally, I felt like I was back among the living again and into my normal routine. It sure felt good to have a few bucks in my pocket after being completely broke.

In early February, 1965, I received an advanced copy of my orders. I was happy and very surprised. I was being sent to Omaha, Nebraska, to be assigned to the Inspector-Instructor staff, and to train the Marine Corps Reserve Unit located there. Wow, what a surprise! A cherished Instructor billet that I didn't even know existed! I figured that my experience as an Instructor at Marine Corps Engineer Schools and as a Drill Instructor had a lot to do with this assignment. However, I wasn't happy to learn that I would be traveling back to the U.S. by ship, which would take approximately three weeks.

CHAPTER 34

MUSIC ON THE WAVES AND COMING HOME TO MY LOVE

On February 15th I boarded the USS Breckinridge, at Naha, Okinawa, to begin my journey. In was somewhat depressing to look ahead to three weeks on this crowded ship. As soon as we got underway, I began to look for something to do to make the time pass more quickly. First, I inquired about whether there were any musical instruments on board, like a guitar that I could check out to use for the voyage. I was happy to learn the ship did have musical instruments for that purpose.

I found my way to the ship's Special Services area to take a look. I was pleasantly surprised to see a selection of nice, quality instruments. I was able to find a good, acoustic electric guitar that I checked out. While I was there, I met an Army fellow who had come there for the same purpose as I. We became acquainted, and I was happy to learn that he was quite a good country music singer and could play the guitar very well! We struck up an immediate friendship and sat there in the Special Services area, playing some tunes. It seemed that we were a very good pair. He could sing a lot of the current popular country songs, and I could play a respectful lead guitar to most of his music.

After several days of getting together at Special Services to practice, we thought, "Why not try and get some other musicians to make up a band?" We were allowed to put out a call through the ship's intercom for a base player and a drummer. Happily, there were some people who responded, and from these, we were able to put together a pretty good country band!

During this time, we also learned that on previous cruises, service members had formed bands and played for the enjoyment of the other passengers. On this cruise, we learned there were a lot of civilians aboard, most of them dependents of military personnel. Also, on previous cruises, ad hoc bands like ours would play for shows in the large dining facilities for military passengers. I was happy to have met this Army fellow, Jim, and he and I really hit it off. Not only was he a very talented guitar player and singer, but he was also an aggressive fellow like me, who wasn't afraid to step out and form a band and play some gigs. We spent several days with the two other musicians we had found, practicing and making a list of songs and instrumental tunes that we could play well. It was a lot of fun, and I spent very little time down in the living area assigned to the Marines.

When we felt confident enough, we scheduled and played a show for the enlisted passengers. I thought we did quite well, and it seemed like they enjoyed it. I had developed perhaps a dozen songs I could sing, and so did Jim. I could also play perhaps ten instrumental tunes. We were quite happy with our band and achievements.

Then, one day, we were offered quite a challenge. It seemed that in past cruises, sometimes the military dependent passengers would have a formal Military Ball and crown the "Queen of the Voyage." The affair would be held in the largest room on the ship, sort of a small ballroom. It would be a formal affair for the attendees. Well, we band members conferred and concluded, *Let's go for it! What do we have to lose?*

A date was set, and we band members held several practice sessions to perfect our repertoire. Also, surprisingly, Special Services had quite a selection of shirts available that could be checked out. We found four brightly colored matching Hawaiian shirts. My Marine buddies down in the Marine living quarters couldn't believe that I was doing what I was doing. They spent their days either lounging on the top deck, in very small restricted areas, playing cards, shining shoes, reading magazines, and telling sea stories. On the other hand, when the pass I was issued, I spent my days going to most every area on the ship, practicing music, talking with people, and having some fun.

The big night finally arrived. It was time for the Military Ball, where female dependents were competing for Queen of the voyage. I never did learn how they selected the Queen. I was too busy making sure that I was ready to play my songs and instrumentals for the dance. I must admit, I was pretty anxious about it. This would certainly be one of the biggest challenges I've ever faced as a musician. All I could do was do my best.

I'm happy to report that the big event went off really well! I was surprised that there were so many dependents. All the officers, Marines and Navy, were in their formal dress, and most of the women wore either formal gowns or similar dresses. First, there was a formal dinner served. Then, after a cocktail period, the chairs and tables were cleared away, and they were ready for the dance. Jim and I and the other band members had previously taken some time to clean and shine up all the musical instruments, so they really glistened under the lights. We band members, in our matching shirts, made an impressive presentation. I learned later that most of the attendees thought we were a professional band who just happened to be traveling on the ship, and they had no idea that we were just an ad hoc group of military personnel.

The entire evening went off better than we had expected. My new music friend, Jim, did a wonderful job and presented himself like a real professional.

There was one anxious moment that I hadn't counted on. After they crowned the Queen of the voyage, one of the party came over and asked us to play a waltz so the ship's Captain could dance with the Queen. Jim turned to me, and we conferred for a moment. We really hadn't practiced a waltz! I dug into my mental food locker of tunes, and the best I could come up with was, "Over the Waves Waltz," which I hadn't played for a long time. I also knew that I couldn't play it like it was supposed to be played. I knew bits of it, however, and so we took on the challenge and away we went.

I played my best rendition of "Over the Waves Waltz." Amazingly, it went off very well! It was a lot of fun watching the Captain in formal Navy dress and a very pretty lady in a beautiful formal gown, dance around the floor to "Over the Waves Waltz" aboard ship. They were very good dancers. I just kept on playing the parts of the tune that I knew. It seemed so appropriate. I think that, in the excitement of the moment, any mistakes that I made were overlooked by the attendees. After that dance, the evening of fun came to a close. I was very surprised when a number of attendees came over and complimented us on our performance. They really heaped on the praise for our music. As for me, I was really happy that people seemed to enjoy my singing, and it made me think that perhaps I could do more of this once I got settled in Omaha and my new job.

After nearly three weeks aboard this ship, I was more than ready to finish this journey. On March 6th, we sailed under the Golden Gate Bridge, and landed and debarked at Treasure Island, just across the bay from San Francisco. It was nearly midnight before we got off the ship and got aboard a bus to take us to the International Airport. As usual, it was difficult to gather all my bags together at the ticketing counter. I found a plane to Pittsburgh, Pennsylvania, which wasn't scheduled to leave until the early morning hours. I would arrive in Pittsburgh just before noon.

This meant that I would have several hours waiting in the airport. The excitement was building. I was nearly home and would soon get to see my beloved Delores, the boys, and my new daughter. I called Delores and told her where I was and when I was arriving in Pittsburgh. It was wonderful to hear her voice, knowing that I would be getting some Delores-style hugging very soon!

I kicked back at the airport to begin my several-hour wait. Soon, another Marine in uniform came up and sat down beside me. He was a black Marine, a bit older than me, and was a Staff Sergeant. We began sharing sea stories and laughing a lot, which made time pass faster. He even broke out a pint of good whiskey, which he shared with me. He left me after an hour or so, and I was so tired and sleepy that I curled up in the chair and dozed for a bit. I remember thinking, *How great it is to be a Marine and able to find companionship anywhere in the world I would go!*

I woke up just in time to board my flight. I had a good seat, and after we were airborne, I was moved into first-class seating. One of the stewardesses told me that it was this airline's policy to move servicemen in uniform into first class if there were empty seats. I thought that was a very good policy! My seat was very comfortable, and I leaned back for the "red eye" flight to Pittsburgh. I couldn't sleep, as the anxiety was building up inside me. The closer and closer we got to Pittsburgh, the more excited I became.

When the wheels of the plane touched down on the runway at Pittsburgh, my long journey, which had begun fourteen months ago, was finally over. I got out of that plane as fast as I could and began to scan the crowd for Delores. *Oh, there she was! And there was Uncle Abe, holding that beautiful little girl baby, Valerie*! We hugged and hugged, and shed some tears together. But these were happy tears, not the sad tears of parting. I could hardly believe it! After all those long, long miles and being half a world apart, we were finally together again! I whispered, *Thank you God; thank you, for making my prayers come true and bringing me home safely.*

Coming home to Delores and the kids in March of 1965 stands out as one of the most exciting times of my life. It was great seeing Delores's family again, and they welcomed me with open arms and a lot of hugs. I also got to again enjoy one of her great family reunions when everybody gathered in the kitchen and dining room of her parent's home where there were lots of refreshments, snacks, beer, some whisky, and a bunch of family stories, with Aunt Helen teasing all the children, as she usually did.

But there was little time to spend doing much partying. We had a lot of things to do! We needed to arrange the date when we would give up the apartment and schedule a moving company to pick up our furniture and other belongings. We also had to arrange and schedule the date when we would depart for Omaha.

We were really excited to be moving to Omaha instead of to a large Marine base. Only the most trusted Marines are fortunate enough to be assigned to this type of independent duty. It was even more exciting because Omaha is only about a three-hour drive north of where my Mom and Dad lived, so visits to the farm would be easier!

When our plans were firmed up, we decided that I would take our car and Bobbie and go on ahead to Omaha to find us a suitable place to live. I would go by way of Kansas City, leaving Bobbie with my sister, Betty, and her husband, Bernard, who had kindly volunteered to take care of him for a short time while I went on to find a home for us. Once I found a decent place, we would schedule a moving company.

Our plan seemed to be going well, and I drove on up to Omaha. I distinctly recall entering the city from the south on old Highway 75. As I was going up through the city and stopping at various traffic lights, I couldn't help but notice numerous taverns advertising live country music. At one traffic stop, there was a club on the corner with the front door wide open, and a country music blasting out to the open street. I made a mental note to find out if I could find an opportunity to play my music. The entertainment bug had bitten me, and I really enjoyed being a performer.

I had already called and established contact with the Inspector/Instructor staff, and I received directions to the training center. I easily located the center, which was located on North 30th Avenue and Fort Street in North Omaha. The training center was a relatively new brick building located on the property of Fort Omaha. Fort Omaha is an Indian War-era installation, and was originally an Army Supply installation. Originally known as Sherman Barracks, it was named in honor of General Tecumseh Sherman, and then was changed to Omaha Barracks. In later years, it came to be known as Fort Omaha, and it occupies more than eighty acres of property. A number of historical buildings are contained on Fort Omaha, including some buildings the Marine Reserve unit used for training. Also located on the Fort was a nice swimming pool and a building that was used primarily for unit parties or some training classes.

I checked in at the training center and met the Marine Staff Sergeant named Jeff, whom I was replacing. All the staff people whom I met were very friendly and helpful. Luckily for me, Jeff suggested that perhaps, since he and his family were leaving, I could rent the house they had lived in! That might turn out to be just what I was looking for! His family had already moved out of the house, so it was easy for him to arrange an introduction with the landlord so we could take a look at the place. Jeff made a phone call to the landlord, and we were invited over to take a look at the place. The landlords of the property, Mr. and Mrs. Nelson, lived on the street just behind the house that we were going to view. She and her husband were elderly folks, and, according to Jeff, were very easy to get along with.

We got the key and went to look at the house. Right away, I knew this was the right place for us! It was a big, old, perhaps turn-of-the-century two-story white house. It seemed to be the perfect place to raise a family. It faced Fort Street, itself a landmark. There was a large front porch with four large white columns across the front. The front yard was pretty big, and there was a back yard with an old garage. Several giant elm trees shaded the property, and shrubs bordered the yard.

Immediately I knew that this was the place for my family. I told Mrs. Nelson that I wanted the house, and I paid her one month's rent. Wow! I was so excited! The house hunting I had been dreading was over! I had a house that I was sure Delores would love. And the house was only about four blocks down the street from Fort Omaha. God must be watching over me. *Thank you, God!*

That first night, I was invited to stay overnight with one of the Marines on the I & I staff. I accepted. They were really nice folks, and

I had an enjoyable meal, and a good night's sleep. They also let me use their phone to call Delores to update her and tell her about the house I had rented. She seemed excited about it.

The next morning, I took the necessary steps to get the house ready to move into. The staff members at the training center were kind enough to let me use an empty office space with a telephone to call and make arrangements for the installation of the phone, water, gas, and electricity service. I also called the moving company that had our furniture and arranged to have it delivered. Everything was coming together quite well.

The next several nights, while I was waiting for the furniture delivery, I slept on the floor of the house. I had brought a blanket and a pillow in the car, and the furnace was on, so I was quite comfortable. The furniture was still being stored in Omaha, and it was only a matter of a few days before it was delivered.

Right after the furniture came, I took a day and drove down to Kansas City to pick up Bobbie from my sister Betty's house. It also gave me a chance to visit Betty and Bernard. While I was there, they gave me some unexpected and very exciting news. Bernard's job was transferring him to their Omaha office! They would soon be moving to Omaha. That was such wonderful news, and I knew that Delores would be happy. I brought Bobbie back to Omaha, where he helped me to get boxes unpacked and things arranged in our new home.

CHAPTER 35

INSPECTOR/INSTRUCTOR DUTY, OMAHA, NEBRASKA

On April 13, 1965, I officially joined the Inspector-Instructor staff at Omaha. I was very upbeat about this assignment and looked forward to a great tour of duty. There were only about fourteen active-duty Marines, like myself, assigned there to train the Marine Reserve unit.

I met the Officer in Charge of the staff, Captain Wall. He was a "Mustang" officer, meaning that he had been an enlisted man before being commissioned. Captain Wall was a stern taskmaster. He was officially known as the I & I, "Inspector/Instructor."

The Reserve unit was actually two units. One of these units trained on the first weekend of the month, and the other unit on the third weekend. An Engineer Maintenance Company was trained to operate and repair various types of engineering equipment. My specific job was to train the unit's Refrigeration and Water Supply people, along with the Electricians. There were only about six or seven of these Marines in the unit.

I was also, from time to time, assigned to teach some general military subjects, like first aid, marksmanship, drill, etc. These were easy assignments for me, and I found out that I had some extra time on my hands. This was great, because thus far, there was never a time in my past when I could say this! It left me with time to play my guitar and consider the idea of possibly joining a band.

After I had found my way around the area and the training center, I began to feel more comfortable. After a weekend of training with one of the reserve units, I had become familiar with what to expect on a weekend drill. The standard operating procedure (SOP) was that the staff members who worked training reserves on the weekend would have two days off the following week. This wasn't always possible, due to unexpected additional assignments such as participating in color guard presentations for various public events, parades, and other holiday happenings.

Also, from time to time, members of the staff would have to participate in a funeral for any Marine death in the area. Such events sometimes prevented us from having the time off we deserved. In fact, sometimes we worked two weeks straight through, without a day off. When some of us spoke up about this seeming unfairness, we were reminded that, as Marines, we could be required to work twenty-four hours a day! Or perhaps we would prefer to go to Vietnam? "No thank you, Sir! I *love* my duty here, Sir!!"

Yes, Sir! I love my duty here.

My leisure time was cut short when, one day, the Captain wanted to see me in his office. When I reported, he told me to sit down and relax, as he wanted to talk personally to me. He said that he was going to officially assign me to extra duty as the Public Relations representative for the Marine Corps in that area, which meant the entire metropolitan Omaha area and a fifty-mile radius around Omaha, including Council Bluffs, Iowa, just across the Missouri River.

He further said he wanted the citizens to know, every day, that there was a Marine Corps present in this area and what the Marine Corps does. He asked if I had any questions. I was too stunned to know what to ask! He told me that he had been observing me since I had first with the staff, and he thought that I had the personality and professionalism to handle this job better than some of the other staff!

Then he reached behind his desk and brought out a large leather camera kit and gave it to me. I knew nothing about cameras and didn't even own one. However, I could easily see this was an extremely old one, a Graflex press camera. Instead of handling me a roll of film, the Captain gave me some old 4" X 6" film sheets that had to be loaded onto film plates in a darkroom. I read all the literature I could find on this old camera until I was able it to take some pretty good pictures. He told me that he wanted me to learn how to use it, as he was not going to spend money to buy another. Then he went on to say that I could use the Marine Corps staff car when it wasn't being used. He also told me that if I used my own car, they would pay me for the mileage! What could I say, but, "Aye, Aye, Sir!" What I really wanted to say was, "I love you! I love you!" But, of course I didn't.

But I really did like this Captain. He was direct and to the point, and I appreciated the trust he put in me. I knew that I'd better not screw it up. I worked for him now, and not the First Sergeant, the Administrative Chief, or the unit Warrant Officer. For their part, it was "Hands off Sergeant Lay. He belongs to the Captain!"

Next he then took me down the hallway in the training center to a small office. He said, "This is your office. This is your workstation." He further said, "You work here, and for me; you report directly to me and no one else. Okay?" Again he asked if there were any questions and when I said no, he said, "Well, then, get to work," and he walked out.

Instructor/Inspector Duty, Omaha, Nebraska.

Whew! This put an entirely new perspective on my job here in Omaha. I sat down behind my desk and gathered my thoughts. I liked having a private office and a phone number of my own. So, I was to report only to the Captain, and my primary job was public relations. I'd had no formal training in this field but was very anxious to learn. I'd had some similar experiences, which I thought might be helpful, such as being an entertainer, teaching at engineer schools, working on the newspaper staff aboard ship as well as on the high school newspaper staff. I realized that I wasn't completely without experience.

First off, it appeared that I had the bare essentials: a desk, a chair, a filing cabinet, and a private telephone line. Next, I had to learn how to use this camera. After I had read everything I could find, I went to a camera shop in downtown Omaha. The people at this shop were very helpful and excited about seeing one of these old cameras that was still in good condition. One of the employees was kind enough to show me how to use it and how to load the film. They said they could also supply me the film and develop the pictures. These folks told me that this camera was capable of producing some very quality photos.

I bought some film and went back to the training center. Going into my office, I turned off all lights and loaded some film plates. I was ready to take some pictures! I had also gotten permission from the Captain to purchase film and develop film at the expense of the Marine Corps. I set up an account for that purpose at the shop. The Captain told me to buy whatever was necessary for the camera and development of the films just as long as it was strictly used for the Marine Corps and promoting public affairs. I thought, *I'm going to really like this new job*!

I began to think about asking for a promotion. I knew I had the time-in-grade necessary to qualify for promotion to Staff Sergeant. And I also believed that I had outstanding performance evaluations. I went to the administrative office and inquired about it. Just a couple of days later, I was asked to come back to the administrative office and then was told to report to the Captain. I went in and reported. He explained that they had made an inquiry with Headquarters Marine Corps and discovered that I should have already been a Staff Sergeant, perhaps two weeks ago! Therefore, he had me stand at attention while he read the promotion warrant to me, shook my hand, and congratulated me. Wow! This was great! I also couldn't help but notice that he was now wearing the Oak Leaf insignia of a Major. He had been promoted also! This was good news, and I congratulated him.

I decided that during my work as the Marine Corps Public Relations representative, I would wear either the Class A dress green uniform or the dress blue uniform everywhere I went on my job. To get to know the Omaha community better, I went downtown to the Omaha Chamber of Commerce and picked up a list of all the social clubs in Omaha. I contacted each of these clubs and offered myself as a speaker at one of their scheduled meetings. I put together about a thirty-minute standard presentation about the Marine Corps and our role in Vietnam.

I soon discovered that I was perhaps the only military person in the Omaha area who had been in Vietnam, and because of that, I soon found myself as a very sought-after speaker. I was invited to speak on a radio program several times, being interviewed about the war in Vietnam. I also appeared and was interviewed on one of the television stations at least three or four times. I would always wear my dress blues.

In the next year or so, I found myself speaking at all sorts of social clubs, either at very early morning meetings, or at luncheons, or in the evening. To name a few, I spoke at the Lions Club, the Eagles Club, Kiwanis Club, Toastmasters, Elks Club, the Seventeen Club, and even to a group of very elderly women's Morning Musical Club. I was pleasantly surprised to find that these elderly women really liked to flirt with me. I was reserved and respectful toward them and ignored their more personal suggestions. I was treated with great respect when I went to speak at these clubs and was always given a free meal.

I pretty much came and went as I pleased with no interference from the First Sergeant's office and staff. Nonetheless, when I went somewhere, I usually went to the office and told the staff I was leaving and when I probably would be back. On very formal occasions

I used the official Marine Corps staff car, which was an early '60's Dodge. It was painted green with yellow markings—a very good car. Every month I submitted a public affairs report of our Omaha area activities to the Kansas City district office. The report listed all the public affairs events that either the staff or I had participated in. One of the measures of our success was how many column inches of newspaper space we filled with articles and photographs of public events. The first several reports that I submitted pleased Major Wall greatly, and he called me in and told me so. In the first annual report, my office was awarded the top public affairs office in the 9th Marine Corps District, which included a large area of the central United States.

In my private life I decided to reach out to play some music in the community. I soon learned that Omaha and the surrounding area were very much into country music. There was a neighborhood bar and restaurant near us named The Ames Cafe. I visited there a couple of times to see what kind of crowd they had. Inside the place, in one corner, there was a small stage where there was enough space for one person, or even a small trio, to play. I also learned that from time to time they would have an entertainer play for them.

I decided to give it a try. I spoke with the owner and scheduled a date. He said my first night would be an audition, and if the customers seemed to like me, he would hire me for perhaps one night a week. I agreed.

It was exciting, and I looked forward to the event. But a million questions filed my mind: *Would they like me? What if I didn't know any songs the audience requested? Will someone actually laugh at me, or heckle me?* (among other unanswered questions). Well, I wouldn't know unless I gave it a try. I was scheduled to play on a Friday night for three hours. I went to the cafe early, got my amplifier and microphone set up, and waited for the time when I would begin to play. I stayed out in the car until just before I was scheduled to go onstage.

I began with a low-key, friendly approach and sang a couple of old favorite tunes that most people hadn't heard in years. I threw in a couple of popular Johnny Cash songs. At that time my voice was very bass and somewhat similar to Cash's voice. Well, to my pleasant surprise, the audience really liked me! I loosened up after that and talked to the crowd over the microphone, told a few jokes that I had preplanned, and sang the songs I had learned. I was having a good time, and before I knew it, the evening was over and it was time to close the cafe and go home. The boss gave me my pay and invited me back the next Friday night. I had earned the enormous sum of $12.00. Well, it was a start, anyway. To tell the truth, I would have done it for free, just for the fun of it! When I got home, I was on a natural high. They had really liked me, and I was invited back. Great!

Thereafter, I performed in numerous other venues throughout the Omaha area.

Performing in the "Hickory Room," Omaha, Nebraska, 1966.

After about two or three weeks of playing at the Ames Cafe, during a break, a lady approached me and introduced herself. She complimented me on my performance and told me that she had a sister who was an entertainer and was trying to form a band. She said her sister would probably like to talk with me.

I gave her my phone number and told her to have her sister contact me. Within a couple of days, a girl named Sandy called me and asked if I would like to come to her house to get together with her and some other musicians, as she was trying to form a band. I happily accepted. I had talked to Delores before about possibly playing music with a band. She was a bit skeptical at first, but after we talked about it, she gave her consent. She knew by now that I had only one other love besides her, and that was with guitars. She knew that I could never be totally happy without a guitar in my arms.

We made an agreement that I would always give her half of the money I earned playing in the clubs, and she could use that money for anything she wished, household items or personal items for herself; whatever she wanted. I could use my half for whatever I wanted. Later on, I was often paid much more than $12.00 per night. There were other times, though, when we had to use all the money for some urgent household expense, or a car repair, or another unplanned cost. My music playing permitted us to enjoy a slightly higher standard of living.

One evening, I took my guitar and went to Sandy's house. She lived near us and had a big, nicely decorated basement that she used for playing music. There I also met Sheryl, a young woman in her mid-twenties. She played electric bass. Another person there was Ken, Sheryl's boyfriend, who was the drummer. They all seemed like really nice people—there weren't any drugs or wild drinking.

We got our instruments tuned and played a few songs. Sandy was a very good singer and also good at playing rhythm guitar to back up her singing. It didn't take us long to determine that we definitely needed to form a band. I thought we sounded pretty good. I could play lead guitar to most of the songs Sandy sang, or I could at least learn them pretty easily. Sandy asked us all if we agreed to be in a band together. Everyone said yes. It was going to be Sandy's band, and she had already picked out a name for it. She named the band The Stardusters.

As it turned out, she was already was working on some bookings. She'd had some colorful business cards made up, and we really felt like professionals. I decided that I would wear some fancy blue-sequined trousers and a vest to match. I believed that I looked pretty good with my fancy Gibson Model 335 guitar!

Our first bookings were two nights a week, Friday and Saturday, at an establishment named, "The Jalo Lounge." It was a bar/dance club. On one side of the club was a bandstand large enough to fit a four-piece band and a nice dance floor. Soon we were building our own following. From time to time, we would play other gigs, such as for birthday parties, weddings, and just parties in general.

After a couple of weeks playing, it was clear that we were going to be a success there at the club. We drew a crowd of people in our age group, twenty-five to thirty-five-year-olds. Over the next two years I worked regularly with Sandy and the band. I got to know her husband, Meryl, very well. A talented finish carpenter, Meryl was a quiet, easygoing fellow. Delores and Sandy, really liked each other, and we remained friends long after we left Omaha. Several years later, when I was stationed in California, she came to visit us. We loved having her, because not only was she a very talented singer and show person, she was also fun to be with.

CHAPTER 36

"THE MARINE'S BALLAD"

During my last year in Omaha, 1967, I got involved with writing and recording two songs. At that time, Army Special Forces Sergeant, Barry Sadler, had written and recorded, "The Ballad of the Green Berets." It became a hit song and was being played constantly over radio stations across the country. I began to think that perhaps I could write a song about the Marines and call it the "The Marine's Ballad." As I struggled with finding the right words and tempo, I discovered that my final result sounded a lot like the tune to "Sink the

Bismarck," written and recorded by Johnny Horton. I thought that maybe I would just try and use the music to "Sink the Bismarck," and insert the words that I had written because they fit together so nicely. But I knew that I had to get permission from the copyright holder, Cajun Publishing Company in Shreveport, Louisiana, in order to legally use the tune of the song.

One day, I picked up the phone and called them. I spoke to an executive of the company and told him the purpose of my call. To my surprise the fellow said, "Well, *Sink the Bismarck* isn't making much money now, so go ahead and send us a demo of your song. If we like it, we'll send you a standard publishing contract." Wow! I could hardly believe it!

I scheduled an appointment with a recording studio in Omaha, and set about to find some musicians to do the recording. I didn't have enough money to hire a lot of professional musicians and a producer. This was going to be just a recording done well enough to give the publisher a general idea of the proposed song done to the tempo and music of "Sink the Bismarck."

I knew that I needed a drummer who could do a drum roll and play a march tempo. I found a Navy fellow who was a good drummer and was stationed at Fort Omaha. Among the musicians with whom I was acquainted, I easily located a bass player. I decided that I would play the rhythm on my guitar. It was really a bare-essentials recording band. Before the recording session, I was trying to come up with a tune for the flip side of the recording. I had several brainstorming sessions, and finally came up with a catchy little tune that I named, "Make a Marine." So, the final recording was a 45 RPM titled, "The Marine's Ballad," with a flip side of "Make a Marine."

The recording itself went well, and within about three hours we had our final product. Considering the time frame and the musicians that I had, I thought it sounded pretty good. I named the record company "BGL Records" (my initials), and had 500 records pressed. I quickly sent a record to Cajun publishing. Within two weeks, I received a nice letter from Cajun telling me they had accepted my song, "The Marine's Ballad," and sent me a standard publishing contract listing me as the writer of the song, along with Johnny Horton and Tillman Franks, who had written the music score to "Sink the Bismarck." I was very happy. I finally had a song published by a major publisher!

The Marine's Ballad, 45 RPM record.

I sent the record to perhaps fifty record companies and publishers asking for their distribution of my record. One record company in Hollywood, California, responded and wanted to distribute the record. They also sent me a standard artist and distribution contract, laying out how much I would receive from each record sold. This was a big deal for me. One of the owners of that company called me to talk about the contract and some of their plans if the record sold really well. It was a very exciting time for me.

"MARINE'S BALLAD", A record displaying the talents of SSgt. Bob Lay, is a regular number on disk jockey Don Denver's show at Radio Station KOOO in Omaha SSgt. Lay is now busy writing songs for an album he plans to cut and release in the near future.

Omaha Marine Signs Contract
With Hollywood Recording C

"Take a little sand, take a little mud.

Take a little sweat, take a little blood."

This, according to a record released by Staff Sergeant Bobbie G. Lay, a member of Omaha's Inspector-Instructor Staff, is what makes a Marine.

Lay made the recording, 'Make a Marine', when he was encouraged by fans to record another of his songs, 'The Marine's Ballad', after they heard him sing it with a combo in Omaha.

the record, listened to it and decided it was good enough to give a distributor to place in the S Diego and Oceanside, Calif., are

Stewart's first reaction to 'Ma a Marine' was, "This thing has it."

"The distributor had har gotten the record out to the reco shops in his area when orders gan pouring in for more copi in about a month more than copies of the recording had b sold," said Stewart.

"The record got its first

In Omaha, I also contracted with a record distributor and signed a distribution contract. As a result of this contract, the record was sold in several record stores in Omaha and some of the smaller surrounding towns. The record was also on some jukeboxes in the Omaha area.

I found it was quite a thrill to be in an establishment and hear my own record playing. I took it to a couple of radio stations where, for a while, it played frequently. I also took a copy of it to the top country music station in Omaha, KOO Radio. I was acquainted with the popular disk jockey there because of my having done public relations for the Marine Corps. His name was Don Denver, and he played my song quite often. One day on my way home from work, when I was just driving into our place, my song came on the car radio. I was so excited! I quickly parked and ran inside to tell Delores to turn on the radio, but by the time I got inside, the song was over. Still, it was a thrill to hear it being played.

Overall, "The Marine's Ballad," although not a big national hit nor a moneymaker, as was the "Ballad of the Green Beret" for Barry Sadler, it was nevertheless, a huge success for me. In the late sixties and early seventies, "The Marine's Ballad" was played on a lot of radio stations and jukeboxes on the west and east coasts, mostly around the larger Marine bases. It was also sold in some Post Exchanges on the bases.

I pretty much lost control of my song. This California record company also distributed records in and around the military bases in Okinawa, Japan, and even in Vietnam without my knowledge. I personally, many times, saw my record on juke boxes in bars and clubs in southern California and in Okinawa.

In my later tours of duty in the Western Pacific area, it was quite a thrill for me to be in a club in Okinawa and see young Marines playing my song on the jukebox.

On one such occasion, some young Marines in a bar, who were partially inebriated, were playing the "The Marine's Ballad" on the jukebox and drilling each other to its marching tempo. It was both funny and exciting to me. I never knew for sure the full extent of the distribution of the record. I'm of the firm belief that a lot of records were distributed and sold for a number of years for which I was never reimbursed.

The company went out of business some time in the 1970s without ever contacting me. In 2010, I resurrected the song, obtained the master tape from Columbia Records in Nashville, Tennessee, and made plans to release the song again. I contracted with a company in Portland, Oregon, to convert the sound to digital and put it on a CD. The sound was greatly improved. I released the CD and contracted with CD Baby for distribution. The song, "The Marine's Ballad," is currently available as a digital download on CD Baby, Amazon, and other digital music sites on the Internet.

In April 2011, "Leatherneck Magazine," the most popular monthly magazine for Marines, ran a major story about the song and about me and my family of Marines. As of the publishing of this book, the song is listed for sale as a download on some of the major online music stores and YouTube. In 2010, Bear Family Records had published, "Next Stop Is Vietnam—The War on Record," an anthology of music inspired by the Vietnam War, with more than 330 songs that cover all facets of the war and its aftermath, featuring The Doors, Bob Dylan, and dozens of other artists. The anthology included rarely heard documentary material including patriotic Public Service Announcements, field news reports, and an intercepted North Vietnamese radio transmission of Jane Fonda and Hanoi Hannah, along with a book detailing the history of the songs included.

My song, "The Marines Ballad," was featured in the anthology. Appropriately, the song and the article about it were adjacent to the song, "Ballad of the Green Berets," by Staff Sergeant Barry Sadler! The article provided the information that Staff Sergeant Sadler and I both performed our songs at the "Take 10" club in Da Nang, Vietnam.

Coincidently, in 1984, my son, Sergeant Mark Lay, was serving at the American Embassy in Guatemala City, Guatemala, where he met SSgt Sadler in a nightclub, and they discussed my song. Sadly, shortly thereafter, SSgt Sadler was shot in Guatemala City, incurring injuries that eventually lead to his untimely death in 1989 at the age of 49. In some Marine Corps circles, "The Marines Ballad" has become known as the "other" Marine song. Of course, the "Marines' Hymn" will always be considered *the* Marine song.

CHAPTER 37

"WHEN SORROWS LIKE SEA BILLOWS ROLL"

In early 1966, my duties at Omaha took on a new dimension. The war in Vietnam was heating up as more and more American troops entered the war. This development also rapidly increased the casualties in the Omaha area, resulting in an increase in the number of casualty assistance calls the Inspector-Instructor and his staff were required to make. This responsibility also included following through with the family members by helping them to make funeral arrangements and any other necessary assistance. As one can imagine, this duty is one of the most solemn and difficult duties to which a Marine might be assigned. The Marine Corps Recruiting Service also had this responsibility. Our I & I Staff and the Recruiting Service created an informal arrangement to rotate the casualty calls so that one unit wasn't getting all of them.

When our unit would receive a casualty-assistance notice from Headquarters Marine Corps, it was required that if at all possible an officer and an enlisted Marine would be a team of two to deliver the notice. The officer assigned would select one of the enlisted staff to go along with him. As it so happened, since I was out in the public more than any of the other staff, I became the person most often selected, because it was said that I "could handle myself well in public." My memories of these calls, and of the families involved, are some of the most vivid and painful ones I have ever experienced. Even until this day, I can remember clearly, and still painfully, most of the calls I assisted on. I'll share only a few of these memories to give the reader an idea of what it may have been like to have been there.

The first call on which I assisted involved the casualty of a young Marine Sergeant who was shot and killed in Vietnam. His wife and three children lived in North Omaha, not very far from the training center. From the man's record, we learned that he was Catholic. We located a priest who was able to go along with us. It was a gloomy, overcast day. We easily located the home of the deceased, but we carefully reviewed our information anyway, just to make sure that we had the correct address.

We were driving the Marine Corps Staff car that I previously described, hoping that it wouldn't be identified and someone might guess or realize that something was amiss before we made the notification. I recall thinking that it might have been better if we had driven one of our private cars. It was too late now. We pulled up in front of the house and parked. Once again, we reviewed our information, as we didn't want to make a serious mistake. We collected our thoughts before getting out of the car and walking up the sidewalk to the old single-story wooden house. I remember thinking about the terrible thing we were about to do. The officer led the way up the sidewalk, followed by the priest, who carried a Bible, followed by me. There was a big lump in my throat and tears in my eyes. This was definitely the most difficult thing I had ever done. As we got closer to the house, the door flew open and three small boys, all wearing Marine Corps dungaree caps, came running out to greet us. They were so excited to see Marines! They were jumping up and down with excitement, and one of them was saying, "My *daddy* is a Marine! My *daddy* is a Marine!" and one of them added, "And he is coming home Saturday!"

We all hesitated for a moment, casting a glance at one another. Then the door opened, and a pretty young woman with long, brown hair, dressed in a nice white dress smiled in greeting. As she began to speak, she suddenly realized the purpose of the visit, hesitated in mid-sentence, put her hand up over her mouth, and said, "Oh no! Oh no!" She screamed, turned around, and ran back into the house. For a moment, we could hear her running through the house, screaming and banging into the furniture.

I immediately directed my attention to these little boys. I knelt down and began giving them hugs and talking with them, asking their names and such. They wanted to know about my ribbons and badges. I talked to them for as long as I could to keep their attention and then asked them to please stay in the yard and play while I went inside for a moment. The officer and priest found the woman kneeling on the kitchen floor of the small house, her long brown hair falling down over her face, crying uncontrollably. Finally, the officer was able to quiet the woman long enough to identify her and officially deliver the message. All of us had tears in our eyes and as he slowly read the message.

As quickly as we could, we were able to obtain the phone numbers of a close friend and some relatives to call, asking them to join us as soon as they could. We stayed with her until some of them began to arrive. Soon, the tragic news had to be conveyed to these precious little boys, as they were beginning to realize something tragic had happened in their family. We left that chore to the mother and some of the relatives. We also learned that the little boys had been correct;

the deceased Sergeant was due to rotate home that coming weekend. How much more tragic can it be?

The I & I Staff followed through with this widow and family, assisting any way we could for her and her family; from arranging for a full military funeral, to helping her apply for benefits due her through the Veterans Administration and other service agencies. This was a tragic event indeed. Most of the public hardly even knew that a war was going on in Vietnam—or even where Vietnam was located. Then, to see casualties of this war coming home in body bags began to chaff the public conscience. To make matters worse, with this particular death, not long after the burial of this young Sergeant, vandals desecrated his gravesite. I went with a couple of other staff members and the widow to put things back together again.

In another case, a Military unit made the initial casualty call, and we were prevailed upon to provide enough Marines to assist in a Military funeral and graveside firing squad. Again, I was one of the Marines chosen to assist. I tried to look upon these assignments as an honor and a celebration of the life of the deceased. However, no matter how magnanimous and honorable this approach, the emotional pain I suffered was almost disabling.

This particular casualty assistance call was in Deadwood, South Dakota. We were flown to Deadwood by an Air Force plane from Offutt Air Force Base, which was just south of Omaha, to an Air Force base near Deadwood. This was in the middle of winter, and it was very cold. We were provided transportation from the Air Force base to the Deadwood Hotel, where we stayed all night, as the funeral was the following day. I believe there were perhaps ten to twelve of us.

After a nice meal at the restaurant in the hotel, true to Marine fashion, we went bar hopping to explore the nightlife in Deadwood.

It wasn't disappointing. There were several very busy bars, and since we were in uniform, we were recognized and most of our drinks were free.

The first bar we visited was the "No. 10 Saloon," where Wild Bill Hickok was killed in 1876. It seems that a cowardly fellow named Jack McCall sneaked up behind him and shot him in the back of the head. There's even a chair there in the bar whose claim to fame is that it was the same chair that Hickok was shot in. It was fun to visit this bar and have some free drinks, thanks to the management and some customers who paid for them. It's this kind of love and respect that really made it fun to be a Marine.

It seemed that the people of Deadwood certainly loved the Marines! It was almost as if most of the people knew why we were in town and were trying to find a way to honor the fallen Marine. We stayed out until midnight when the bars closed. After that, we went to a large cafe that stayed open late, and we all gathered there for a late night snack. We were quickly recognized and likewise honored with free drinks. While there, some arm wrestling contests ensued between the Marines and some lumberjacks who happened to be in the place. It was great fun, and I'm happy to say I won my arm-wrestling match! However, my right arm and shoulder hurt pretty badly for a couple weeks after that. Maybe I wasn't really the winner!

As we made our way back to the hotel, snow began to fall, quickly covering Deadwood and the surrounding mountains in a blanket of three inches of new snow, with large soft flakes still drifting slowly down. All the bars were closing, and customers and bar girls were just coming out into the streets to go home. Some folks playfully threw some snowballs at us, and the game was on! A large snowball fight ensued, quite a contrast compared to the gunfights back in the gold rush days! That snowball fight after midnight in the streets of Deadwood, South Dakota, while wearing my dress blues, is another special memory for my mental footlocker.

The following day we prepared for the funeral service of the local Marine killed in Vietnam. The service was held in a church in the suburbs of Deadwood. I was assigned to be at the graveside services and also act as a member of the firing squad. As the services began at the church, a funeral car took those of us in the graveside detail to the cemetery and dropped us off. The cemetery was on the side of one of the surrounding mountains. From there, we could look down and see most of Deadwood, which was now steeped in mourning for their Marine who had been consumed by the war.

Almost as soon as the vehicle that brought us up to the cemetery departed, we realized just how cold it was—partly because a noticeable wind and some snowflakes were blowing around us, dropping the wind chill to far below the temperature down in Deadwood. There was no shelter for us to get in out of the wind. We all learned just how inadequate the Marine dress blue uniform is to protect a body from the cold. I believe there were seven of us—seven very cold Marines, jumping up and down, stomping our feet, clapping our hands—anything to generate some body heat. If someone had observed us from afar, they would have witnessed what seemed to be some kind of strange dance celebration. Of course, the Marine Corps has a nice, long overcoat that's available to wear on such occasions, but none were ever issued to us.

It felt as though the funeral was taking forever, and we were nearing the point of frostbite on our ears, hands, and toes before we finally saw the funeral procession coming up the road for the burial. We checked our weapons to make sure they were ready to fire.

The graveside service was very sad. Many people were crying. Their young warrior, an American Indian lad, had came home to rest. When we fired the volley, the sharp cracking sounds jerked everyone physically, and the sounds echoed throughout the valley. The solemn folding of the flag, and its presentation to the family, was one of the saddest events I had ever witnessed. There, in a lonely grave on a mountainside, in the middle of winter, a grieving family had laid their son to rest, and all that was left was a feeling of emptiness. And that was just a fraction of the cost of that terrible war.

After all the services were concluded, we were invited to a dinner at the church honoring the fallen Marine. There was a lot of good food, which we were ready for. Practically everyone at the dinner made it a point to introduce himself or herself and thank us for our service and for being there for the funeral. It was heartwarming to see the large number of people who came to honor this fallen Marine. I will never forget these people. Later that day, we went to the nearby Air Force base and were flown back to Omaha. Just another day in my life as a Marine.

It began to dawn on me that most of the casualties were young Marines. On one occasion, however, the deceased was an older Marine, a career man. In this instance, the initial death notice was delivered to his wife, a pretty woman in her mid-thirties. I recall that there were several children. The deceased lived in a small town south and west of Omaha. I didn't attend the initial death notice but was called upon to assist in all follow-up activities for the funeral and graveside services.

It was clear that the deceased Marine and his family were well known in the community. This was a picturesque little town, in the full bloom of midsummer. On the day of the funeral and services, the temperature was hovering near one hundred degrees. The services were held inside a quaint old white church. For some reason, the family had requested that during the services they wanted one Marine standing at the foot of the casket and one at the head.

The casket was displayed right in front of the altar. I was chosen to stand at the foot of the casket facing the crowd. The casket was open, and the deceased was in dress blues and facing me just a couple feet away. He seemed too close to me. The small church was packed with mourners, and there was no air conditioning. As the services got underway, I was already sweating profusely. The Marine's family, wife, and several children were seated right on the front row, just a few feet away, facing me. They were trying to be brave, but most were crying. During this service I remember feeling so hot that for a few moments I thought I was going to faint. I could feel the sweat running down my back and down my legs. The sweat running into my eyes blinded me.

The sadness of the scene was almost overwhelming. I could feel hot tears filling my eyes, and I tried hard not to cry. I remember how glad I was when these services concluded and we went outside and to the cemetery. I was one of the Marines at the graveside who stood by the casket during the services and helped to fold the flag. I passed the folded flag to the Marine officer who presented it to the widow. What made this event especially memorable was the sorrow of the children. It was pure, raw emotional pain. Their daddy was gone, never to be seen again, killed in a war far, far away. And for what? For no clearly defined purpose.

I realized that these same scenes were playing out clear across our country nearly every day. And I'm sure the unanswered questions were the same. Why was our country in this war? Was the reason important enough to justify the killing our country's finest young men? During this funeral, seeing the deceased lying there in his dress blues caused me to visualize myself lying in a casket just like that. I couldn't get that scene out of my mind. Then I began to picture how the scene would look with the funeral car coming up the old gravel road at home, going to cemetery where I would be buried, and the faces of Mom and Dad crying like these people were doing. It was difficult, and sometimes impossible, to shake these pictures from my mind.

In the winter of 1967, I was called upon to go to North Platte, Nebraska, to assist in a funeral for a Marine who had been killed in Vietnam. North Platte is a four- or five-hour drive west of Omaha. The weather was threatening, and there were warnings not to travel. However, someone senior to me had made the decision that we were to go anyway. There were six of us in the Marine Corps sedan. We planned to make it out there in time for the afternoon service, then attend the burial in the local cemetery, and then return to Omaha.

However, by the time we arrived, the weather reports predicted that a dangerous blizzard was virtually upon us and warned people not to travel. The funeral was cancelled and would be scheduled at a later date. So, what were we six Marines to do? The two or three motels in North Platte were already filled. A decision had to be made. The Captain made the decision to leave for Omaha right away and try to outrun the blizzard, and, if necessary get a motel along the way.

We started off for Omaha and were only a few miles out of North Platte when the blizzard caught us. It hit with a fury I had never seen before. There was snow and high winds coming out of the northwest, blowing crossways on the road. The snow and wind were hitting the north side of the car with enough force to make it shudder, and the windshield wiper blades, coated with snow and ice, were standing up and waving in the wind.

Sometimes it felt and sounded like someone was throwing a constant barrage of snowballs against the car. With the windshield wipers iced up, we could hardly see. It was very uncomfortable for the six of us jammed in the car. Visibility ahead of us was reduced to about twenty feet. There was a large truck in front of us, creeping along. We followed it, using it as a sort of guide through the snow and wind.

As we struggled down the road, someone said he had to pee. Well, now how were we going to arrange this? We decided that if we stopped, we all needed to answer nature's call with one stop. We pulled over and fought the doors of the car to get them open. Then we lined up along the edge of the road with the wind at our backs. It was probably a sight never seen before nor since: six Marines decked out in full dress blues, standing side by side in a blizzard, all facing the same direction—peeing. Indeed, it was almost impossible to stand up in the wind and pee. Somehow, we all managed to get relief, though we speculated that most of the pee was either on us or had been blown to Kansas and Oklahoma. Whatever. The relief was what was important.

When we got going down the road again, the truck we had been following had long since left us behind. We were on our own. We decided to try and catch him because he was a good guide. We started off again, taking it very slowly. Visibility was still nearly zero. We came to the edge of a little town. It was getting dark, and it appeared that the town was deserted. No one was out, and we began to look for a motel or a place where we could get something to eat. Every place seemed closed, except for one. It was a bar and pool hall in the town square.

We stopped there and were delighted to learn that they did serve hamburgers, soup, and sandwiches. We went in. There were several people like us there—travelers, looking for food and shelter. The storm still raged, and some of the town appeared to have lost all its electrical power. This business owner was running his place on an emergency generator.

I ate a large burger and fries and washed it down with beer. After talking to the people there, we concluded, without a doubt, that we were stranded in a fierce blizzard. All the power lines were down, and the road ahead was closed. We'd have to find a place to sleep for the night. Well, at least we had shelter for the moment.

Soon, however, the owner of this place said that he closes at midnight and that we couldn't stay beyond that. As the clock neared midnight, we started to get downright worried. All six of us may have to sleep in our car.

One more idea hit us. There was a local fire department building only one block away, and we knew there was always someone at the fire department! We decided to go for it. We struggled through the deep snow down the one block to the fire station. There was one man there, and he would be there all night.

Upon learning of our problem, he said, "Well, you're all welcome to stay here, but there's only one bed," and that was his. However, there was at least a seat in each of the two trucks, and one of them had a jump seat behind the main seat. He said, "The rest of you can just look around and find a corner or sofa to sleep in or on," and he had several old blankets that he gave us. I grabbed one of the seats in one of the fire trucks, and I don't know where the others slept. Wherever it was, no one got much sleep. It was bitterly cold, and I heard the wind raging outside until it slowly died down as daylight drew near. My feet were *very* cold, and I almost got frostbite on my toes.

When morning came, we all began to wake up, trying to figure out what we were going to do. We were stiff and sore and in need of some food and hot coffee. The fireman had made us a big pot of steaming coffee. It seemed that the storm had blown itself out, and citizens were out and about, opening up their little town. We dug out our car, and, taking a tip from the fireman, made our way to a small cafe about two blocks away. There we enjoyed a hot breakfast and more coffee and discussed what course we should take. Should we look for a motel to stay another day, or just try and push on toward Omaha? The national news was reporting on this blizzard and suggesting that everyone stranded should just stay put to allow enough time for the snowplows to clear the road.

We hung out in this café, drinking more coffee until noon, and then, based upon information from a couple of truckers, we thought we could probably get through by taking it very slowly. In early afternoon, we headed east to Omaha. The snowplows were out, working on getting the roads open. Progress was slow, as in some places there was only one lane open.

I shall never forget this scene. There were cars off the road and down in a ditch that were totally covered by snow. Many cars had been abandoned along the road. What had happened to the passengers? According to news reports, several people had lost their lives in this storm. We were lucky we had made it out unscathed. I don't know what happened to the funeral of the Marine that we were supposed to bury. I know that I never made a trip back out there. My lesson learned from that adventure was not to travel if a blizzard is forecast *anywhere close* to us when in that part of the country. And I always keep emergency provisions, like water, food supplies, and blankets in my car. In the winter months, I try to keep abreast of the local weather news. I don't want to ever go through such scary and dangerous experience again!

Early in the winter of 1967, not long before when I was due to receive my orders, I was called upon to assist one of our officers in a death notification. This time, the deceased lived quite a ways west and north of Omaha, out on the windswept plains of northwest Nebraska. There was snow and ice on the ground, and it was very cold. The officer and I were to notify an elderly mother and father of the death of their son, a Marine officer killed in action in Vietnam.

I drove the staff car, and the closer we got to our destination, the sadder I felt, and I had that old familiar lump was in my throat. The officer and I hardly spoke as we drove along, and when we did, it was in hushed tones. We found the man's home. It was an old two-story wooden house sitting on level ground with some outbuildings around it. The scene was bleak, stark, and cold. The officer and I sat in the car in the driveway for a few moments, trying to muster our courage and collect our thoughts. Finally, we got out of the car and walked up to the door, with the snow and ice crunching under our feet. We knocked on the door.

The door opened, and we were greeted by a motherly-looking woman. Standing behind her was an older man in bib overalls. As soon as they saw us, the woman's face puckered up, and she put her hands to her breast and said something like, "Oh no! No-o-o!" and she began to cry. The old man's face clouded, and he put his arm around his wife and hugged her. He tried to say something, but his voice failed him. They opened the door a little further and motioned for us to come in. We were invited us to sit down.

The officer began by asking them if they were the folks we were looking for. They were. He went on with his solemn duty of reading the message to them. It was so awful, seeing that elderly mother and father crying together, holding each other. Their pain cut to the bone and put a burr in the pit of my stomach. Their baby—yes, the one that had suckled at her breast was gone, dead, killed in a war thousands of miles away. For what reason?

After a few moments of letting things sink in a little, we asked them if there were any friends or family we could help them call. The officer with me made it clear that the Marine Corps would assist them in any way they needed and gave them our contact information. The father began to take charge, and picked up the phone and began calling people, likely family members. He never told them why he was calling. He just told them to come quickly— something bad had happened to "Jimmy."

People began to arrive until the room was soon filled with grieving family. I remember thinking, "This is what happens, Mr. President, when you send our young men off to war. This is what happens! I wish you could see this, Mr. President." I wish all presidents could see this.

As soon as we saw that family and friends were getting things under control, the officer and I excused ourselves with clear instructions to the family about how to get our help with the funeral and others services, and asked if there was anything more that we could do.

We departed and made the long drive back to Omaha without saying much. I could tell that the officer was feeling very emotional and near the point of crying himself. I don't recall participating in any further assistance requested by this family. A lot of folks prefer to have a private funeral with no military services. As 1967, was coming to a close, I felt like I just shouldn't take part in any more military funerals and death notices. I couldn't get rid of the visions of myself in dress blues, lying in a casket, and my family grieving. My commanding officer, Major Wall, was very understanding about it and for a while I was relieved from these duties. Needless to say, I was very grateful.

One of the more popular events the Marine Corps Reserve participates in is the Toys for Tots program during the Christmas holidays. Again—lucky me! Because I was good at public relations, I was assigned to be the I & I staff member to be in charge of the program when Christmas time rolled around. It was a lot of work! I had to contact all the major businesses in Omaha and the surrounding area that in the past had participated in the program and contributed either cash or donated toys to children who otherwise wouldn't get any at Christmas time. The Marine Corps provided a lot of promotional material, such as posters, pamphlets, short videos announcements for TV, and radio spot announcements, etc.

Although the Marine Corps Reserve sponsors the drive, the reality was that I had to do most of the actual work, as reservists have civilian jobs during the day. They only worked on weekends when they were attending drill and most businesses are closed.

I really didn't mind doing the work. I liked working with people, and I was becoming very well connected around the town. It was a great publicity mechanism for the Marine Corps, and the people in Omaha were very generous, especially to Marines.

For one business in particular, the program was very beneficial—the five McDonalds restaurants in the greater Omaha area. We designated the McDonalds restaurants as drop-off places for people donating toys. Of course, what generally happened was that since people were there dropping off toys, they usually purchased McDonalds food. It was a big boon for McDonald's every year. McDonalds reciprocated by giving a free meal to any Marine in uniform who visited one of their restaurants during the Christmas period. Needless to say, my family ate a lot of McDonalds food during that time period. During the last promotional period in 1967, McDonalds management somehow found out that I was about to receive my orders overseas back to Vietnam. It touched my heart that during that period of time, all of the McDonalds' marquis in the Omaha area displayed the message, "Good luck Sgt. Bob Lay."

On December 31st 1967, I received my orders from Omaha to the Western Pacific area, with a delay at Camp Pendleton, California, for processing. Just as Delores and I had done in 1964 when I was scheduled to leave for overseas duty, we determined to have the best Christmas ever. So once again we began the countdown of how many days before I had to leave.

Yes, Daddy was going away again. I had to do the best I could to get Delores and the boys ready to live without Daddy once more. We decided that Delores would stay in Omaha while I was gone. We loved the old house, she was all settled in there, and the kids were in school. After that decision was made we were relieved of lot of stress.

We took a trip down to Kansas to see my Mom and Dad before I had to go. After the holidays were over we began to again count down the days until I had to leave Omaha. Time passed so quickly, and way too soon it was time to go. I would fly from Omaha to Camp Pendleton, California, and from there, on to Vietnam.

The day before leaving, we began to count down the hours, then the minutes, before I had to walk out that door and head to the airport. That day arrived, and, just as it had been before when I had to depart from my family as I headed to Vietnam, the sky was gloomy and overcast. Delores and the children went to the airport to see me off. It was so hard to go! *A Marine's life isn't easy*, I reminded myself.

The plane was parked on the tarmac about a hundred yards from the terminal. A number of times in the past three years I had been with a grieving family here at this very airport when their deceased loved one came home. However, when a deceased Marine comes home, his remains are shipped in a metallic looking casket inside a large wooden crate, and this crate is delivered to another place at the airport called Freight Terminal instead of the Passenger Terminal. I recall waiting out there in the cold and seeing a tractor pulling a trailer with a huge wooden crate on it heading our way. Usually the deceased's escort, a Marine in uniform, would be riding seated on top of the crate, or in the seat with the driver. This scene always brought a lot of tears. I was very sad when we'd see the large crate on a cart being pulled by a tractor coming to the cargo area. It certainly was a possibility that I could come back that same way. I whispered a prayer that I would not.

I kissed and hugged Delores, then knelt down and hugged each of the children. Then I stood up and began that long walk out to the stairway to board. Just before I walked up the stairs, I turned and waved. My sunglasses hid the tears in my eyes. I nearly stumbled on the step because my vision was so blurred by my tears.

I sat down in a seat from which I could look out and see my little family standing there, waving at me. The plane started its engines, and, as it moved, it turned and headed toward the runway. I waved from the window for the last time. I was on my way for the second time to that land of war on the other side of the globe. I would be gone thirteen to fourteen months. It seemed like an eternity.

CHAPTER 38

CAMP PENDLETON, CALIFORNIA, INFANTRY TRAINING COMMAND, 1968

When I arrived at Camp Pendleton and was in the process of checking in, I anticipated being there only a few days. I would get any required vaccinations and there would be a review of my records to bring everything up to date, such as life insurance, dog tags, a will, the correct address for my dependents, and a review of my pay records.

People who check in there and are en route to an overseas assignment are sent to Staging Battalion. When I turned in my orders they took one look at my records and asked me to step aside. I was taken to a nearby desk, where a sergeant invited me to sit down. He told me that because of my past assignments in troop-handling experience, such as having been a Drill Instructor, I'd had been selected to become a leader of a unit going through Infantry Training School before they were to be sent to Vietnam. This training is the same as the training recruits are sent to after boot camp, and the same training I had struggled with at Camp Geiger, North Carolina, in 1958. It's considered the best of any infantry training in America.

The training is constantly being updated because of new information coming from Vietnam.

I was really surprised and, needless to say, not happy with this news. I offered some words of protest, telling the sergeant that I had already been through the Infantry Training School almost twice at Camp Geiger, North Carolina, and that he should also consider the fact that I was an engineer, a Utilities Chief.

The sergeant was adamant. I had been named as the leader of a unit that was forming at that very moment, and was due to begin their training schedule in two days. I had no recourse. This is what Marines do. The sergeant told me there were other Staff Sergeants in this unit, but I was the senior Staff Sergeant, and would be the Acting First Sergeant. There would be 165 men in my unit. I was to form them into a Marine Rifle Company, with platoons, squad leaders, and platoon sergeants, etc. The unit would also have an officer who would function as Company Commander, and whom I would meet that afternoon. When I did meet this captain he explained that he was a supply officer and had never been in the infantry. He told me that he was going to count on me to take charge and carry out the training schedule, and if I needed him, give him a call. He certainly was neither encouraging nor helpful.

Wow! This was a difficult pill to swallow. All of a sudden my plans for a few easy days relaxing at Camp Pendleton, hanging out at the Staff Club, and taking some liberty in Oceanside, had all changed. Now, not only was I going to have to go through Infantry Training School, but I was also going to have to lead the unit of 165 men. This was going to be tough. I was really out of shape. I hadn't done any physical training or exercise for at least three years while I was at Omaha. I'd been drinking and smoking, playing the guitar, and having a good time. Now, all of a sudden I'm the Acting First Sergeant of an infantry company going through a torturous training cycle. Could I do it? I had to. I was a Marine! I must admit that sometimes it's very difficult to claim the title, "Marine."

Before I left the check-in building, I met with an officer—a captain, I believe. He handed me a roster that contained 165 names. He told me that these were the men assigned to this training unit, and it was my job to take them through the training cycle, ensuring that the unit is present at all scheduled training. He told me the date on which the unit was scheduled to complete this training and board an airplane at Marine Corps Air Station, El Toro, for a flight to Okinawa.

The captain also told me that there were 165 men starting the training, and they wanted 165 men to complete the training and board the flight to Okinawa. He said they realized that some men would be dropped out, but other men would join to make sure there was a full component boarding the plane. He went on to affirm that I was the senior man in the unit, except for the captain, and they must follow my orders. He told me that the captain and I could decide what time reveille would take place each day, which would be governed by the training schedule, and also when we would be scheduled to be in the first class or activity.

The captain asked if I had any questions. I wanted him to confirm that I was the senior person and that I was completely in charge. He said, "Yes, as of this moment, you are in charge of these people," handing me the printout of names. He went on to say, "You let me, or any member of my staff here know if you have any problems. We will support you one hundred percent." He finished by saying, "As you may or may not know, things are not going well in Vietnam. Our Marines are kicking ass over there, but these men who are training are badly needed in Vietnam right now." He went on to say that there weren't many people who had the leadership experience that I had, and who were capable of doing what they're asking me to do. He added, "What you are going to do is extremely important to the Marine Corps and to our country; in reviewing your record, we know we that we can count on you." With that statement, the captain stood up, shook my hand, and said, "Good luck!"

A jeep and a driver were assigned to take me to the barracks where my unit would be billeted. Already, there were a lot of Marines with their gear in front of the building, and others were inside, claiming the racks where they wanted to sleep. The driver helped me into the building with my gear and then up to the second deck to a room. I had a private room with my own shower and head. There were four other similar rooms.

I closed my door and sat down to collect my thoughts. My thoughts, which were spinning like a whirlwind. I sat down and had a talk with myself, assessing my situation. First of all, there was no doubt that I had to do this, no matter what I wanted. I could think of no valid reason why I should be excused from this job. Secondly, could I do this? Yes, I believed that I had the knowledge and the command presence to be a First Sergeant of an infantry company. Thirdly, could I physically do this? Well, that's a big question. I'll just do the best I can. There may be a lot of blisters and sore muscles at first, but I can work through that. I'm going to have to present a strong presence and demonstrate full confidence to be successful.

But I was also going to use the other staff sergeants to their full extent and delegate the authority to them to be platoon sergeants and totally responsible for the actions of the men in their platoon. This was something they should be capable of doing.

I pulled out the unit roster to review it. I picked out the four staff sergeants and wrote their names on a notepad. I was happy to learn that all the staff sergeants were infantry people. I decided that it was time to get this show on the road.

I stepped out of my room and found one of the men. I introduced myself and told him to round up the other staff sergeants and tell them to come to my room right away for a meeting. He looked a bit surprised, but he hesitated only an instant and took off to look for the others. When they had all gathered in my room, I introduced myself and told them that I had been assigned as the acting first sergeant of this unit and would be responsible for making sure this unit was present for every training event on our daily training schedule for the next month. I asked them point blank if they had any doubt that I was in charge. No one questioned it. I told them that I was assigning each one of them as platoon sergeant, and they would be responsible to me for all the men in their platoon. I then assigned each of them to a platoon. Giving them an extra copy of the full unit roster, I told them that by 17:00 I wanted them to form this unit into a company, ready for inspection, in front of this barracks, and we would have our first roll call for the entire unit.

So far, so good. I sent them on their way.

I unpacked my utilities uniform, combat boots, and changed from my Class A greens to the utility uniform and combat boots. I wanted to look sharp for my first appearance before the unit. I had also contacted the captain and told him of the formation of the full unit I had called, in case he wanted to attend. At 17:00, I looked out of my window and saw the unit was assembled on the deck in front of the barracks. Grabbing my clipboard, I sucked in a big breath, and said to myself, "Okay, Lay, show time!" and walked outside.

I walked with as much poise and confidence as I could to a place in the center of the assembly area, and, in a loud commanding voice, ordered, "**Fall In!**" Most of the men hurriedly took their positions and stood at attention. I waited a moment while they all found their places in formation. It was their first formation as a unit, and I thought they did pretty well. When I saw that the platoon sergeants were in place, I called them to attention and gave the command for the platoon sergeants to report. They did well with their report and responded that all were present.

I hesitated for a couple of moments and told them to stand at ease. Everyone relaxed. At this time, I gave a short speech. First off, I thanked them and the platoon sergeants for their cooperation in quickly bringing this unit together for the first time. I told them, among other things, everything I knew about the schedule for the training and how important it was to take this training seriously, as things were not going well in Vietnam, and they needed this unit and a lot more very badly. I told them the training they would get would be based upon the latest lessons learned in Vietnam and that their lives, or the lives of others, could depend on what they learn here at Camp Pendleton.

I told them that we would be drawing field gear and a weapon tomorrow, and then we would move out to another training area, Las Pulgas, where we would live while in training. I encouraged them to fully engage themselves in the training, and the importance of developing team spirit. Finally, I told them that if they cooperated, it would make all of our jobs easier, but if they made my job difficult, I would make *their* job difficult.

The next day, we drew field gear and weapons and were transported to Las Pulgas, where we moved into the old World War II era Quonset huts. I was issued an M1911A1 .45 caliber pistol for my weapon. I loved this pistol and was good with it. We staff sergeants had a hut of our own. The captain, the staff sergeants, and myself had a meeting in the late afternoon. We had a copy of the first day's trading schedule. First, and most noticeable, was the schedule for chow the next morning. We were scheduled to eat at 04:00. This meant I had to establish reveille at 03:30. Then, after chow, the schedule indicated that we were to depart for the first training area by forced march at 04:30. When I saw the schedule for the first day, my heart dropped. Maybe this training would prove to be too much for me, a non-infantry Marine. I knew that I'd just have to give it my best shot.

The next morning after chow, as per the schedule, at 04:30 we departed for the first class of the day, which was to be weapons training. It was being held at a firing range that was about a two-hour march from the chow hall. The captain and I took the lead, and at my command of "Forward March!" we moved out. We all wore helmets, field marching packs, weapons, and full canteens. My pack was riding easily on my back, but I knew it wouldn't be long before the straps would begin to cut into my shoulders, and the helmet would feel as heavy as an iron anvil on my head. The captain had a map of the area and the day before had attended a training briefing, even touring some of the training areas, including the one we were going to this morning. He was supposed to know how to get to the training range.

When we got away from the lights of the Las Pulgas area and started up an incline, it was very dark. As we marched, the old familiar sounds of men on the march came back to me: the jingling of the rifle slings, the squeaking of the web gear, the swishing of trouser legs, the coughs and heavy breathing, and the crunching of boots on the dirt trail. Somehow, it gave me a feeling of security and camaraderie. After about twenty minutes hiking up a long hill, the captain asked me to halt the men and give them a break. He got out his map, and we studied it by flashlight. Much to our dismay we discovered that captain had led us on the wrong trail! If we continued on the trail we were on, we would be entering an artillery impact zone.

While the troops were taking a break, the captain and I looked at the map and found a shorter route that we could take without turning around and going back. We cut across a rugged valley area through some sagebrush and cactus to get to the road we were supposed to be on. It all worked out, but it made our march to the training area nearly a mile further. We pushed the men hard and made it to our destination at the scheduled time. I was really wiped out. My leg muscles were burning, my pack straps were cutting into my shoulders, and my lungs were gasping for air. But I had made it, and that was the important thing!

For the next approximately three-and-a-half weeks, I took my unit to every scheduled training event, participating in each one with them. I wouldn't ask these men to do something I couldn't do. Each day, the march to the training areas grew longer. I focused on only one day at a time. As the days and the training rolled on, I became more and more comfortable with my command of the unit. Most of the time, it was only I who was doing the training while the captain was involved with other matters. It wasn't my job to question his whereabouts.

I thought we had a very good unit. All the men were very attentive to the classes and training events. They knew what was going on in Vietnam. Every day, the news media reported on the operations in Vietnam and the American casualties. Every day the casualties mounted. These men accepted the fact that perhaps what they learned here at Camp Pendleton could very well save their lives. It was a somber time for all of us.

During the first few days of training, more and more men complained of blisters on their feet and wanted to go to sickbay for treatment. I couldn't refuse a man's request to go to sickbay, but I didn't want them to miss any training just for blisters. So, one day, early on during a break in a class, I stood in front of the men and held an impromptu class. I sat down and told them to gather around me and listen up. I told them that I was going to show them how to treat blisters. I took off one of my boots and my sock and pointed to a large blister on my foot. I invited any of them who desired to come up and look at it. I took a needle, sanitized it by heating the tip with a cigarette lighter, and showed them how to open the side of the blister with the pin and drain the fluid from it by just gently pressing the top of the blister. I told them that they could just leave the drained blister as it was, or they could pour a bit of alcohol or aftershave lotion on it. I then put on a pair of clean socks. I told them that most of the time, the blister will harden and eventually a callus would form where the blister had been and would likely need no further treatment. They needed to check the blister every day, and if it appeared that it was getting infected, they should report for sick call and have a doctor look at it.

Although these men had most likely had this instruction before, I knew that it wouldn't hurt for them to have it again. I also believed that it would be a powerful reminder if they saw that their leader had a large blister, just like many of them probably had, and then I demonstrated once again how to treat it. I reminded them that the more they could stay in class and learn, the better off they'd be when they got to Vietnam. Requests to go to sick call for treatment of blisters diminished and then stopped altogether.

At some point during this time, I began to recall and remind the men of how many famous Marines in past wars had climbed these very same Camp Pendleton hills and had left their sweat here, mingled with the dust. Just to mention a few, there was General

Chesty Puller, General Ray Murray, General David Shoup, General Ray Davis, and Gunnery Sergeant John Basilone, along with many, many others. Now it was our turn to leave some sweat in these Camp Pendleton hills. In later years, three of my children would also leave their sweat mingled in this same Camp Pendleton dust. My family is proud of this history.

As our training was nearing its end, Delores and I talked and decided that it would be great if she could come out to Camp Pendleton and spend a couple of days here over a weekend before I left for thirteen months. Our good Marine friends Mac and Dorine were now living in San Diego, and they would be a huge help in making this happen.

Delores flew into San Diego. Dorine picked her up at the airport, brought her up to Camp Pendleton, and picked me up. We checked into a nice hotel in San Diego for a weekend of bliss. We also found some time to spend with our friends. Mac was again serving as a drill instructor, this time at the Marine Corps Recruit Depot in San Diego. It was exciting for me to once again visit the Recruit Depot from which I had graduated in 1953.

It was wonderful to spend some time with Delores again. We repeated our expressions of love for each other, and she brought me up to date on how the children were doing. But the weekend flew by quickly, and soon it was time to say goodbye again. On Sunday evening, Dorine and Delores took me back to Camp Pendleton and on out to the lonely old Quonset huts at Las Pulgas.

Our goodbye was bittersweet. Delores flew back to Omaha the next day to resume the care of our family. I don't believe a sweeter, more loving, and more trusting woman than my Delores has ever lived. The memory of her sweet face kept my spirits charged until the time when I would see her again.

A few days before we would be leaving to go overseas, a couple of the staff sergeants and I decided to go out to Oceanside, a California city just outside the main gate of Camp Pendleton, for a few hours, just to get some cold beers and relax for a little bit. We all were very proud of our training unit, and we thought that we had earned a brief respite from our labors. Those bars in Oceanside have been the lifeblood of this city for many, many years. Oceanside hasn't changed much. The street names and the names of the bars don't change much, but the girls change frequently. The bar clientele remains the same: Marines who've had a few drinks just looking for girls to have a good time with—not necessarily to take as a bride. Many were the Marines before us who went to Oceanside to drink a couple beers, and maybe get lucky with one of the bar girls before shipping out. We were no exception, except for me. I wasn't looking for a girl.

It was almost like a ritual for Marines going off to war. In one bar where we sat down for a drink, I noticed my song "The Marine's Ballad" was playing on the jukebox. What a thrill for me! I could hardly convince my two friends that it was me singing my song! While sitting at the bar, scantily dressed pretty young women were dancing on the bar and serving drinks. On the spur of the moment, I thought that I would try to impress one of these girls. So, while the song was playing, I asked one of the girls what she thought of the song, thinking that if she said she liked it, I'd tell her it was me and maybe impress her. Much to my chagrin, the girl said, "I hate that damn song. Did you ever try and dance to it?" She added, "They play it all the time."

Well, taken aback and speechless I hunkered down on the bar stool and took a drink of my beer. My friends and I had a good laugh about it, though! During the course of the evening, we visited several other bars, and in all the bars we visited, my song was being played. Here we were, Marines, getting ready to be deployed to Vietnam, and the lyrics of the song played:

In March of 1965, in the land of Vietnam.
Things were going badly, and the enemy wouldn't run.
Then, from the halls of the Pentagon, there came a cry for more.
The president sent those mighty men of the U.S. Marine Corps.

From their landing craft that early morn, they stared into the dark.
Soon the sun would rise, and the time to disembark.
Their rifles at the ready, their bayonets held high.
On that hostile enemy shore, many a Marine would die.

The story spread for miles around, the Marines had come ashore.
They hit the beach a-running, as they did in wars before.
Those mighty, gallant men, with their rifles and their packs,
They will charge right through the enemy, and never will turn back.

Through the rice fields and the jungle, the enemy fled that day.
They left their rifles, they left their food, they left their dead to lay.
The Marines had won the battle, and they never did turn back,
Those mighty gallant men with their rifles and their packs.

On the shores of many foreign lands, afar across the sea,
The Marines have always won their fame, against the enemy.
They have always won their battles and they never have turned back.
Those mighty gallant men with their rifles and their packs.

When my buddies and I thought we'd had enough to drink, and we knew it was time to get back to our Marines, we caught a cab to Las Pulgas. By the time I got back to my rack, I was ready for a few hours sleep. My face was feeling numb and I was a bit dizzy. I slept well and woke up refreshed early Monday morning with a lot of things to do. We were scheduled to fly out of El Toro in a couple of days.

On the night before we were scheduled to leave, it appeared that our barracks was in a state of chaos, as all the men were busy, packing their gear, cleaning the barracks, and saying goodbye to loved ones. During this chaos, one of the platoon sergeants brought a young man to me and told me, "This man is refusing to pack up and go with us." He went on to say that the man was an immigrant from Central America with a green card, and said that he wasn't going to go and perhaps die for this country. This enraged me, and in a loud, angry voice I said, "So, you coward, you can come here and enjoy all the benefits of being an American, but when it comes to defending America you turn your back, you coward?" The anger I displayed, and the tone of my voice, really scared the young man. He stood stiffly at attention and, wide-eyed, replied, "Yes, sir."

I then bellowed at him, "You coward! Get out of my sight, you coward!" He turned and took off running out of the barracks. In my rage, I threw my clipboard at him as he turned and ran out the door. I never saw him again. Now I had to call Battalion Headquarters to report this matter, as they would have to supply another man to make up for this one who had dropped out.

In times of war, emotions are raw, and people have to quickly make life-changing decisions. Later on, I thought that perhaps I should have handled the situation differently. But, if this man had these kinds of thoughts about fighting for America, no one would want him fighting beside them, so he may just as well bug out. The next morning, the man was missing from morning roll call, and Battalion sent another to take his place.

In late February 1968, as we were making final preparations to depart for Vietnam, shocking scenes of the violence and horror of the fighting in Vietnam was portrayed nightly on television in millions of Americans' living rooms. Although Americans and South Vietnamese troops had blunted the January Tet Offensive, the ferocity and strength of the Viet Cong guerrillas shocked the American forces. The American commanding general in Vietnam was requesting more than 200,000 more additional troops.

The time for our departure had finally arrived. One hundred sixty-five solemn-faced, combat-ready United States Marines, including myself, stood at the ready in the bright sun, silently gazing through squinted eyes at the huge aircraft that would soon whisk us away to a land of war. Here, on our last morning, the hot Southern California sun tormented us, as black blisters of tar oozed up through the cracks in the asphalt, as if in protest of the sun's wrath.

The aircraft, a long, sleek, Continental jetliner, was parked on the shimmering asphalt some two hundred yards from us, facing us at a forty-five degree angle. It loomed in front of us like some huge monster waiting eagerly to gobble us up and disappear into the sky, indifferent to our fate and unspoken protest.

There was a nervous shuffling of feet among the men as the door of the aircraft opened and a stewardess stepped out and stood at the top of the loading ramp. Some fifty feet behind us behind a chain link fence was a gathering of family and friends of us departing Marines. Most of them were silent; the goodbyes had all been said, the tears had all been shed. Now, only a murmur and occasional sob broke the silence. Mothers lifted their small children up above the fence to wave goodbye to their parting fathers—women who knew that some of these men would be swallowed up in the war.

Upon a signal from the stewardess, I gave a marching command, and the first column of men moved forward, single-file, toward the loading ramp. The file of men moving forward was similar to a huge green serpent slowly crawling across the asphalt, up the ramp, and into the belly of the greater monster that leered at them.

Finally, the tail of the serpent disappeared into the aircraft. The door was closed, and the ramp rolled away. As I settled into my seat, the gentle whine of the engines gradually became an ear-splitting shriek as the big machine turned slowly from its parking place and rumbled toward the taxiway. I could see from the window that some of the family and friends had already begun to slowly depart. Most, however, stayed and likely watched until the huge machine was only a speck in the pale blue California sky.

As the plane climbed, making a long, sweeping arc, the panoramic view of the California coastline, awash in hazy luminance, slowly faded from our view. Except for the powerful growl of the great engines, the cabin was eerily silent. A thick blanket of sadness had settled on the shoulders of these young Marines, each lost in their private thoughts of home, family, and an uncertain future, while the great plane continued to carry them away to a distant land of war and their rendezvous with destiny.

I reclined my seat back as far as it would go, pulled my cap bill down to hide the tears that filled my eyes. I solemnly swore that I would not allow this war to consume me, and that I would return someday; I *would* return to my family and this great land, America! *Oh, so help me, God!*

After a stopover for fueling at Anchorage, Alaska, we landed at Kadena Air Force base, Okinawa, Japan. It was midmorning, and it was hot and humid. We were bussed to Camp Hansen, an infantry base in the northern part of the island. I had all the men unload and fall into formation. I was still responsible for them, and I wanted to turn them over to someone else as soon as I could.

I went into the reception center and found the right people to take over. Of course they were expecting us. They came outside, took the roster, and began to call out the names. When it was clear that all were accounted for, one of the men signed for acceptance. What a relief! It was time to drink some of that Japanese beer and eat some fried rice. I was back in the Orient again!

A couple of the other staff sergeants and I quickly changed clothes and went to Kin-Ville, the little village right outside the main gate, that was composed of dozens of gin mills, pawn shops, souvenir shops, and clandestine whore houses, and catered mostly to the Marines at Camp Hansen or to anyone who had some money. We celebrated our success in bringing these 165 men through Infantry Training School, a job of which we were very proud.

I was at the assignment center for only a few days before I flew out, bound for Da Nang, Vietnam. Camp Hansen was an exciting bustle of activity, a feeling of electricity in the air, with hundreds of Marines either on their way back from Vietnam or on their way to Vietnam—all talking about Vietnam. Their uniforms varied from weathered and faded cammies to newly issued ones. Some of those travelers were burnt brown by the Vietnam sun and their were boots were caked with red Vietnam dust. It seemed that everyone was in a hurry. It was a pleasant surprise to hear that my "Marine's Ballad" record was on the jukebox in the Staff Club at Camp Hansen and was being played a lot. It was also on a couple of the jukeboxes in bars in Kin Ville, where it was also popular. I thought to myself, *Well, Bob, there's no time to celebrate any fame now. It's time to go to Vietnam. Fame, if any, can come later."*

I wrote Delores a letter telling her how very much I loved her and missed her and the kids, and I updated her on my destiny to go on to Vietnam, very likely to the same place I had left four years ago. By this point, we'd already been separated for more than a month, and I would be gone another thirteen months. It seemed like forever.

CHAPTER 39

RETURN TO VIETNAM, 1968

When our plane touched down on the runway at Da Nang, I could hardly believe I was back there again. As we taxied in, I could see familiar sights from the window. The sights brought me no joy. We debarked and once again I stood on Vietnamese soil. It was gloomy and overcast, and the old familiar stench of Vietnam saddened my already gloomy mood. A fine mist hung in the leaden air, making it seem that we were living in a world of grey flannel. The plane's crew informed us where we were to wait for transportation to our unit. I was being assigned to MWSG-17. This designation stood for Marine Wing Support Group, number 17. Essentially, this unit provided all types of support activities for the men and also the maintenance activities for Marine tactical aircraft. There were perhaps a dozen of us waiting for transportation. I dropped my gear in the sand beside a bunker and sat down in the sand to wait. Sitting there, with all my gear stacked around me, breathing that putrid air and facing thirteen months here, was a real low point. Just thinking that I would *still* be here next year at the same time caused my spirits to sink to the bottom of an unknown black pit. I just sat in that pit in my mind and brooded over my situation for awhile, until someone said, "Hey, buddy, our ride is here."

I got into the truck, which took me down a familiar dusty road to the headquarters of MWSG-17. I reported in and was gladly received, as they'd been waiting for their utilities chief. Someone in the office said something about a lot of stuff being broken down that needed fixed, meaning refrigeration gear at the mess hall. This seemed like a familiar story to me.

I was welcomed with a handshake from the first sergeant. The squadron commander, a colonel, dressed in his flight suit, also came out of his office to greet me with a handshake. The first sergeant assigned one of the office clerks to take me to where I would be billeted. The clerk took me through a large sandy area, where several squadron buildings stood, and to the staff billeting area, which consisted of a row of huts built of plywood that were up on stilts, covered with screen wire and topped with tin roofs.

I was assigned to a hut with other staff sergeants and sergeants. None of the other men were there, so I took the only rack available as mine. When I sat down on my rack to collect my thoughts, a Marine came in and introduced himself as a person from communications. He said that he was instructed to install a field phone beside my rack. I asked him, "Why me?" He told me that only key staff, people who needed to be called in an emergency, get to have a phone installed. I thought, sarcastically, *Oh, aren't I the lucky one!*

When evening rolled around, I met my roommates. There was Ray, a crew chief on a flight crew that sometimes had night missions. Ray was a true hater of Vietnam and the Vietnamese. He had a wife and children at home in Pennsylvania, and he missed them with every fiber of his being. I notified Delores that Ray's wife lived very close by, so maybe they could hook up for a visit while we were gone. They did get together, and Delores later said they had a really good time. Ray and I thought it was great that they were able to get together.

I liked Ray, and we got along very well. He bought a lot of souvenirs during his time in Vietnam, making several trips to Bangkok, Thailand, where he found a lot of items. When it came time for Ray to rotate back to the states, he made a trip to the large postal facility operated by the U.S. to ship his items home. Sadly, he carelessly left his purchases in his jeep while he went in to make a quick inquiry about shipping. Although he was gone only a few minutes, when he came back the jeep was empty. Everything he had purchased in thirteen months was gone—stolen—and the thieves were nowhere to be found.

There was no recourse. It would be impossible to find the thief. There were dozens of Vietnamese in and around this area constantly. Ray came back to the hut a crushed man. There were no words adequate enough to describe his hatred for these people.

Another man, Steve, was a nice quiet guy from Nebraska. Steve had a very pretty girlfriend back in Nebraska. He showed me her picture a couple of times. He was faithful to her and said that he sure wanted us to meet her when we all got back home. Sure enough, once we had returned home, he brought her to visit Delores and me. They had married and looked like the perfect, happy couple. They both had that fresh-scrubbed, wholesome Nebraskan look. Steve and I were so grateful that we had survived Vietnam together. We reminisced, sharing with our wives our experiences, including the many nights that we had sat hunkered down in our bunker, listening to rockets and mortar fire bursting near us, as we cradled our rifles, hoping that we wouldn't have to use them.

And then, there was "Ski." Ski was a Polish guy in his mid-fifties. He had served at the end of World War II and had been discharged for a couple of years when he came back in for the Korean War. After that was over, he again got out of the Marine Corps but came back in for the Vietnam War, trying to accumulate enough total active duty time to retire.

We all liked Ski, but we soon concluded that he was a bit crazy. He was always teasing the housemaids and playing pranks on people. Somehow, he got his hands on a woman's wig. Sometimes he'd put that wig on with his utility cap on top of it. He looked very comical, and the housemaids and we cracked up laughing at him. He never got completely out of line and was fun to have around.

He was still just a staff sergeant, and that didn't seem to bother him. He just liked the camaraderie of being with Marines. Ski was a construction chief, which meant that he was put in charge of the carpenter shop in the utilities section. He was subordinate to me and was good at his job, so I didn't have to worry too much about

316

carpenter work orders not getting done right. There were perhaps six Vietnamese civilians working for him in the carpenter shop.

Ski also became known as the true "dirty old man" by his language and some things he did. For example, he taught the Vietnamese who worked for him in the carpenter shop all the dirty words and curse words that he knew, which was a lot. But the Vietnamese didn't know these words were foul language, so they used them frequently in their everyday chatter as they worked. On a daily basis, we could hear all of this foul language coming from the carpenter shop. It was pretty funny, but it certainly wouldn't have been tolerated back in the States.

One time, the unit chaplain sent in a work order for us to build a new altar for the chapel. I passed it on to Ski and suggested that he contact the chaplain to get any specifics. Several days went by, and one day, the chaplain stopped by to see me. He had been over to the carpenter shop to check on the progress of the altar. He said that the altar was going to be beautiful, but the dirty language shouted back and forth between the Vietnamese in the shop did not amuse him. In fact, he was downright shocked and angry when one of the Vietnamese workers (not realizing that it was a terrible way to address a chaplain or anyone else) referred to him as an old "SOB." He thought that we Americans should be teaching these Vietnamese who worked for us not only correct English but also the good things about America.

I promised that I would talk to Ski about it, but I knew there was no way to stop it now. Also, of note, Ski would not salute the chaplain, even though the chaplain is an officer and rates a salute. When Ski happened to meet the chaplain on the street, rather than saluting, Ski would walk up to him and put his arm around the chaplain and say, "Hello, Bro, how you doing today?" or something to that effect, and continue to walk down the street with his arm around him.

Yes, Ski sure was a memorable person. I've always wondered what happened to him after the war. He certainly kept us amused in Vietnam.

As a part of my check-in process, I had to go to the unit armory to draw a weapon. To my surprise, they issued me an M1911A1 .45 caliber pistol, the standard issue for Marines my rank and in certain duties. I also asked for an M-16 rifle, because I felt that the pistol wasn't adequate as a primary defense weapon for what was going on in Vietnam at that time. They told me no, I wasn't eligible for an M-16 rifle.

This armorer told me that if I were a platoon sergeant for the reactionary platoon, then I could be issued an M-16. He went on to say that MWSG-17 had a reactionary platoon, which consisted of people from units such as motor transport, supply, and utilities sections, and supplied people to form a platoon that would be called upon in case of an emergency, such as an attack on our perimeter fence.

Consequently, I went over to the unit office and volunteered to be one of the platoon sergeants! They were happy, because they needed a platoon sergeant. I volunteered and was given a roster of the names of the people in my platoon. I was told that I needed to muster these people at least once a week to make sure they had their weapons, ammo, and knew what they were suppose to do in case of an emergency. I was given a letter of authorization to be issued the M-16 rifle.

I went back to the armorer and was issued the rifle along with six full magazines of ammunition for it. I returned to my quarters, proudly carrying my rifle and feeling much more confidant that I could at least defend myself in case of an attack. I planned to muster this platoon the next day to get them all briefed, and know who they were and what they were supposed to do. I realized that this was going to be both extra work and another responsibility for me, but I wanted to have the best chance I could at defending myself in case of an attack. I was determined to live through this tour and go home to my wonderful little family.

Da Nang, Vietnam, 1968.

After I got checked in, I went to the utilities shop to assume the responsibilities of utilities chief. By this time, I had been promoted to gunnery sergeant, a cherished rank in the Marine Corps. But with the rank came the responsibilities of the rank. And, as a gunnery sergeant, I was expected to know a lot of things about a lot of subjects. For example, it was expected in the Marine Corps that if no one else knew what to do, just ask the ole "Gunny." I was surprised and happy to see that the utilities section had some nice buildings to work from. Some Gunny before me had seen to it that the Utilities Section had adequate buildings and space in which to operate. Thank you, Gunny, whoever you are.

The utilities building contained an office for Utilities Officer, Captain Marks, and myself. There was a refrigeration-and-electrical shop, a carpenter shop, a lumber storage area, plus a nearby space where several pieces of equipment were stored. It took me several days to inventory all the utilities gear and get a grasp on our operations.

Essentially, our services were accessed when someone, or some unit in our area of responsibility, would submit a work order to our Unit S-4 office. The S-4 would review that order and either approve or disapprove of it, then forward it on to the Utilities Section if approved. These work orders may run the gamut from someone who wants a packing crate built, to someone whose electrical socket has no power, or perhaps a power line is down. I would review and assign these work orders to the appropriate person or persons to complete. It was a very busy operation, and we had a large backlog of work orders waiting to be completed. The Utilities section had most of the things that make people happy or comfortable in a situation such as ours. We could run electrical wire, build most anything, had lumber of all kinds, and were able to fix or find an air conditioning unit for someone, if they had been authorized to receive one. Shortly after I arrived, we received a work order to install an air conditioner in the Squadron Supply Officer's office. I thought that I had better go and personally talk to this supply officer, as he wasn't technically authorized to receive an air conditioner. The supply officer was a Lieutenant Colonel. He invited me into his office to have a chat. His office was extremely hot inside, and without an air conditioning unit, he, like everyone else, sweated profusely here in Vietnam. I asked him where I was supposed to get the air-conditioner to install in his office. He told me that he, as the Unit Supply Officer, along with the fact that we were operating in a combat zone, had the authority to purchase almost anything on the open market in Okinawa or Japan, or even have them shipped from the States.

He went on to say that if I would install a unit in his office, he would purchase one for my office also. I told him I thought that would be great. We shook hands, and he thanked me for coming to see him and said that he would notify me when the air conditioners were received.

Within just a few days he called and told me that the air conditioning units had arrived. They were large-capacity window units and would surely be able to keep the offices cool, even in this hot, sultry weather. I assigned two refrigeration mechanics to install one of the units in the Colonel's office. It didn't take them long, and when they returned, they installed the unit in my office. From then on, it was really comfortable and cool in there. I believe that the Supply Officer and I had the coolest offices in our entire operating area! I was very grateful to the Colonel, and I still don't know how he got approval to purchase those expensive units. As for me, the nice, cool office was great, but now I found it difficult to keep my office from becoming a gathering place where some high-ranking officers and staff would constantly drop by to say hello to me, sit around and shoot the shit for a while, and just enjoy the cool air. I didn't really mind, but I had a lot of work to do, and it was sometimes downright annoying. I was already well known by then because of my record, and now I had become even better known for having the coldest office of anyone around.

Meanwhile, I received a call from the Colonel thanking me and telling me how wonderful it was to have air conditioning. He said that my men had done a great job installing the unit, and invited me to stop in and see him anytime, letting me know that if there was ever anything I needed, I was to let him know. I thought, *Well, he's certainly the right person to know over here, where practically everything people want is in short supply*

Meanwhile, Marines from the entire surrounding area were always stopping by, looking for items like lumber, wire, bulbs, etc. For me, it meant an opportunity to trade what I had on hand for whatever they had to offer. A lot of times they were simply looking for a handout, which I freely gave if I had what they wanted. We had Marines come by from units all over the Da Nang operating area—grunts looking all beat up, dirty, scruffy, and hollowed-eyed. There were even people from other services stopping by. Sometimes all it took to make the grunts happy was to give them a couple pieces of lumber and a handful of nails. My men and I tried to help all that we could.

I reviewed the work orders that we received and assigned them to my Utilities people to complete according to the priority of the request. Sometimes the S-4 office would assign priority, and if they didn't, I did, based upon my judgment of what was really necessary, and not someone's pipe dream to decorate his office or living space.

One time I received a priority work request from the Colonel to paint the officers' head. This obviously was not a priority compared to all the other work requests I had waiting. Nevertheless, I had been in the Marine Corps long enough to know that I had to give this request a priority. When the "old man" wanted something done, we'd better do it!

I called in a couple of Marines from the carpenter shop and assigned them the job of painting the officer's head. The head was just a common four-holer made of plywood, like all the other heads in the area. When I gave the work order to the men, one of them looked at it and asked what color it should be painted, as the work order didn't specify that. They asked if they could choose the color.

I thought about it for a few seconds, and then told them, "Sure, why not? Paint it whatever color you want."

Well, they came back an hour or so later and told me the job was done. Not an hour had passed until I received a call from S-4, who told me that the Colonel was not happy with the color, and it had to be repainted *immediately*—and to paint it Marine Corps Green.

I walked over to the Officer's living area to look at the newly painted head and immediately realized why the paint job was unsatisfactory. My men had used a little bit of every single color of paint in the paint locker and had painted it in a bright, psychedelic pattern. It was the most beautiful, colorful four-holer in Vietnam—and it stuck out like a sore thumb. That would make it a choice target for a sniper or a mortar or any other enemy fire to zero in on.

I went back to my shop and called in the guilty painters. They both had sheepish expressions on their faces. I told them that they had to go back and repaint the head Marine Corps Green. I didn't chastise them, as I knew they had a good time doing it, and it would become one of their favorite sea stories of their Vietnam tour.

After working at this job for a while, and based on my past experience, I had developed a philosophy of priority assignment. The Captain one day asked me how I made assignments for work orders. I told him that, contrary to the old adage, "Don't put off until tomorrow what you can do today," my philosophy was, "Any work order that can be delayed until tomorrow should be delayed until tomorrow." When he looked puzzled by my response, I told him that I had discovered that sometimes when I assigned some of my people to complete a work order, the ones who had submitted the order didn't know what the hell they were talking about. In one case, it seems that the guy who submitted the order had rotated back home and hadn't told anyone why he wanted this or that done. Since that guy was gone, they didn't need the work done now and were told to just cancel the order.

This kind of thing happened frequently, where the person who submitted the order had either died or been transferred, and the work was no longer necessary or the situation had changed. I had discovered that due to the overall nature of the operations in Vietnam, things change a lot, and consequently, so do needs change. So, I'd just pick and choose those requests that seemed truly necessary at the time or try to discover some other way to solve their needs. I realized that I *had* to do this, as I didn't have the personnel and supplies required to fix everything that was either already broken or may break. When I explained this philosophy to the captain, he thought about it a moment, chuckled, and said, "I see what you mean, Gunny. Just keep on doing what you've been doing."

One hot day I received a knock on my door, and a young staff sergeant came in to see me. He looked very squared away and was polite. He introduced himself as Staff Sergeant Paul Smith. He said that he was the new Squadron Embarkation man and he wanted to talk with me for a few minutes about our embarkation readiness status.

I was immediately impressed by this man. He was articulate, professional, and had a friendly smile. We visited for quite a while, and, looking back, I believe I knew right away that I wanted this Marine for a friend—for a buddy. His personality was so engaging that right away I could see that he was a good person. He could speak intelligently on any subject, and without using foul language or curse words. He was a country boy from Maryville, Tennessee, and had been in the Marine Corps about ten years.

I got to know Paul quite well over the next few weeks while he helped me to get my embarkation requirements up to date. We often went to evening chow together and afterward we liked to just to sit on the sand bags around the old bunker talking about our families, our time in the Marine Corps, and old buddies we had known. He had heard my record, "The Marine's Ballad," on the jukebox at Okinawa and in Oceanside. He liked my song and said he was honored to meet me.

In one of the old buildings nearby where our unit was established was a small recreation room of sorts. There was nothing much there but an old weight bench and a set of weights. Some evenings, if no operations were going on, and we weren't on alert, Paul and I would go to the weight room and do some light weightlifting. It was a good place to visit and tell stories while we worked out. We felt close enough to share our personal information. Of course, it was very hot, and we were drenched with sweat after a workout. A cold beer sure tasted good!

Then Paul received word that he'd been selected for a commission to 2nd Lieutenant. That was great news for Paul, and I was very happy for him. As far as I was concerned, the Marine Corps couldn't have made a better decision. He would make a great officer. But I was also worried that he probably wouldn't be able to be my close friend any longer because of the expectation that officers shouldn't fraternize with enlisted people. I also expected that he would be transferred to another unit that had an opening for a officer with his MOS.

That didn't happen in this case. Our unit retained him and put him in the position of embarkation officer, assigning him a number of additional duties, such as officer in charge of the Mess Hall, Special Services, the Officer's club, and others. These aren't fulltime jobs, but they do require an officer to accept the overall responsibility of the daily operations.

True to form, Paul assumed these responsibilities without showing any stress or feeling burdened. He made the move from enlisted to officer very smoothly. These were marks of Paul's natural leadership abilities, which is what his superiors saw in him and which caused them to recommend him for a commission. One day he was a staff sergeant, and the next day, a 2nd Lieutenant, wearing those gold bars instead of staff sergeant stripes. It was a memorable moment for me to salute him for the first time.

Paul and most of the other men, including me, were looking forward to taking a five-day R&R and meeting our wives in Hawaii. He was very excited, counting down the days until he could leave, reunite with his wife, and also celebrate his promotion.

When Paul came back from R&R, instead of being happy and somewhat rested from relief from the daily grind, he seemed a bit down. It was unusual to see him like this. We talked about it that evening while we were working out with weights. Paul said that when they were in Hawaii, he and his wife weren't getting along very well and he thought they might have to get a divorce when his tour was over and he returned to California. But after a few weeks, he seemed like his normal self—upbeat, excited about life, and performing his duties as a good Marine officer. (On a sad note, I later learned that when Paul returned from his overseas tour, he filed for divorce.)

One day, Paul mentioned an opportunity for me to go to Okinawa for a few weeks to attend embarkation school. This gave me a chance to get out of Vietnam for a while and get an education in another subject. He told me that when I returned, he would get me appointed as the squadron embarkation non-commissioned officer as an additional duty. He pointed out that although it would be more work and responsibility, I would become better known by the command staff and enhance my opportunity for promotion. I agreed, and told Paul to submit my name for the school. Sure enough, I was selected to attend embarkation school.

In August, I received orders to proceed to Camp Hansen, Okinawa. It was great to get out of Vietnam for a while. The class wasn't very big—perhaps twelve people, all with the rank of Staff Sergeant and above.

The atmosphere was very relaxed. Class was from 08:00 to 16:30 every day. We were essentially learning how to load ships for the movement of troops along with their equipment to any place on the globe in as short a period of time as possible. We had to learn to plot out on paper where every person and every cubic foot of property of a unit would be stored for shipping and in which cargo hole on the ship it was to be kept. To do this we had to know the total cubic feet, square feet, and weight of all property of a unit and where on the ship it was stored. It was also necessary to load the ship according to the mission of the unit being shipped out, taking into consideration whether the move was from one place to another with the mission of conducting an amphibious landing, or if it was simply moving the cargo to another location in the world.

Although the daily class activity was low key, the subject matter was very difficult. Each student had an old, bulky adding machine on his desk. These machines, although very helpful and necessary, were also a burden to operate. With each entry of numbers, in order to get the total, one had to press the total key and then pull a handle, much like on a slot machine. The paper on the roll fed out, giving the answer and providing the very useful written record of the total.

On a busy day in class, the sounds of twelve people punching keys and pulling those levers, with rolls of paper feeding out of the machine and onto the floor, created a pretty interesting atmosphere. If a person isn't comfortable working with numbers, they should probably avoid this school. We had to learn how to create the written plan to load a ship and calculate the numbers, using addition, subtraction, division, and percentages of very large numbers accurately. The correct answer one was looking for was how many ships and what kind of ships it would take to move this unit or units from one place to another. That number along with the loading plan was provided to each unit and to the upper commands.

Although I found the classes difficult, it was still better than being in Vietnam! It was also a great relief to not have the daily stress of running the Utilities Section.

During the time that I was gone, Captain Marks took over the daily operations. The Captain was a good man, a good officer. Meanwhile, I enjoyed my evenings, sipping a cold beer and dining on the famous Okinawan and Japanese food offered here.

As usual, time seemed to pass too quickly, and soon the class was over. A brief and simple graduation ceremony was held. Now, I had another Marine Corps diploma under my belt and in my service record book. In addition to my other titles, I was now a Utilities Chief as well as a certified Embarkation Specialist.

On September 25th, I returned to Vietnam and my job as Utilities Chief. Believe me, it's no fun returning to Vietnam, where the smells, heat, humidity, and, hanging over everyone's head at all times, the possibility of being shot by a sniper or blown up by a grenade or stepping on or in a booby trap. These concerns were on everyone's mind continually.

As expected, when I returned from Okinawa, I was called to the office of Admin Chief, who told me that I was being assigned as the Squadron Embarkation NCO as an extra duty. With this title came the responsibility of ensuring that every unit in the squadron had their required boxes for shipping every piece of gear, their equipment correctly marked, and with up-to-date embarkation lists. Paul was the one who was responsible for getting all of these new assignments for me. With him being the Embarkation Officer, and I the Embarkation NCO, together we had the responsibility of inventorying all the Squadron Embarkation reports and lists.

He and I worked many hours, visiting every unit and digging through boxes in hot supply buildings, reviewing their embarkation reports, and making sure everything was up-to-date. It all was extra work for me, additional duties above and beyond that of Utilities Chief, but I really enjoyed working with Paul, and our friendship deepened. We developed the kind of trust and friendship in which both of us were comfortable discussing the most personal information about ourselves.

At this period of time during the Vietnam War, our government had a very popular program called the Rest and Recuperate (R&R) program. All military people serving in Vietnam were eligible. Additionally, the military assistance command helped to coordinate the visit of each serviceman's wife to Hawaii as well as to several other sites in the far eastern theater, including Australia, the Philippines, and Hong Kong. The most popular site was Hawaii, where the U.S. Army provided support at the Army base, Fort DeRussy, situated on the waterfront at Waikiki Beach. It was a great location.

As soon as I found out about the program, I began to get all the details and to figure out what timeframe would work for Delores and me. It was very difficult on Delores's part, because she had to make arrangements for someone to watch the children in addition to making her own travel plans.

We decided that October would be a good time. Now the countdown began toward the day we would finally be together again. It took a super- human effort for Delores to make all arrangements, along with the fact that she was dealing with a nasty cold. But, I reminded myself, this woman I had married was a tough one, born into a very tough Slovakian family from the old country. I knew she could handle it—and she did.

She arranged for the kids to stay with my Mom and Dad out on the old farm. The kids were excited about it, as were Grandpa and Grandma. She kept me updated with letters as the time drew near. We were both really excited and hoped and prayed that nothing would happen to cause us to cancel our plans. And nothing did! The time finally arrived and we were on our way, with her flying west and me flying east to meet up in Hawaii.

Delores arrived before me and was already there at the R&R center at Fort DeRussy to greet me. She and a long line of other wives were anxiously waiting, waving at us from the reception area in the terminal. The excitement was explosive when we finally got together in the reception area! Some of the women were disappointed because some husbands had been bumped from their flight. I felt so sorry for them. But the good news was that if someone was bumped, they were almost certain to arrive on the next plane, with several planes arriving every day.

Delores and I met, and we hugged and kissed amid many happy tears. We were so happy and excited! We quickly found our bags and got a taxi to take us to our hotel. Another Marine and his wife who were going to the same hotel shared the taxi with us. They were lucky—they got to the back seat first, while Delores and I had to sit in the front seat with the driver. We were all excited to be together, and the couple who had grabbed the back seat quickly seemed to lose control of their passions, and continued their struggle until we pulled into the hotel.

We stayed at the Reef Hotel right on the waterfront of Waikiki Beach. For both of us, with Delores coming from Nebraska and me from Vietnam, meeting in beautiful Hawaii was like coming out of a black and white world into a Technicolor one! It was such a contrast to come from hot, muggy, dirty, smelly, dangerous Vietnam, to beautiful, fragrant, clean, refreshing, peaceful, and friendly Hawaii, with its white sandy beaches and deep blue waters. We could hardly believe that we were together in our beautiful hotel in Hawaii. Wow! It was just like a second honeymoon!

Our room overlooked the beautiful Pacific Ocean, the beach, and the hotel pool. Our room had a small private patio outside our sliding door. Delores and I liked to sit out on that patio, sipping a glass of champagne.

I went to a music store and rented a guitar. I felt like I always had to have a guitar in my hands. Playing guitar was part of me, and I loved sharing that part with Delores. Our love for one another and the bond between us grew even stronger during this time. We rented a car, a Volkswagen bug, and drove around the island visiting a lot of beautiful places. We were comfortable and relaxed, just enjoying each other.

We visited several nightclubs and restaurants while we were there. At one of the nicest clubs, the entertainment consisted of one fellow playing a guitar and singing. The stage was on an elevated platform behind the horseshoe shaped bar. The songs he played were mostly all the songs I knew and played. He was quite good. After we'd listened for a while, I excused myself and went to the restroom. While I was gone, Delores, unbeknownst to me, went up and spoke with the manager, telling him that I was also an entertainer and that we were there on R&R. She asked him if I could come up and play.

To my surprise, when I returned from the restroom and sat down, the entertainer was calling for me over the microphone, asking me to come up to the stage. Delores had a sheepish look on her face. I never would have thought that she could be so bold. I went up to the stage and introduced myself to the fellow. He gave me his guitar and turned the stage over to me. This was definitely going to be an impromptu performance. Wow, there I was, on the stage in a nice place on the boulevard on Waikiki beach in Hawaii, and was about to sing in front of people!

I took the guitar, sat down, introduced myself, and received a rousing applause. I told them that I was a Marine on R&R from Vietnam and here with my wife. I pointed Delores out, and they cheered for her also. I was pretty confident of myself at that time and knew that I had a good repertoire. I played about half-a-dozen songs, which were well received. The applause made me feel good. When I gave the guitar back to the other musician and left the stage, the crowd gave me a good round of cheers. What a boost of joy that brought me! I returned to the booth where Delores was sitting, all smiles. She gave me a little kiss, and said, "You were really good. I'm so proud of you!"

These lazy, wonderful days in the sun, along with the warm nights, walking on the beach, holding hands, and the sound of the surf, came to an end all too soon. We spent our last night together just holding on to each other and saying sweet things. It was time for us to leave this world of dreams-come-true and go back to the real world of earning a living and caring for our children. My flight back to Vietnam left before Delores's flight, so she came to the airport to see me off. It was so hard to pull ourselves apart, and I once again made that difficult walk to the plane, leaving her there, waving at me. I told myself that it was time to go be a Marine again. That was my job—being a warrior for my country.

It was a sad flight back to Da Nang. We stopped at Guam for refueling. Most of us went into the PX and purchased some things, including several bottles of really good whiskey, which was very inexpensive there. Again, I landed at the Air Force base at Da Nang and went inside to try and find transportation back to my base and living area. It was late in the evening and very hot and humid. I was quickly able to find transportation back to within one-half mile from my living area.

I had to walk that last half-mile up a dusty road in the swelter- ing heat, carrying my bags. That was a walk I'll never forget. I was exhausted and sad and had such a pain in my heart, missing Delores. I shuffled along the hot dusty road to my hooch, sweating profusely, knowing that I faced at least five more months before I left this place. I cursed Vietnam, Ho Chi Minh, and the Viet Cong, over and over. As I walked, I prayed to Jesus for comfort and for God's blessing. It was good to finally get to my hooch and drop my bags. Ray, Steve, and Ski greeted me, and I felt better.

I got out of my dirty, sweaty clothes and went to take a shower. When I returned, I opened one of the bottles of Johnny Walker Black Label Scotch for a couple drinks to help me relax. I shared that good scotch with my hooch buddies as I told them of my experiences with Delores in Hawaii. Those memories of Hawaii with Delores while on my R&R will be among my best memories, stored deep in my mental footlocker forever.

In my daily routine, after evening chow I'd come back to my hooch and relax, write a letter, and often play the guitar I had purchased in Da Nang. Often Paul would stop by to just to talk and to listen to my playing. One evening when Paul came over, he was excited because he had some happy news for me. It seems that now, as officer in charge of the Officer's Club, he was responsible for booking the entertainment for the club. There were quite a few traveling bands and acts around Vietnam. They found it quite financially rewarding, as most of the clubs, being on military bases, had little or no overhead expenses, like rent or utilities. Consequently, the clubs could pay the acts and bands quite well.

Well, Paul came up with the idea of having me do an hour-long performance at the Officer's Club. He went on to say that he would hire one of the best country music bands to play with me and back me up. At first, I was skeptical of the idea, as I would have to perform before many of the officers, perhaps some of the highest-ranking Marine officers in Vietnam. I didn't know how they would accept a singing gunnery sergeant. Weren't gunnery sergeants supposed to be out there pushing troops, belching fire, and getting things done?

I needed some time to think about it. Paul finally talked me in to it. He reminded me that I was already quite well known because of my song, "The Marine's Ballad," and he told me that our officers also thought of me as a tough old Utilities Chief who got things done. He believed that the officers would likely be very receptive of me. I finally told Paul to go ahead and book me, but to give me a couple of weeks or so to pick out my songs and practice them, and to find and hire a band to back me up. I told him that I wouldn't do it without a good band. So Paul set about finding me a country band.

A few days later, he told me that he had found a band to back me up if I played at the Officer's Club. The band was made up of guys from the Air Force, and they were reputed to have the best country band around. I believe they called themselves The Gunfighters. Paul also had arranged for me to meet the band and have a practice session sometime before the booking. That pleased me very much. One evening Paul got us a jeep, and we went around the runway to the Air Force living and operating area. We met the band in a vacant building. The Air Force guys were there already and had their instruments and amplifiers set up. We all introduced ourselves. Just before we began our practice session, I gave them a list of the songs I planned to do and the key in which I wanted them played. To our surprise, they gave *me* a list of the songs *they* were going to do!

When they handed us their song list, Paul stepped up and said there must have been a misunderstanding. He told the band that he was hiring them to play backup for me only—not to perform their own songs. So, they all had a brief conference, came back, and said, "Sure! It's okay."

We were all good with that. I was happy that Paul had stepped up and made sure that we all had the same understanding. Then, for the next couple of hours, the band and I went through my song list and practiced my songs until we could perform them really well.

Paul scheduled the gig, and I began to get myself mentally prepared. This, to me, was a pretty unusual opportunity. Not many gunnery sergeants in the Marine Corps at that time would be in a position to be booked to perform country music at the Marine Corps Officer's Club at Da Nang, Vietnam. During my practice times, I sang each song over and over again until I was sure that I had memorized it completely and correctly. I searched through my memory banks for all the appropriate jokes to tell, all the one-liners, and the small talk that I was accustomed to using when I performed. I memorized the lead-in and introduction for each song. I was very nervous about this gig. Paul kept telling me that I was going to do just fine and that everyone would like me.

When the night of the performance arrived, Paul came by my hooch to get me, and we walked to the Officer's Club together. He asked if I was nervous, and I told him that I was. When we arrived at the club, we saw it was really packed. I then learned that I was playing at a good-bye party for one of the well-known squadron commanders, so this was an even bigger event than I had thought.

We entered the club through the side door that went backstage. There were several artists' private rooms. Paul and I took one of them. Paul asked me if I wanted anything. I said that I did, adding, "How about a drink?"

Paul summoned one of the waitresses. I knew what I needed. I ordered five shots of Jack Daniels and a beer chaser. Paul looked at me a bit skeptically, but I assured him that it was okay. I knew what I needed. I took a peep from behind the curtains and saw a full house, with many Marine officers. All were close to being intoxicated. It was really loud out there.

I noticed that a large table surrounded by the highest-ranking officers in the I Corps area was situated right in front of the stage. They had prepared a special seat for the officer who was departing and being honored. They had taken one of the bar stools from the bar and made it to look like a cockpit of an aircraft, complete with seat belts and helmet.

This officer, a Lt. Colonel, was seated in his "cockpit." On the bar and in front of him were dozens of drinks. These men were having a great time. *Wow,* I told myself, *Bob, you have really gotten yourself into something here! You'd better be good!*

To excite the crowd even further was the performance just before mine. It consisted of some song-and-dance girls in very skimpy costumes, like a Las Vegas showgirl show. They were just completing their dance routine and leaving the stage when Paul and I arrived.

There was a huge roar from the crowd when the girls left the stage. Paul looked at me skeptically, and said, "Well, Bob, are you ready?" By this time, I had already drunk all the whiskeys except for one, and my gut felt like it was on fire. But that was just the feeling I wanted. I felt very bold, my face was numb, and I was anxious to get out there on the stage and get on with the show. I didn't care who was there.

The band members were busily setting up their instruments on the stage, and were soon ready to go on. When it looked like it was time, Paul went out on the stage to introduce me. He gave me an outstanding buildup, told them all about my song, "The Marine's Ballad," and announced, "Here he is, Gunnery Sergeant Bob Lay!" I tossed back my last shot of whiskey and got ready to step out onto the stage.

Hearing the rousing applause, I felt like they all really loved and welcomed me. It was a wonderful feeling! There was standing room only in the club, and I glanced over at the table of high-ranking officers right in front of the stage. At first glance I didn't recognize anyone, but I noticed a lot of "brass" on those collars. I could honestly say that it was the top Marine Corps brass in Vietnam at that time. I walked onstage acting like I was kind of lost, went up to the microphone and tapped on it, as if testing it. Then I spoke into it, "Could someone please tell me where the head is located?"

Thankfully, they all really laughed, and I knew then that I had them in my hand. I approached the mike like Johnny Cash, turned, and said, "Hello, this is not Johnny Cash."

I did an imitation of Johnny Cash's "Folsom Prison Blues." It went over very well, and the band did a great job. Now that I'd had a good start, the rest of the program was even better than I had expected. The hour passed quickly, and soon it was time to close the show. Paul was signaling me from behind the curtains. I wrapped it up and left the stage to a large applause. It was over! What a great feeling to have finished it successfully.

Paul told me that I had done great. He had already ordered a burger and fries for both of us. We sat outside on the patio and ate while the rest of the show went on. When we finished eating, it was time to go back to my humble hooch—back to being the utilities chief and away from that world of being a celebrity of sorts. This was an experience that I'll certainly put in a secure place in my mental footlocker—a good memory for later times. I wished that Delores and the children and Mom and Dad could have seen me. This was the best performance of my lifetime.

Time seemed to drag. The workload at the Utilities Section was always heavy. A number of times I was awakened in the middle of the night for some emergency, like power lines being down due to wind storms, damage from incoming mortars or rocket attacks, or a generator that was down—any one of dozens of things could happen. When these emergencies arose, I had to get up, sometimes in a driving rain, go to the utilities shop, possibly assess the damage and call out the appropriate repairmen or set up some additional generators to ensure that operations could continue. I usually slept very lightly. At the slightest noise, my eyes would pop open and I'd be instantly awake. There were frequent rocket and mortar attacks fired at random on the big airfield and living areas. When the attacks were nearby, a siren in our area went off and we were all up in an instant, grabbing our weapon and ammo and running out the door of the hooch to crawl into the bunker beside it.

Only a direct hit on the bunker would have injured us. Sometimes the rounds hit close to us, but most of the time they landed in and around the airfield. On one occasion, some rockets or mortars hit so close that some of the shrapnel shards were embedded in the plywood of our hooch. On this occasion, I didn't head for the bunker; I just threw myself out of the rack quickly onto the deck of the hooch on my stomach, covering my head and ears with my hands. Steve and the others ran out to the bunker, and, on his way out, Steve stepped on me. No one in our immediate area was injured, and when it was all clear, I acted like I was really mad at Steve. I told him, "You stepped on me, and then went on out, not even stopping to see if I was injured!" I teased him about it for a long time afterward.

On one occasion, when I had staff duty NCO for the twenty-four hour period, our area was hit pretty hard with rockets. During this same twenty-four-hour period, an officer was also serving as Officer of the Day. That night, we slept on cots at our squadron office near the command bunker. We were responsible for answering any urgent matter that might arise.

This attack came about 05:30, when one of the rockets blew up near the Mess Hall. It was quite an explosion. The Officer of the Day and I happened to be sleeping. The concussion of the explosion lifted both of us off our racks and onto the deck. I quickly shook it off, grabbed my weapon, and headed for the command bunker. The officer beat me there.

Several other explosions occurred nearby before the attack was over. I strapped on my pistol belt, flack jacket, and helmet, and went out to assess the damages. There was no loss of life or injuries in our unit, but the explosion was so close to the mess hall that food, trays, and broken glass were scattered all over the dining area where some people were eating at early chow call. It was rumored that one U.S. Army man was killed and several injured in an Army barracks near our area. I was never able to confirm that. I had enough to do finding and reporting on the damage done in our own area.

This kind of attack was a constant threat, and we were aware that danger was hanging over our heads every day and night. Although we were the ones who were "in the rear with the gear" and considered by some to be safe, in truth, the word "safe" was a relative term used to denote the likeliness of being killed or wounded in a particular area.

One night around midnight the sergeant major of the squadron shook me awake. I knew immediately that this was serious. He whispered to me that one of my utilities men had shot and killed another Marine. "Come with me," he said.

I dressed quickly, grabbed my gear, and went outside. The sergeant major told me that it appeared to be an unintentional killing. He described what it looked like had happened. Apparently, my utilities man had pointed a .45 caliber pistol at his friend and work buddy, not realizing that it was loaded, and pulled the trigger. The round hit the man in a vital organ, and he died immediately, right there on the steps of his hooch. The Military Police had already arrived and had my man in handcuffs. He was sitting down in the sand, his head bent low, weeping, when I got to the scene. They had just removed the body of his friend, and he was sobbing almost uncontrollably.

The event was indeed a terrible accidental shooting of a fellow Marine and friend. These two men had worked together every day— my man, who was a corporal and a water supply man in my utilities section, and his friend, the victim, who worked as a driver for the Motor Transportation section. Every day he would drive a large tanker truck filled with water, accompanied by my utilities man, to various places delivering water. Somehow, they had acquired a .45 pistol and kept in under the seat in the truck. According to their rank and job duties, neither of them was eligible to have a pistol. We surmised that they had either bought it or traded something for it. After that day's water run, they had returned to the utilities section and hung around the office for a little while. The motor transport man went to turn in the truck and go to his hooch. Not long after that, my utilities man wrote a standard entry in the logbook, as he was required to do after a successful water delivery, and headed to his hooch.

For some reason, he had the pistol with him, wrapped in a rag. The route that he took to his hooch took him past the hooch of his buddy, the motor transport man. As he approached his buddy's hooch, his friend appeared in the doorway and said something to my man in a joking manner. My man, also in a joking manner, raised the pistol, and aimed it at his buddy, and, thinking the pistol wasn't loaded, pulled the trigger.

Tragically, the pistol *was* loaded. He shot his buddy in the chest, and he died immediately. The deceased Marine was due to rotate home in a few days. The Military Police and Criminal Investigation Division, (CID), began to investigate the shooting. A couple of months went by, and I was called to testify at the General Court Martial for my utilities man. When I was called to the witness stand, I was asked to describe what kind of Marine my man was: was he a hard worker and a disciplined Marine? I felt comfortable testifying that he was, indeed, a good, hard-working, and well-disciplined Marine in his work for me.

I never found out what happened or how the case turned out, as I was rotated home before it was resolved. It was indeed a sad event for all of us who knew about it. But it was somewhat similar to many unintentional and tragic deaths that occurred in Vietnam. These seemed even more tragic and sad than death in combat. Dying in combat is expected, although unwanted, but an accidental death means that a person loses his life for no justifiable reason.

I myself was almost shot one night. It was such a stupid event that I'm reluctant to even write about it. I've decided to include it here to demonstrate the inherent dangers of just being in Vietnam, where everyone carries a weapon and ammunition. Sometimes, the combination of loaded weapons and alcohol can be deadly.

On one occasion, I woke up in the middle of the night to find another Marine sitting beside my rack in my chair, and I could see in the dim light that he had his .45 caliber pistol in his right hand, pointed upward. Instantly awake, and frightened when I saw the pistol, I started to get up.

The guy was a Gunnery Sergeant we knew as "Speedy," and he lived in the hooch across from mine. I quickly lay back down. I didn't want to startle him, as I could tell by his slurred speech that he was drunk. I asked him in a friendly way to put the pistol down and to go back to his hooch and go to sleep.

He responded that *no one* could tell him what to do. He continued to wave the gun around in a threatening manner, saying that he thought he might just go ahead and shoot me. I reminded him that if he shot anyone, he would go to prison for many years. I also reminded him that I had a wife and kids back home. He said he didn't care.

This conversation went on for fifteen or twenty minutes, as he kept waving the pistol around, repeating that he "might just shoot" me, and threatening to shoot a hole in the roof of my hooch. He finally just got up and left, going back to his hooch. I quickly got up, put my boots on, and was about to leave my hooch and go somewhere for the rest of the night. But then I began to wonder what might have happened to the other men who lived in his hooch.

After a while, I could tell that it was quiet in his hooch, and I later found out that when he had threatened these men, they'd all left. I could hear him stumbling around in there, and then I heard a pistol shot. It scared me! Did he shoot somebody or himself? But then I heard him moving around some more. Another shot—then all was quiet.

I waited for quite awhile and finally lay down and tried to sleep. I correctly guessed that he had passed out and someone from his hooch went back and took away Speedy's pistol.

Early the next day, I went to the Squadron office and reported the event to the first sergeant. He already knew about it. They had already called Speedy in and had him turn in his pistol and any other weapons he might have. He was brought up on charges and transferred to Okinawa.

Sometimes under stressful conditions men drink to help them cope. And, being always armed, they present a real danger to others working and living with them. Speedy was a hard-working, friendly, likable Marine, but when he drank, he turned into someone else. When I think back to that event it, still gives me chills. It was a harrowing event and has left a very bad memory.

CHAPTER 40

CHRISTMAS IN VIETNAM, 1968

I used to dread it when Christmas time grew near. Now I'm always reminded of our men and women serving overseas who won't be with their families and loved ones for Christmas. Being on a lonely outpost on the other side of the world at that time of year brings on a special kind of sadness that only those who have experienced it can understand.

As a career Marine, this would be the second Christmas that I would be away from home and in a war zone on the far side of the globe. The plywood huts with tin roofs, surrounded by sandbags, dust, or mud, depending on the weather, may seem luxurious to grunt Marines in the battle zones, but in reality, our cheerless area, devoid of strings of colored lights and Christmas music, was a pretty gloomy environment.

As Christmas drew nearer, my hut buddies, Steve, Ski, and Ray, began to feel that peculiar kind of sadness creeping in, getting worse day by day. It seemed as though Ray was particularly sad. He seemed to miss his family even more than the rest of us, if that were possible.

Ray's wife had sent him a small plastic Christmas tree about a foot-and-a-half tall, complete with lights and a little star on top.

Ray set the little tree on a crude table made from a packing crate and with some Christmas wrapping paper around the bottom. Each of us bought several small presents for our Vietnamese housemaid and put them under the tree. Despite the language barrier, by using a rough form of sign language we were able to make her understand that the gifts were for her, but she couldn't have them until Christmas. She seemed to understand and bowed and thanked us. The little Christmas tree with presents under it seemed to ease some of Ray's sadness and gave all of us something to smile about.

On the day before Christmas, all the Vietnamese workers were released at noon, as were most Marines who weren't on duty. Steve, Ski, and I were in our hut at noon that day when the housemaid gathered up her personal things to depart for the holiday. Ray was on a flight crew and wouldn't be back until evening.

As the maid was preparing to leave, we told her that she could take her presents now and motioned toward the tree. We watched, at first happily, as she scooped up the presents and put them in her bag, and then, to our dismay, she picked up the tree and backed toward the door, bowing and thanking us all the way. And then she was gone!

It had all happened so quickly—and it was so hard to believe that none of us had made a move to stop her or at least tell her that the gifts didn't include the tree! We just sat there and looked stupidly at each other. "Why didn't you stop her?" we asked each other. No one had an answer. The housemaid was gone; so was Ray's Christmas tree. What were we to do? What would we say to Ray when he got back that evening? Oh, how we dreaded his return!

It was nearly dark when Ray returned. He came into the hut looking weary, tossed his weapons, belt, and gear onto his rack, and then noticed the empty spot where the tree had been. He stopped in his tracks, and, with his hands on his hips, said, "*Okay, you guys this isn't funny! Where is my Christmas tree*?!*"

We tried lamely to explain what had happened, while Ray raged about the hut, throwing his gear around and cursing us, the war, the Vietnamese—but especially us, his buddies, who let somebody walk off with his Christmas tree right in front of their eyes!

Ray was a genuinely nice guy—one of those kinds of people whom you always remember as a decent, friendly, sincere person. After a little while and a few drinks of holiday cheer, Ray finally was able to laugh it off as we speculated about how much the housemaid's family might be enjoying that little tree.

I have a photo from that long ago Christmas Eve that shows me and a couple of other buddies gathered around a small makeshift barbecue, drinks in hand, appearing half-tanked, smiling, and apparently feeling no pain as we celebrated Christmas Eve in Vietnam, laughing about the "stolen" Christmas tree. But no matter how fond the memories of those friendships and the camaraderie we shared, nothing feels as good as being home with one's family for Christmas in the good old United States of America.

As the time was nearing for my tour of duty to be over, I, just as thousands of others in this situation, began to get anxious about leaving and hoped that nothing happened to delay that day. I'm pretty sure that in the back of everyone's mind was a fear that we were going to get killed in some way before we left. That fear really intensified once we received our orders and flight date. This flight date became the most important thing in our minds.

I learned the hard way that this fear can actually make a person physically ill. Shortly after I received my orders and flight date, I began to feel sick one morning and went to sickbay. My stomach was upset, and I thought like I might vomit at any moment. I was extremely tired, and felt like I was running a fever. The doctor examined me and I described my symptoms. I was surprised when he asked if I had received my orders and flight date. I told him that I had. He asked when I had received them, and I told him that it was perhaps two weeks ago. Next he asked how long I had felt sick, and I told him, "About two weeks."

The doctor then told me that they, the Medical Department, had realized that the symptoms that not only I, but many others, had were closely tied to when they had received their orders and flight date. He went on to explain that they believe that when people receive their orders, and especially their flight date, there's a heightened state of anxiety. Then, when they begin to count the days, and even the hours, before they leave, the anxiety level begins to affect them physically, actually making them sick. He said there was really nothing he would prescribe for my symptoms.

I received my orders to MWFS-3, (Marine Wing Facilities Squadron-3,), at the Marine Corps Air Station at El Toro, California. Yes! Yes!! I was very happy with this assignment! The flight date was March 18, 1969. I quickly wrote Delores a letter with the good news. I knew that she, as I, would be happy to move to sunny southern California and away from the snow and cold winds of Nebraska.

Next we had to make all the arrangements to move our family and belongings to California. But there was little we could do ahead of time to find a home in California until we actually got there. Nevertheless, we weren't worried about that, as we were now becoming old hands at moving. Besides that, any possible anxiety we had about that was overshadowed by our excitement of seeing each other again!

When I told Paul about my orders and that we were going to sunny California, he was happy for us. His tour was over perhaps two months behind mine, and he said that he, too, was requesting orders to Camp Pendleton, California. Paul promised that he would look me up when he got back to the States. He was that rare kind of Marine Corps friend whom you just never forget.

In the meantime, I was going to be very busy—moving across the country, finding a home, and checking in at a new unit. Paul and I shook hands, and then I backed up a step and saluted him. In return, he gave me a perfect, classy salute, and said, "Good luck, Gunny Lay." I replied, with a firm, "Thank you, Sir!"

It was an exciting day when I walked across the tarmac to board that huge aircraft, now nicknamed "the Freedom Bird," that would carry us out of Vietnam and onto the first leg of our long journey home. That word, "home," had become almost magical to me, encompassing all the good things we had dreamed about: family, good food, our home, children, manicured lawns, shopping malls, TV, new movies, and freedom from the fear that had hung ominously on my shoulders and in my mind constantly.

It's a long way back from the far side of the world. The sights and sounds seem a bit overwhelming. We made a couple of stops for refueling, but there weren't any layovers. When I finally landed at Eppley Airfield, Omaha, it looked the same as when I had left there fourteen months before. Delores and children were there to greet me. Wow! I was thinking, *After all these long months, weeks, and days, I'm finally home again*!

What a wonderful bunch of hugs we all had! What a wonderful family to come home to! We were so excited on the drive to our place. The kids were trying to tell me something all at the same time. When we got to the house, Rusty, our collie dog, greeted me. He jumped up on me and was so excited! During the time I was gone, he had grown up and was now a full-grown beautiful Collie.

It was a wonderful homecoming, and the big old house on Fort Street looked so inviting! I felt truly safe. There was no sniper sighting in on me, nor a hidden bomb to blow me up. Here, I was surrounded by nothing but love and affection, and that feeling just brought tears to my eyes.

CHAPTER 41

JOURNEY TO CALIFORNIA

We all were excited to be moving to sunny California. However, this old house had now been our home for four years, and it really felt like home. It was spacious and comfortable, and it was hard to leave. After our homecoming excitement had wound down, we began to plan to move. We had to determine when the movers should come to get our furniture and things, and then we would begin our journey late that same day once the house was empty. Since the government was paying for our move, all we had to do was to gather everything we would need for our trip and find a temporary place to live after we arrived in California until we had a permanent home.

We planned that we would first go south to Kansas and visit my Mom and Dad. After that, we would head south and west, picking up the now-famous Route 66 in Oklahoma City, and then southwest across the great American desert and into California. It was exciting to think about the trip, but I was concerned about our old station wagon. I questioned whether it was up to such a long trip, fully loaded, with two adults, three children, a large dog, a guitar in a case, and all of our suitcases.

The station wagon was an early '60's Dodge. Like several other name brand vehicles of that vintage, it was very large and had a powerful motor. I had the old vehicle serviced and a mechanic checked it out to ensure that it was in top running condition. I had two retread tires put on the rear. In retrospect, I should have bought new tires instead. I didn't know it then, but retreads have a tendency to come apart in high heat and load conditions. Not a good thing on a long trip.

Moving day came too soon, and our furniture was picked up as planned. We swept out the house and turned in the key to the landlady. She was a sweet, older lady, and she and Delores had developed a friendship while I was gone. We all parted with hugs, kind words, and best wishes.

Thus we began our long journey that day, heading south out of Omaha. This was a very familiar road to us, as we had driven it many times going to the farm to visit Mom and Dad. By late evening, we entered the small town of Holton, Kansas. A problem had developed with the car. The alternator wasn't charging, and the battery was running down. Since it was late and we were tired, we got a motel room and decided to address the problem the next day. It wasn't a big problem, and I wasn't too worried.

On the way to California, 1969. Car trouble, naturally.

I brought some food to our room. We ate, kicked back, and relaxed until morning. We soon learned that a big dog is hard to manage in a small hotel room, but we managed to solve all our problems, and the motel management even provided an extra cot to accommodate sleeping places for all of us.

The next day I found a local mechanic who brought us a new alternator and installed it. On the road again! We arrived at the farm in the early afternoon, and it was sure good to see Mom and Dad and family again. Even so, there was a bit of sadness in the air because we were moving so far away and there would be fewer visits.

Nevertheless, we were anxious to keep moving because we were excited about California! We only stayed two or three days, then we packed up and headed west and south out of Kansas.

The miles behind us were adding up, and by mid-afternoon we were somewhere in a small town outside of Oklahoma City, when a serious clanking, clicking sound developed coming from beneath the car. We made it to a service station, where a mechanic checked it out. He put the wagon on the lift, raised it up, and found the problem. The universal joint in the driveshaft was coming apart. A new joint had to be installed. The mechanic said he could fix it, so we all had to just hang out for a couple of hours while the mechanic went to a parts store, picked up the part, and installed it. By the time it was ready, it was suppertime. We drove for a few miles until we found a nice motel and restaurant. I hoped and prayed that the old station wagon would hold out until we got to California. Thankfully, the motor was still running fine and strong. We couldn't have had a better vehicle considering what we were doing and the load we were hauling.

The next day, we were on our way down across the Texas panhandle and into Gallup, New Mexico. We all began to really enjoy the scenes of the great Southwest. When we'd stop to eat, I'd put Bobbie in charge of our dog, Rusty, to take him out to do "his business" and make sure that he got water and food.

One particular stop still lingers in my mind. We had stopped at a nice restaurant to eat. We went in to get a table while Bobbie took Rusty out. This restaurant had a large picture window where customers could look outside and enjoy the scenery while they ate. We got a booth along the side with the window, and, like a lot of customers, were looking out the window. Well, guess what sight greeted us just outside this big window— nothing less than Bobbie holding Rusty while Rusty was pooping! Rusty did a *huge* pile, right outside the picture window while we all watched! I heard a couple of remarks, "Oh no. Geez, that's awful! Don't look, Martha!" and other comments from the diners. When Bobbie finally came in to eat, we asked him why he took the dog there to do his business. Bobbie replied that he wouldn't do it anywhere else. Well, such is life. We all finished eating and continued our journey.

The next afternoon we were outside Kingman, Arizona, on a long stretch of road through the beautiful desert scenery. I had been doing all the driving up to this point and was beginning to get weary. Delores volunteered to take over. Bobbie got up in front while I got in the back with Mark, Valerie, and the dog, Rusty. I wiggled around in the back, carved out a little space for myself, lay down, and tried to get some sleep.

I hadn't been back there long and was just beginning to doze off, when I heard a bumping sound coming from underneath the car. I tried to ignore it for a while, but soon it got worse. I got up and asked Delores to pull over and stop. She did, and I got out to inspect the car. I quickly found the problem. On one of the rear tires, the tread was coming loose and hitting on the car fender. I *knew* I shouldn't have bought those retread tires! In these driving conditions, they were dangerous. This was a foolish mistake that would now cost us more money to buy a new tire, not to mention the delay of our journey.

I decided to proceed at a low speed off on the side of the road until we came to the next stop. Looking up and down this lonely stretch of road, nothing was in sight. I drove on slowly for several miles, hoping that I wouldn't hear the horrible sound of a blowout. Thankfully, after a few miles, I could see a large service station up the road, looking like an oasis in the desert and an answer to our prayers.

We made it to the station and had someone inspect the tires. Of course, the only thing to do to so that we could safely continue our travel was to purchase two new tires for the rear. They had the size I needed in stock, but they were the most expensive tires I've ever bought. When you're in this situation, however, you have no options. You have to do whatever it takes to keep on going, and be thankful about it.

I learned my lesson; I'll never buy retread tires again! We drove on past Flagstaff and stopped for the night. We were all tired from our long and expensive stop for new tires. We found a nice motel with a swimming pool. That was our only consideration for the kids when deciding where we will stay. I must admit, Delores and I also enjoyed the pool, which was a real treat after traveling across Arizona.

The last day of our journey we crossed the Mojave Desert and on into Barstow, California, where we stopped for lunch. We continued on south through San Bernardino, stopping in Santa Ana for a room. The El Toro, Marine Air Station was just south of Santa Ana a few miles. We were really tired and needed to rest before going on to the base.

Wow! We had actually made it to California! Even though we were tired, we were all very excited at being in sunny California, a place we had all been dreaming about. We were finally here! We all put on our swimsuits and took a dip in the very welcoming swimming pool. Delores and I both had the feeling that we were just beginning a great new adventure.

CHAPTER 42

MARINE CORPS AIR STATION, TUSTIN, CALIFORNIA

I was required to check in at El Toro, May 1, 1969, on the day following our arrival at Santa Ana. The next day we drove down to El Toro, just to take a quick look at the base and to go to the base housing office. We loved the look of the base, with the boulevards lined with towering Eucalyptus, and palm trees, and the tropical landscaping. The housing office told us there was a several-months waiting list for base housing, but they gave me some contacts to help us find suitable housing in the meantime. I put our name on the waiting list, and we went back to our motel room to look over the recommendations they made.

As we considered our options, we recalled that our old Marine friends, Mac and Dorine, had been transferred to Marine Corps Recruit Depot, San Diego, where Mac was again working as a Drill Instructor. It seems that while I had been attending Utilities Chiefs School, they had moved to San Diego! We decided to call them and perhaps go down to visit them and possibly save the cost of a motel for a few days. I called Mac and asked if it was all right if we came to stay with them for a couple of days. They were happy to hear from us and said, "Sure! Come on down!" We looked forward to swapping old sea stories again and were assured that they would be happy to see us.

We drove to San Diego to visit our friends for several days. How great it was to again see Mac and Dorine again! I loved it that Mac and I had been friends for a long time—long before I had even met Delores. I was a corporal and he was a sergeant at Engineers Schools, where we were instructors before we were D.I.'s at Parris Island. Now, we were both gunnery sergeants. Mac had always been one of those really gung-ho disciples of the Corps. Now, the Marine Corps was a way of life for us, and we all tried to help each other when we could.

We returned to Santa Ana and again checked in at the motel where we had been before. From the information provided to us at the housing office, we contacted a Real Estate agent. This agent said he had a place just a few miles south of the base in the little town of El Toro. We were directed to a fairly new housing project, and the house was situated in a cul-de-sac. We'd have loved to have enough money to buy this place, as it was for sale. We were able to make a deal with the owner to rent it for several months until we could get into government housing. The rent was just barely within what we could afford on our frugal living expenses. But I planned to form a country music band where I might be able to make some extra money to help pay the expenses. I'd just have to wait and see what my job duties would be when I got checked in at the base.

Our new home was a large, three-bedroom, ranch style house. It was landscaped with a desert motif. No mowing in the front yard! We had a very nice, private back yard with a good-sized grassy area. After we moved in and were mostly settled, we learned that we had some very friendly neighbors. The ones next door to us had a nice swimming pool in their backyard. The neighbors across the cul-de-sac reached out to us as friends. He was the general manager of the hardware store in Tustin. His wife was a stay-at-home mom, and they had two small children. Our dream of sunny California life was coming true!

I checked in at El Toro, anxious to get started and see what my new job would be. When I checked in, I learned that I was being assigned to Marine Wing Facilities Squadron-3 (MWFS-3) as the utilities chief. It felt good to check in and assume my duties. I found the job to be exactly what I had been trained in.

The Utilities Section was located in one of the old aircraft hangars that were positioned alongside the main airstrip. Consequently, just as it had been in Vietnam, we were never without the sound of aircraft, either preparing to take off, taking off, or warning up. It's just something a person has to live with when serving in the Marine Corps Air Wing.

I got settled into my office and was just getting a handle on the duties, when, one day, I got a call to come to the squadron office. The major, the squadron commander, wanted to see me. When I reported to his office, he explained to me that the unit was without a first sergeant, which I knew, and they didn't know when the position would be filled. He said there were several master sergeants (a pay grade equal to mine, gunnery sergeant), and a couple of master gunnery sergeants in the unit, who were senior to me, but none of them wanted the job.

Then he asked me if I wanted to be the squadron acting first sergeant. I immediately said, "Yes, it would be an honor!" The Major said that he would issue an order that day making me the First Sergeant. It's typical in the Marine Corps that if a position is vacant and no one with the rank that is specified in the Table of Organization, (OTA), is available, that they must appoint a lower-ranked person to the position in an "acting" status.

Marine Corps Air Station, Tustin, C.A. At the time I was a Gunnery Sergeant, but was filling the position of First Sergeant, senior enlisted Marine of the squadron.

The Major went on to say that this order would make me the senior enlisted man in the squadron, and if any of the master gunnery sergeants or senior master sergeants gave me any trouble, he wanted to know immediately. He said, "You're the man, the senior enlisted man, in this squadron, and the person I'm looking to as my first sergeant." We shook hands, and, as we walked out, he pointed out my office, which was a very nice one, right outside his office. He told me that he wanted me to assume my new position the next morning.

I liked this major, who I learned was a helicopter pilot by trade but wasn't now in flight status. I left the office very happy and could hardly wait to get home to tell Delores. It seemed that this tour of duty may be even better than I had hoped for!

The next morning, I took my place in the squadron first sergeant's office. I cleaned and organized my desk and placed my custom-carved nameplate, made out of granite from "Marble Mountain" in Vietnam. I settled back, ready to carry out the duties assigned to me. I felt comfortable in this position of authority, and, as such, I was also responsible for all the administrative work and discipline of the squadron. There was a staff sergeant, however, with the title of Administrative Chief, who supervised the daily work of the staff, and he reported to me. I called him in, and we discussed what I expected of him, and, in return, told him what he could expect of me.

After getting settled, I took a couple of jaunts at night around the area to see if there was any potential for a country band to play in the local dance clubs. I learned that there seemed to be a real need for a band. At that time in California, the culture was still that of the hippie generation. It was a time of freedom of the spirit, free love, and happy times.

I didn't see any other full country music bands playing in our area, so I decided to put together a four- or five-piece band. I ran an ad in the Santa Ana newspaper for musicians. I got a good response and scheduled interviews and auditions for various musicians—a drummer, a bass player, and a lead guitarist.

The weekend of the auditions was a lot of fun, and I met some interesting people. From my ad I found an outstanding drummer. He was a sort of hippie fellow, with long hair, wearing a tie-dyed tee shirt and sandals. He said that he was a hippie, and country music was not his kind of music, but he knew how to play and needed a job. I hired him.

I also hired a man-and-wife team. He played lead guitar, and his wife played steel guitar and also did some singing. Not really a good fit, but I hired them. I also hired an older man who was a good bass player.

I scheduled a practice session with all of these musicians in my garage. I thought it was a pretty good sounding band. I made it clear that this was only a part-time job, and we'd all only get paid when we played a gig.

With a band hired, I proceeded to book us at a club in Costa Mesa. It was a large dance club, with a nice stage that had curtains if we wanted to use them. Our first gig was on a Saturday night. I had told the band members that I would like for them to dress like entertainers, and not like hippies or grease monkeys. "Look sharp!" I told them. I was very happy to see that the band members did look sharp, showing up in western-style garb. Even the young man I had hired as a drummer came to work dressed like a hippie but he'd brought along a fancy western shirt and some cowboy boots, which he changed into when we started our show. We had a good perfor-mance that first night.

Performing in a dance club in Costa Mesa, California, 1969.

After the gig was over, the hippie changed back into his hippie garb. His wife was also a true hippie. She came with him and usually sat by herself at a small table near the bandstand. He was very jealous of her and wouldn't let her dance with anyone.

I learned that this dance hall had been here for a long time, so they had a lot of established costumers. I talked afterwards with the manager, and he told me to plan on coming back every Saturday night until notified differently. I collected our pay for the evening and paid the band members.

I kept this gig for quite a while, but I also found another one as just a single act in a popular lounge named "The Walnut Room." It was owned and operated by a man and his wife. They had a piano bar on Saturday nights, and they hired me for Friday nights.

Along one side of the Walnut Room was a bar, and in the back was a pool table. On the other side was a small U-shaped bar with a piano behind it and a number of stools around the bar. There was also an area for tables and chairs.

The manager and his wife hired me as a single act to play guitar and sing behind the piano bar. It was quite a challenge at first, but I soon began to enjoy it and actually looked forward to Friday nights. My program consisted of my playing and singing some popular songs of the day, tell some jokes, and interact with the audience. I realized that I was pretty good at doing this sort of thing and was able to draw a following from the kind of people who enjoyed that kind of entertainment.

I had to modify the way I would present a song sometimes. I couldn't sing it as if I had a full band behind me, so I'd sing it in kind of a talking fashion, which was more easygoing. I soon realized that the audience wasn't expecting a big-band sound from a lone entertainer. All in all, it worked out well. I continued this gig the entire time that I was at El Toro, and I became like a fixture at The Walnut Room.

The base newspaper, *The Flight Jacket*, carried a weekly advertisement for The Walnut Room, listing me as a Friday night attraction. Over the years I had a number of Marine customers.

After about three months, the husband-and-wife duo of my band grew tired of the gig and quit. They said that they weren't making enough money. Then, as if on schedule, I came across another man-and-wife team. These folks were real professionals and had played on some of the big shows back East, including WWVA Wheeling, West Virginia, which was a popular stage show. The wife, Vickie, was a very good bass player and an outstanding singer. Her husband was a talented musician. He played both a steel guitar and a standard electric Gretsch lead guitar. He would bring both instruments with him and have them both tuned and ready for whatever tune we were going to play. It was really a great setup, and adding these two to the band gave us a sound as good or better than any band playing in that area.

In our presentation, Vickie and I would stand on the front of the stage with two standing microphones. She played the bass and sang. She also harmonized with me on a lot of the songs I sang.

Vickie was pretty and had a good figure. Many of the men in the audience were attracted to her. She usually wore a fancy dress with fringe all over it, and when she sang, the fringe gave the impression of her wiggling her body.

We sounded good! With this new sound, I booked us to play at two of the service clubs on the base. One night, we were playing at the base Enlisted Club. Vickie and I were out front singing, and I was dressed in a fancy sequined western suit, when I recognized one of the men from my squadron dancing.

On one occasion, he and his girlfriend danced right in front of the stage. He happened to look up as he passed by and suddenly recognized me. He did the most startling double take I have ever seen. He could hardly believe his eyes; that mean old first sergeant was actually a country-western singer—and doing a pretty good job of it! He stopped dancing for a moment, came over to the stage, said some kind of greeting, and expressed his astonishment that his first sergeant was actually a human, doing normal human things. I will never forget that look that he had given me.

We had several other bookings from time to time, but mostly we played on Saturday nights at the club in Costa Mesa. This gig, and my Friday nights at The Walnut Room, satisfied my musical appetite. However, once in a while, I was invited to do something extra. For example, I was asked to play some music for the children's Christmas Party in the base theatre. I accepted the job and did this one as a single act. I had to dig down really deep to learn some of the ordinary Christmas songs so that I could lead the singing. I thought I was going to be a complete flop, but as it turned out, they all acted like they loved me! I had a great time. I received a nice letter from the El Toro commanding officer, thanking me for my performance.

Occasionally, I was asked to play for private parties. I played at some officer's houses, as well as at some residences off the base for events such as birthday parties, anniversaries, and going away parties. It was all a lot of fun, and I became quite fairly well known around the El Toro area.

Meanwhile, California living did not disappoint us. We realized that we could get to the ocean in about twenty minutes, and the kids enjoyed it. We all agreed that we loved California more than any other place we had lived. Delores and the kids made it to the beach a lot more often than I, but, I also loved the beach and especially enjoyed Laguna Beach, which I considered my favorite city in all America, with its art stores and laid-back atmosphere right on the beachfront. I never tired of visiting there.

Disneyland was also close by, and we spent some quality time there. The kids loved it. Delores took them often, even when I couldn't go. My wife never let anything stop her. When her heart was set on doing something, she did it! She was a tough but sweet lady—a better life partner I could never have found.

It was soon time to move again, but, this time, we didn't have to go far. I was notified that I could get a two-bedroom place on base housing for a very low cost. The housing was on government property near the base, but on the west side of Interstate 5. It wasn't a difficult move, and the government paid for it!

We were sad to move from El Toro, especially as we'd made some good friends on the cul-de-sac where we lived. But we weren't moving far, and we would still be close enough to visit easily. We liked our new home on the base. It was located in a nice, clean area, and all our neighbors were Marines like us. It didn't seem to take us long to get settled again and meet some new friends.

About this time, my friend, Lt. Paul Smith, contacted me. He had rotated back to the States, and as he had hoped for, he was stationed at Camp Pendleton. It was great to hear from Paul and he made plans to visit us right away. I was anxious to see him again and to introduce him to Delores. When he came to visit a few days later, he was looking sharp. I believe that becoming an officer was good for him, and certainly for the Marine Corps. He said that he was becoming more and more comfortable with his new rank. During Paul's visit we shared stories, caught up on events, and I cooked some steaks on the grill. He made a good impression on Delores, and she liked him.

Visiting with Lieutenant Paul Smith. Marine Corp Air Station, Tustin, C.A., 1969.

Paul also gave us some bad news. He and his wife of many years had divorced, but he was given custody of his two small children. He didn't seem particularly sad about the breakup. Sometimes, a divorce makes people happy rather than sad. Paul promised that he would bring his children up to visit the next time he came up.

The months passed by quickly, and soon we were moving into 1970. At some point in the early 1970s, Delores broke the news that she was pregnant again. The baby was due somewhere around Thanksgiving. Now we had another happy event to look forward to! Would it be a boy or girl? Valerie was happy, as she would have a little baby to play with.

Also, through Paul, I met another guitar player, Chuck Hatcher, who lived in the Fallbrook, California, area, a community in the desert to the west of Camp Pendleton. I became very fond of Chuck, and he was an excellent singer and guitar player. He asked me to play in his band and said he had some gigs booked in the Fallbrook area. Chuck not only sang a good song himself, but he could harmonize with me on a lot of songs. I really enjoyed playing gigs with Chuck, but I dreaded the drive home up Interstate 5 after the dance. It was a dangerous road at any time, but it was especially dangerous after playing music for four hours and drinking a beer or two. I never had a problem, though, and I can thank the good Lord for that.

When we left California, I lost track of Chuck. Sadly, however, a few years later I learned from a mutual friend that Chuck had passed away due to a heart attack. The news grieved me greatly, as I really liked Chuck, and we made such a good pair musically. This mutual friend also told me that Chuck and his wife, who was from Guam, had moved back there to be near her family. That's where Chuck died. I still have fond memories of him.

In early summer we decided to go to Kansas and visit my Mom and Dad. I had traded the old reliable station wagon for a Volkswagen Camper Van. It had a pop-up top, and a bed in the back, a sink, and a small refrigerator. We thought it would be the best and most comfortable vehicle to ride in for the long trip to the farm with the kids.

In addition, Delores's niece, Donna, a teenager who lived in North Braddock, PA, made plans to come visit us for a while that summer. Since we were going to be in Kansas, it was decided that Donna could fly into Kansas City, where we would pick her up, and she could ride back to California with us after spending some time at the farm. It all worked out well, but we were pretty crowded in the van on the return trip to California. One thing I did note, however, was that the engine of the Volkswagen, while a remarkably engineered air-cooled engine, was not nearly powerful enough for this large of a van. Most of the time I had to run the engine at full throttle all the way to Kansas. Even then, I could only achieve about 55 miles per hour, and not even that if we were on any kind of grade.

We had a lot of fun at the old farm and got to see all the rest of my family. What a great gang of people when we all got together! We were sad to see that Mom had broken her arm not long before we got there. She had fallen down and reached out to catch herself with her arm and had broken it in the process. She had her arm in a sling when we were there. She couldn't do much but be the boss of the other family members when fixing meals, cleaning up, and washing dishes. But Delores and my sisters sort of took over those chores while we were there.

While living in California, we took a trip to visit my folks at the farm in Kansas. My four sisters and their children were all there. It was a wonderful gathering. Pictured: Dad, sister Dorothy, and Mom, with her arm in a cast.

Visiting folks 1970 at folk's farm. Pictured: Me with sisters Judy, Dorothy, Margaret and Betty. Niece Kim, Margaret's daughter, and nephew Marty, son of Dorothy in tree.

It was an additional great adventure for Donna during her vacation on the farm. Being there was something she hadn't counted on. We all were sad when our time was up and we had to leave the old farm and Mom and Dad. As always, it is so hard to part.

We took a southern route on our return trip to California, going through western Kansas and into southern Colorado on Highway 160, which took us over Wolf Creek Pass, which really tested the Volkswagen—and me. I believe I drove full throttle in first gear for two hours going over that pass, which has an elevation of 10,480 ft. In this heavy van camper, which was fully loaded with people, it was very scary. If I had known about Wolf Creek Pass, I would have taken another route.

On our way up the pass, I saw several cars pulled over with their car hoods raised and steam coming from under the hoods. The small Volkswagen air-cooled motor was operating at full throttle for more than two hours, and it didn't overheat, but it was terribly slow and made for an agonizing journey.

When we finally reached the summit, we stopped for a rest and a chance to get out and stretch our legs. The kids got into a snowball fight. Then, we started downhill, which was also very scary at times. I prayed that the brakes on the Volkswagen were designed for these conditions. I took it easy and didn't let it get going too fast. The steep, sharp curves were difficult to manage, and there were always large trucks behind us trying to pass. What a relief when we dropped down to a more level road.

We crossed over a corner of New Mexico and on into Arizona, where we arrived at the Grand Canyon late in the evening. What an awesome sight awaited us as the blistering hot Arizona sun beat down upon us! We were all very tired. We were anxious to find a motel and be able to sleep, but there weren't any motels in that region of the southern rim of the Grand Canyon. We decided that we would just sleep in the camper. I parked the van in a remote area of the parking lot, backed up to the curb, with the rim of the Canyon about 50 feet behind us.

We converted the van to a sleeper, for which it was designed. I popped up the top for my bed. Delores and Donna would sleep in the bed, and I hung a hammock over the front seats for Mark and Valerie, while Bobbie found a place between the seats on the floor. It was dark by the time we all got settled.

Just about the time we were all drifting off to sleep, I was awakened by a Park Ranger, who was knocking on my window with a flashlight. When I responded, he told us that no one was allowed to park and camp there. He said that we would have to move to a place off the boundaries of the Grand Canyon park area. I asked for an exception, as we all had just gotten settled. The ranger was adamant; we would have to move—*now*!

We all had to get up, take down the hammocks, put the top down, and drive away from the park area, which was only two or three miles. As we left the park area, we saw there were perhaps six or seven other parties who had found a place off the road in a lightly forested area. We found a place to park and set up the camper again for sleeping. There were no rest rooms, so when nature called, one would just have to take a flashlight and go out in the woods.

When we finally all got settled again, we noticed that it was very cold. I was the first to notice it, since I was up higher in the "pop top." I had forgotten how cold it gets at night in the desert and can then be very hot during the day. I felt like I had frost on my backbone. Delores invited me down from the pop up to sleep with her and Donna. Wow, it felt good to get warm! Then I drifted off to sleep.

By the time daylight came, we all felt like we had been beaten up, were sleepy, and hungry. So, I fired up the old Volkswagen, and we went back to the park and found a nice restaurant that overlooked the Canyon and ate breakfast. After eating, we headed south on Highway 64, into the town of Williams, Arizona, and then headed west on Highway 40. We crossed some very beautiful desert, but the temperature was well over one hundred degrees. We felt like we were being baked in an oven.

At the same time, we all decided that we were too tired and too hot to travel any longer! We decided that we would find a motel that had a swimming pool and sleep through the heat of the day. Then we'd get up very early and travel across the desert in the wee morning hours.

When I first suggested the motel idea, everyone said, "Yes, yes, let's get a motel!" That decided, we kept an eye out for one. We didn't have to go far before a nice, big motel loomed in the horizon, looking like an oasis. We checked in and immediately hit the pool. It was great!

After we cooled off, we turned the air conditioning on high in our room and went to sleep. We headed out again in the wee hours of the morning and made it through Needles, California, across the Mojave Desert, and into Barstow. We stopped to eat, then took off for the final leg of our journey.

At last we arrived at our destination. Home always looks so good after being gone for a while! This was a journey we will always remember with fondness—more good memories for the old mental footlocker.

In late summer, I became aware of a music event in which I wanted to participate. It was titled the Worldwide Armed Forces Music Festival, and was sponsored by the Bristol-Myers Corporation.

Talent contests were to be held at Armed Forces bases in the United States and around the world. The winners would be scheduled to appear on a special Ed Sullivan show early the following year. I submitted my name and was scheduled for the contest that would be held at El Toro. A Marine Sergeant and I were selected to represent El Toro in the large West Coast event that was scheduled for October 24, 1970, at the base theatre at Camp Pendleton. According to all the advertisements, this promised to be a big event. I planned to do only one song, "The Marine's Ballad." I thought it was unique enough and was somewhat well known at the time. I took extra time to practice the song and planned to do it without a band.

I also thought it would be a good idea to contact the person who was handling the production and distribution of the 45 RPM record of my "Marine's Ballad" song, who was located in the Hollywood area of Los Angles. I was thinking that in the event I did win the contest and was scheduled to appear on the Ed Sullivan show, they might want to know and do some extra distribution. I called and talked to Al Stewart, the agent handling my song. He was quite interested, and I made an appointment to visit him at his home in Hollywood. I had, on a number of occasions, spoken with Mr. Stewart by phone in the past couple years, but I had never met him personally.

I went to his home in the Hollywood Hills area. Al Stewart was a middle-aged, likable man. He gave me a tour of his house, which was a large and obviously expensive home with a lot of posters from movies he had been involved in and other mementos showcasing a successful career in the entertainment business. It appeared that he had been involved with the production of a number of famous films going back to the 1940s and 1950s.

He offered me a drink, which I accepted, and we sat down and talked about the upcoming talent contest at Camp Pendleton. He seemed very interested in the possibility of me winning the contest, and if I did, he thought that it would be a good idea to press a number of records and have them available for national distribution. Then Mr. Stewart said that he wanted me to meet a certain guy who could provide the money for the distribution. He picked up the phone and called someone. Within five minutes, this other man drove up in a cream-colored Lincoln convertible. He was a man of about forty, dressed in flashy clothes and with gay mannerisms. Al introduced him to me, poured us all a drink, and we sat around for about thirty minutes talking about the Camp Pendleton talent contest and music in general. This man seemed interested but didn't commit himself at that time. He was friendly to me, and I think it's fair to say that, according to what we discussed, if I won the contest, they would put out money for a national distribution of the song near the time of the Ed Sullivan Show in the spring of the next year.

I agreed to keep in touch with Al and to let him know if I won the contest. He said that if I did, he wanted me to come back up to see him again right away. It was an interesting meeting, and now there was really a good incentive to win the contest. Personally, I didn't think there was much of a chance of my winning, however, because I knew that there would be a lot of talented people competing. And I was right.

When the big night rolled around, I went down to Camp Pendleton early in the afternoon, and Delores and the kids were going to drive down in time for the show. I was required to be there early to participate in a rehearsal before the show. It all went well, and after the rehearsal I went over to the staff club for some supper and a couple of drinks. I began to feel a bit of anxiety, so I had more than a couple of drinks.

When it came to show time, I was backstage with all the other contestants. This very large base theatre was packed. A couple of platoons of Marines in utilities, probably trainees from the Infantry School, took up a lot of space in the back. They were all gung-ho and really cheered for me.

Since this was being filmed for television to be aired at a later time, there were large, and very bright lights, and TV cameras had been set up facing the stage. It was difficult to even see all the audience, but I did spot Delores and the kids sitting right up front. I wasn't the first performer, and as the show progressed, my anxiety began to build. I sort of hid myself behind a curtain and took a half-pint of Jim Beam from my guitar case and drank about half of it just before I was called. The whiskey put a fire in my gut and relieved my anxiety very quickly. It also gave me the courage to walk out on that stage, face that huge audience, and do my song the very best I could.

When it was time, the master of ceremonies, Louie Nye, the famous actor/comic, called my name. I walked out like I owned the place. I was in uniform. Mr. Nye made some funny remarks, one of them about my baggy trousers. He got a laugh. I stepped up and did the song the best I could do, without any glitches. I received a great ovation and was happy when I left the stage. Those Marines in the back really cheered. Wow, it felt so great to get backstage and relax, and it was also time for another visit with Jim Beam.

Performing in the Armed Forces World Wide Music Festival, Camp Pendleton, C.A.

Well, according to the local newspapers, the show was a great success. I didn't win and was disappointed about it. I saw all the other performances, and there were some very professional acts and a lot of talent. I met up with Delores and the kids after the show, and we talked before we all headed north on Interstate 5 to Santa Ana and home. By the time I got home, I was dog-tired and just wanted to sleep. Although I hadn't won, I was still glad that I had participated in the show. It was just another good music event that I could put in my mental footlocker of good memories.

Time marches on, and as Delores's due date approached, we found ourselves really anxious and hoping and praying that all would go well. She had been sick with a bad cold for several weeks that summer, and she was having a hard time getting her strength back. Then, during the daytime, on November 29th, she began to have labor cramps, which got progressively stronger as the afternoon passed. It was an unusual day in southern California in that it was raining—and raining really hard. By seven in the evening Delores's labor cramps had become stronger and more frequent. She decided that it was time to go to the hospital.

As planned, I took her to St. Joseph's hospital in Santa Ana. She was examined and told that shes wasn't far enough along to be admitted. They advised her to go back home and come back when the labor pains were more frequent. We drove home in the rain. There, we waited several more hours until Delores said she was certain that it was time to go back to the hospital.

This time, when they examined her, she was admitted. Delores told me to go back home and wait, as she saw that I was nearly a nervous wreck, which was making *her* more nervous. I drove back home again through the still-driving rain.

When I got home, I lay down and caught a quick nap until Delores called and told me that we had a beautiful big baby boy, born just before midnight on November 29, 1970. She said that all had gone well and that after I left, things had begun to happen very rapidly, and she had a quick delivery. She said that she was fine, and they had put her in a beautiful private room. She sounded so happy! She told me not to come right away, because she wanted to just rest a while.

Wow! What a relief for both of us. It's always exciting and a such a blessing when you learn that your baby appears normal: ten fingers and ten toes, and healthy. Good job, Delores!

When the new day arrived, it was with bright sunlight and no rain; everything smelled fresh. I went to the hospital to see Delores and our new baby. Delores looked radiant, and that big baby boy was awake and smiling! We thanked God for this blessing. We had to decide for sure on a name for this little boy. We had already talked about it and decided his first name would be Quentin. Then, for the middle name, we liked the name Bernard, after my sister Betty's husband, Bernard Guilfoyle. Bernard was happy when he heard about this.

So, our new little family member was Quentin Bernard Lay, a strong name, we thought. Delores was in the hospital five days before I brought her back home. We all were thrilled to have this new little guy to play with. He was a happy, healthy baby. Valerie loved having the little baby around and was happy to take care of it of instead of a doll.

With my son Quentin,

All in all, 1970 was a great year! We had taken our long trip to Kansas with our Volkswagen camper, and had had a great time on the farm. Donna had visited several weeks during the summer, and Uncle Abe had come to visit.

When Christmastime rolled around, we had a wonderful celebration. It was our first Christmas without snow, and it seemed strange. Looking back at pictures from that year, we're reminded of what a fun time it was, living and playing in sunny California. We had a large kid's pool set up in the back yard, and all of us, from time to time, would get in it to cool off. I remember one occasion when we were in the backyard playing around, I picked Delores up and, clothes and all, carried her to the pool and dropped her in it. At first she was as mad as an old wet hen at me! But her anger quickly cooled off, and she gave me a hug and kiss to prove it.

I had great fun playing music and I met some wonderful people. My gig at The Walnut Room was the best experience of all. I realized that playing as a single gig was more fun than playing with a band and all that it entailed: booking gigs, keeping the band members together, and always wondering if everyone would show up for a big performance.

I knew when I left here that there would be no more Walnut Room gigs. It was such a special and popular neighborhood lounge, where people could have a drink, socialize, and where there were never any fights or trouble. It would be hard to give it up. But, such is life.

At my job, I had also been very fortunate. For most of my tour I had held the job of acting first sergeant. I only went back to the utilities section for a couple months, but for some reason, every first sergeant who came in was due to retire. When a first sergeant took the position, I would go back to utilities. Then when they would leave, I would go back to being first sergeant. Being first sergeant was a most difficult job, but I liked the authority and responsibilities of the position. The experience would surely help me in my promotion to first sergeant.

CHAPTER 43

RECRUITING DUTY

As the spring of 1971, rolled around, I began to think about where my next duty station would be. It could be that I would receive overseas orders again, perhaps soon. It had been about three years since I had returned from overseas in the spring of 1969, and that's about as long as one might remain on any assignment. I knew that I didn't want to go overseas at this time, that's for sure. I thought that perhaps I should submit a letter to my monitor in Headquarters Marine Corps in Washington, D.C., requesting Recruiting Duty. If accepted, I could avert another overseas tour until after Recruiting duty has ended. And, it might even be possible for me to do that until I was eligible for retirement and then I'd never have to go overseas again!

Every Marine has a monitor in Headquarters Marine Corps who governs their career and overseas assignments. It takes an effort to make sure that rotations overseas are done fairly and that people are assigned to the benefit of both the Marine Corps and the individual. I thought it was worth a try, so I submitted a letter requesting that my next duty would be recruiting. Delores and I discussed this and decided that it might be nice to live in Nashville, Tennessee, where I could get involved with the country music scene there. Then, perhaps I could retire there. And thus, we set our hopes of getting recruiting duty in Tennessee.

Around the end of April in 1971, I received orders to Recruiters School at Parris Island, South Carolina. We both were just giddy with excitement, especially knowing that I wasn't going overseas. On May 5, I flew from California to the airport that was closest to Parris Island, which was Savannah, Georgia. I checked into a nice hotel and caught a shuttle bus to Parris Island the next day.

What a treat to be in the Old South again! It was a big cultural shock, however. California, with its crowded freeways, seemed like a fast-moving, modern way of life, while in the South, everything was laid back and slow, and hadn't changed much, perhaps, in the past one hundred years. I really enjoyed it. At the hotel, when the bellboy, an older black man, helped me take my luggage up to the room, he just came on in like it was his duty to pull the curtains, make sure the air conditioning was turned on, and check the bathroom to make sure everything was in order.

Then he sure surprised me when I handed him a tip, and he asked, in a deep southern drawl, "Would the gentleman like some company tonight?"

I was shocked. Then he added, "…black or white is available."

I said, "No thanks," but he said, "If the gentleman changes his mind just call me." And, he handed me his card. I had been in a lot of hotels, both overseas and in the States, and I had never seen anything quite this brazen!

I took a short walk down the old historic streets of Savannah, where I hadn't been for several years. I found a cozy restaurant and enjoyed some of the South's legendary seafood. I was very happy to go to Recruiters School, and these little side experiences are just like frosting on the cake of being a Marine.

The next day I checked in at Recruiters School and learned that there were more than one hundred students enrolled in this class. I also found out that the duty stations at the end of the class would be assigned according to the availability of openings, and also dependent upon one's class standing at the end of school: the first in class would get first choice, second in class, the next choice, and so on. Clearly, it was advantageous to work hard and come out in high standing. I wanted to be stationed in Nashville, so I set about to be first in class, and if they had an opening when we graduated, I wanted to be the one to fill it.

The classes were held in the same training area on the base where I had attended Drill Instructor's school back in 1961, and it was all very familiar to me. I liked the palm trees and palmetto trees, the well-manicured lawn behind the barracks, and the boat dock that was close by. I had, and still have, a great nostalgia associated with that area and Parris Island in general.

After the first day of class it had become clear what the focus of the school would be. We were primarily being instructed on the importance of personal appearance in uniform, military bearing, and the ability to make public appearances, such as giving speeches to high schools on career days, or speaking to other social groups, and even how to appear and speak on television.

Marines on recruiting duty are required to be absolutely immaculate in the uniform at all times. Overweight students must meet a certain weight goal or be dropped from class. And recruiters must learn all of the administrative details involved in getting young men and women qualified and sent to induction centers for physical examinations, then shipped to San Diego or Parris Island for training. And, although physical fitness classes were not on included on the schedule, recruiting students were urged to do a physical fitness program on their own.

I studied hard and maintained a standing at near the top of the class throughout the course. Periodically, after a written test or personal inspection, several students would be dropped from the class. It became very clear that the Marine Corps wanted only the very best out there in the public eye.

Time passed quickly, and soon it was time to graduate. There was one final written test and inspection that took place the day before graduation. These test scores would determine the class standings. Apparently my dedication to my studies paid off; I was number one in class standing out off 102 graduating students! There were only a few points difference between the first three or four standings, but I was clearly at the top of the class.

On that same day, we learned where we would be stationed. The available duty stations were revealed and we chose the one we wanted. Well, just as I had hoped, there were positions available at Nashville! I very happily made that my choice. Later on, however, I was a bit disappointed to learn that Nashville was a *Main* Recruiting station, but under Nashville were sub-stations in other places, where I might be assigned.

There were recruiters stationed in Nashville, but there were also several substations under the main recruiting station, in places like Chattanooga, Knoxville, and others, which all came under the command of Nashville. The Recruiting Station would assign the sub-station. Therefore, new recruiters coming into Nashville would be assigned to one of sub-stations, which may or may not be the Nashville sub-station. It was the same throughout the U.S., central large cities had Recruiting Stations and sub-stations. I wouldn't know until I checked in at Nashville to which of the sub-stations I would be assigned. That meant that I wouldn't know where we would be living until I checked in at Nashville.

The next day, June 18, 1971, I graduated from Recruiters School. I was surprised when I was presented with a beautiful, regulation, Staff Non-Commissioned Officer's Ceremonial Sword, with scabbard. It had beautiful engravings on its highly polished stainless steel blade. I hadn't realized that the top graduate of the class in every Recruiter's School is given such a sword. It really was an honor, and I still consider the sword one of my most prized possessions, and it is proudly displayed on a wall in my home to this day.

Graduation from Recruiters School, Parris Island, S.C., 1971. First in class.

I had made reservations on a flight from Savannah to the Orange County Airport in California the next day. I'd learned about a Marine Corps friend with whom I had worked in Omaha, who was stationed at the Marine Corps Air Station located near Beaufort. He came and picked me up, and we went to his house in the outskirts of Beaufort. His wife prepared us an excellent dinner. It was great seeing him and his wife and talking about our good times in Omaha. He also committed himself to take me to the airport the next day.

The next day, before my friend arrived to take me to the airport, I had some free time and decided to place a call to North Carolina to talk with my old friend, Lt. Paul Smith, as I hadn't spoken with him for several weeks. Someone else answered the phone where I normally could reach Paul. When I asked to speak to him, there was a long pause before the person said, "Perhaps you should talk to the Commanding Officer."

Then, when the CO answered and I requested to speak to Lt. Paul Smith, there was another pause, and this person asked me if I was a friend or relative of Lt. Smith. I explained our friendship to him. He then told me that he was very sorry to inform me that Lt. Paul Smith was deceased. He was the victim of a double murder-suicide a couple of weeks ago. I was so shocked I could hardly speak. The gentleman with whom I spoke told me that he couldn't give me much information and again expressed his sympathy and told me that I could probably get a copy of the Jacksonville, NC, newspaper that had reported a full story about the event.

Essentially, what happened was this: Paul was dating a woman who had been previously married. He had told me in our last telephone conversation that he had a new girlfriend of whom he was very fond and that she had been married before. Paul had been at her house the evening of the shooting. Apparently, this woman's previous husband had come to the house and shot both her and Paul. He then went back to his own house and shot himself.

What a terrible shock! I could hardly believe it. This was devastating, to say the least. There was no one else I could call to get more information. I didn't have the phone number of his previous wife in California. Plus, I wasn't sure if I should even try to reach her.

The only thing I could do at the time was to carry on with my life for the moment until this terrible information could settle in my soul. Paul was one of my very best friends and like a member of the family. It was a tragic event. Paul had his whole life ahead of him. With his intelligence and love for the Corps, he would have definitely reached a high rank before retiring. What a tragedy!

Later, when my friend showed up and took me to the airport in Savannah, I had a problem boarding. They considered my sword a weapon and weren't going to let me board with it. Finally, after a discussion with one of the senior security personnel, they let me board, but they took the sword and kept it in a secure place in the front of the plane. I congratulated the security personnel on their strict vigilance. I also had an old guitar without a case that I had bought from one of the students. I wasn't allowed to board with that, either, so I had to leave it with my buddy. I never saw the guitar again.

Delores and the kids picked me up at the airport in the Volkswagen camper. It's always so good to get home again, no matter where you have been or how long you had been gone! Every time I came home from an assignment, there was always a homecoming atmosphere, and everyone celebrated that Daddy was coming home!

Our primary focus now was to arrange for a moving company to pick up our furniture and other belongings and transport them from California to Tennessee. It was, however, a huge job to get everything packed for the movers, excluding any clothing or other items we would need for thirty days and during the trip.

My orders required that I check in at Nashville no later than July 18, 1971. I had also decided that I would trade cars and get a large station wagon instead of the Volkswagen Camper. I began my search for a suitable family vehicle, because we had a long trip ahead of us. According to the road atlas, it was 2,006 miles to Nashville, and we wanted to stop by the farm to visit Grandma and Grandpa on our way to Nashville.

I located a wonderful, large Chrysler New Yorker station wagon with very low miles. It was a beautiful light bronze color. I don't remember the dollar amount, but I do recall that it stretched our budget pretty tightly to buy it. It was a beauty, though, with leather upholstery and all the amenities—top of the line for Chrysler. It was, in my opinion, the best-looking station wagon I had ever seen and just what we needed to move a family of five across country.

We decided that we would have to sell our second car, the Volkswagen Karmann Ghia. I hated to sell it, but it would cost too much to keep and move across the country. I had considered it my "poor man's sports car." I had driven it to work every day and loved cruising through the orange groves, with the windows down, sucking in the wonderful fragrance of the orchards. It wasn't hard to sell, and I admit that I felt like crying when the new owner drove it away. I've always regretted selling it, even to this day. I really enjoyed that little car and cruising around Southern California. Its value would have doubled or tripled by now, but I'm glad that I still have the memories.

Our move got off to a very good start. We packed the station wagon with our suitcases, a guitar, and four kids, and we still had room to spare. Soon we were cruising east across the desert at 75 to 80 miles per hour, in perfect, air-conditioned comfort, with the large motor purring along so quietly that we couldn't even hear it. Delores and I were off on another great adventure—living in Tennessee!

We stopped in Kansas for a few days to see Mom and Dad. It was always so good to see them! We introduced them to their new grandson, Quentin. It was summer again, and Kansas was in full bloom. Sunflowers lined the roadways, and Mom and Dad's garden was still producing yummy lettuce, tomatoes, and green onions. It would have been great to stay longer, but we were anxious to learn where we would be living and get settled. We packed up again, said goodbye to Mom and Dad, and headed for Tennessee.

We finally got to Nashville and found our way to the Recruiting Station. I left Delores with the kids and the car so they could get out and stretch while I went into the building to check in. I was greeted professionally and waited for a few minutes to see the Commanding Officer, Major Smith. When the Major was free, I was invited into his office. He greeted me with a handshake and asked me to sit down. We engaged in a few minutes of small talk, and then he said, "I'll bet you want to know where you'll be stationed." He then said he was assigning me to the sub-station in Chattanooga.

I guess he could see my disappointment and went on to tell me why he needed me in Chattanooga and what a great place it was to live. I was very disappointed. I had worked so hard to get to Nashville, not knowing that Nashville would then assign me to a sub-station. But I accepted the orders and went to tell Delores. I tried to console myself by acknowledging that Chattanooga was only a two-hour drive from Nashville.

As I expected, Delores was disappointed, but she said that she had been reading about Chattanooga being a beautiful place to live, right at the foot of the Great Smoky Mountains. We were actually pretty flexible, so we hugged and got back into the car headed south for Chattanooga, approximately a two-hour drive. We stopped outside of Nashville for lunch and studied the road map.

The closer we got to Chattanooga, the more mountainous it became and the more beautiful the scenery. When we exited the freeway, we soon realized that we had taken the wrong exit. We found ourselves in the downtown area in one of those dangerous, blighted areas of Chattanooga.

After a bit of anxiety, we found our way out to the recruiting sub-station in the Federal Post Office building. I left Delores with the kids while I went upstairs and checked in. I met the Marine in charge of the station, a Master Gunnery Sergeant, and two other recruiters. I didn't stay long, and then Delores and I went to find a place to stay for the night.

Well, we had made it to Tennessee, and everyone was healthy but tired, and we concluded that our journey had indeed been a success. Next we needed to find temporary living quarters until the right home showed up. We went on out to the eastern side of Chattanooga and found a nice motel room at a reasonable price.

Upon the recommendation from one of the Recruiters, we contacted a real estate agent. We decided to buy a house! Delores and I had invested in a mutual fund shortly after we were married. That fund had done well, and we had enough to make a down payment, and, using my VA benefits, we were able to buy a house. Within a few days, we found one that we liked and signed a contract to buy it. We learned that it would take approximately 30 days for the loan to be approved, and then we could move in. The house was in a very nice subdivision in the Northeastern area of the Chattanooga metro area.

Since we wouldn't be able to get into our house until after the 30-day loan approval period, we decided it would be best if Delores and the children went to her old home in North Braddock, Pennsylvania, where they could stay until our new home was ready. I headed north to Pennsylvania to drop off Delores and the children at the home of her brother, Abe, and then returned to Chattanooga.

I decided that I would go ahead and report in to the Recruiting office, thus ending my leave time, and then look for an efficiency apartment for a month. It wasn't difficult to find a small apartment and move in with my belongings.

I checked in and met all the recruiters. I learned that there were five and sometimes six other recruiters working out of Chattanooga. I met them all and was happy to find something I liked about each of them. The Marine Corps recruiting office was in the Post Office in an area with the other services, Army, Navy, and Air Force. It seemed like the recruiters of each service knew each other and cooperated in reaching our goals of a certain number of new enlistees per month. Sometimes it occurred that an enlistee might not qualify for one service but would qualify for another. Young men and sometimes women would come to the Post Office and shop around each service, looking for the best deal.

After I checked in, I was assigned an area in which to recruit. Generally speaking, I was assigned to a large mountainous area north of Chattanooga. I was also assigned a vehicle, a very old Chevy Suburban. It was painted a faded Marine Corps green. This was not a favorite vehicle among the recruiters, and it had been assigned to me because I was the newest recruiter there.

One day, shortly after I had arrived at Chattanooga, the main office at Nashville notified me that my enlistment was due to expire and I would have to re-enlist or be discharged. Well, obviously I was going to re-enlist. A date was set when the Recruiting Officer, Major Smith, would come to the Chattanooga office and swear me in for six more years. The Major had set a time of 09:00 when he would arrive at Chattanooga. When he wasn't there at the specified time, the other recruiters and I waited around patiently for his arrival.

While we waited, MGySgt (Master Gunnery Sergeant) Bailly took a phone call. The caller asked to speak to me. I took the phone, and the person on the line said, "Gunnery Sergeant Lay, this is Major Smith, and want to apologize for being late. I can't be there as planned, so I want to swear you in on the phone, and we can do the paper work later."

I said, "Yes Sir, it's okay with me!" (What else *could* I say?) So, he said, "I want you to stand at attention with your right hand raised." He also told me to have MGySgt Bailly on the phone as a witness. Then he told me to repeat after him, and he administered the oath of office.

At the end, he said, "So help me, Hanna," instead of, "So help me, God." I hesitated a bit, and then said, "So help me, God."

He asked me why I had said that. I mumbled something like I thought I was supposed to. He then said, "Congratulations! You have just been sworn in by your Air Force recruiter, Sgt. Joe Smith."

There was a moment of confusion on my part, and then we all lost control, laughing, for a few minutes, as I realized that it was the *Air Force* recruiter from his office next door who had sworn me in. There was a hilarious outbreak of laughter, as all the recruiters were in on the prank, and it went off just as they had planned. As it turned out, I didn't have to be sworn in that day after all. I went to the recruiting office in Nashville the next day to be *officially* sworn in.

Well, it was certainly a good prank, and I soon learned that this group of recruiters was a fun-loving, easygoing bunch of people. I also learned that it was good to be ever on the alert to prevent one of them from playing a prank on me.

Two of the recruiters were really into fishing, and the area in and around Chattanooga was a haven for fishermen. I went out several times, fishing and camping overnight with them. Several times we camped on the banks of the Chickamauga Lake that had been created by the Chickamauga Dam on the Tennessee River, a fisherman's paradise.

I began my recruiting in the areas north of Chattanooga, and was constantly surprised by both the beauty of the rugged area and by the level of the poverty in which some of the people lived. A lot of time was spent trying to find a potential enlistee who had completed an information request card picked up at the post office or other venue. The hills were rugged, and oftentimes addresses were vague. I found that some inhabitants were reluctant to provide me with any information about someone. Many of the people didn't trust anybody who worked for the government.

One time I found myself in front of what appeared to be a general store, which must have been there for untold decades. When I walked into that store wearing my full dress blues, the room grew completely silent. No one said a word to me. I asked for help with directions to find a potential enlistee who had sent in a card requesting information about the Marine Corps. Several old men were sitting around an old pot-bellied wood stove, whittling, or picking their teeth and smoking. I clearly wasn't welcome here.

After attempting to recruit for a while in this area, I concluded that this particular area of Tennessee was several decades behind the rest of the world. The last time I was up in that area looking for an enlistee, I stopped by that store again. They had apparently come to trust me, because when I told them I was looking for this young man who had sent in a card requesting information, one of the old men sitting around responded. He said, "The boy you're looking for is sitting alongside the road about a mile that way," and he pointed his finger in the direction. The old man went on to say, "That boy and his dog have been sitting out there since early morning waiting for you." From this, I concluded that it must have been well known in the community that I was coming up there that day.

I thanked the old man for the information and left the store. I got into my vehicle and drove slowly down the road in the direction the old man had indicated. Sure enough, about a mile ahead, sitting on a bank behind the ditch on the right side of the road was a blond-haired boy with a big dog. I stopped, got out, and approached him, introducing myself. He seemed excited but nervous. I interviewed him right there while we were talking. He wanted to join the Marines and was ready to go. When I asked him when he would like to leave, he said, "Now." I was somewhat taken aback for a moment, but I concluded that he was basically qualified if he could pass the written exam. He wanted to take the test right there, now.

I invited him over to the vehicle where he took a seat in the passenger side. I pulled out the test and gave it to him. Exiting the vehicle, I walked around a bit as I timed the test.

The boy finished the test in good time. I graded his exam, and told him that he had passed. Again, I asked him when he wanted to leave, and he again said. "Right now!"

I thought about it for a couple of minutes and concluded that there was no reason why he couldn't leave then. I asked him if he wanted to go back home and say goodbye to his family. He said that he had already said goodbye. So I said, "Well, let's go!" and started the old Chevy.

Suddenly, he said, "Wait a minute." He got out and went over and hugged his dog, which had been sitting patiently while all this was taking place. The boy then told the dog to go home and pointed to the driveway behind him. The old dog obeyed, reluctantly, stopping a couple of times to look back forlornly, and the boy again told him to go on home. It was a heart-wrenching moment for the boy and the dog, and it was a scene that I'll never forget.

I took him down the mountain to the little town of Spring Hill, Tennessee, bought him a bus ticket to Knoxville using a government credit card, and gave him some meal tickets for the hotel where potential enlistees stay overnight. The next day he would be given a physical examination and a more comprehensive written test. If he passed the test and the physical he and the others would be shipped to Parris Island, unless they were going into the delayed entry program. If they failed either of the tests, they would be sent back home.

I never found out if this young man had made it or not. I did learn that he passed all the tests at the induction center and was shipped to Parris Island. I could picture how happy his dog would be to see him whenever he did go home. This was only one of dozens of similar situations that occurred in my recruiting out of Chattanooga.

I soon realized that recruiting is a hard job, contrary to the belief some people may have that recruiting is a cushy job. All recruiters who worked out of Nashville at that time were required to enlist five recruits per month. This means that an enlistee must take and pass the exams given at the Induction Center and are sworn in to the Marine Corps. It doesn't count how many potential recruits a recruiter sends to the induction center—only the ones who pass and are sworn in count. It's a very frustrating way to gauge ones work performance. A recruiter might work all month going out to high schools, or trying to locate potential enlistees, and send perhaps ten potentials to the induction center, and they all fail or change their mind. In this instance the recruiter, at the end of the month, comes up with a zero. It's a very frustrating situation. However, I understand it, and I haven't been able to come up with a better system that I could recommend.

After we got settled a bit in Chattanooga, we realized that it was a very nice place to live. It was a good place for picnicking and sightseeing. The areas around Chattanooga are rich in Civil War historic sites, including Look Out Mountain. Because there were so many historic sites, there are also lots of tourists the year around. We also realized that it was a great place for our families to come and visit. We had no more gotten settled when they began to arrive for a visit. Thankfully, they didn't all come at the same time. We had relatives come to see us, many of whom I hadn't seen in many years, including Harold Dean Lay, my first cousin. We enjoyed their visits, but it made a lot of work for Delores. I couldn't get away from work to take them sightseeing, so it was up to her. What a trooper she was! God bless her.

I even learned that one of my old Marine friends, GySgt. Tom Singletary, whom I worked with at Omaha, was on recruiting duty out of Atlanta, Georgia. He was employed out of the sub-station in Marietta, Georgia, and we were able to cross paths now and then, and we stopped to chat once in awhile. One day, Delores and the kids and I were guests at Tom's house, and we all had a great time reminiscing about our duty in Omaha.

One of the good things about recruiting was that I got to meet and talk to a lot of the local people. I enjoyed stopping in at various businesses and making it a point to be friendly and socialize with people. In the beginning, I was usually met with a bit of skepticism and withdrawal. But after a good conversation, I found them to be very friendly, and good patriots.

In Cleveland, Tennessee, there was a music store that I stopped in and visited quite often. I'd sit down and play some of their guitars. Sometimes, another player would sit down and join in. I guess you could call these impromptu jam sessions. It wasn't every day they got to see and hear a Marine in full dress blues playing some good boogie and country music!

After several months of recruiting in the area north of Chattanooga, I learned that I had been selected for promotion to First Sergeant. Wow! This was exciting news to me. After all these years of struggling, I was finally going to be promoted to the position with the honorable title of First Sergeant. I had served as an Acting First Sergeant in California for almost two years, but that was nothing like becoming a true First Sergeant. Those stripes and that diamond on the sleeve commanded a lot of respect.

I was ecstatic, but I kept it low key. I didn't tell Delores about it yet, but I knew that at some point in the not-too-distant future we would be transferred. I anticipated that either Master Gunnery Sergeant Jim Beaty or I would be transferred if I became a First Sergeant. Being supervised by a Master Gunnery Sergeant would be troublesome. That's because a First Sergeant is normally considered the senior enlisted person in a unit, but the Master Gunnery Sergeant has senior rank over First Sergeant.

To make this situation livable for both persons, I was assigned to take over a one-person recruiting office in Cleveland, Tennessee, which also fell under the supervision of the Nashville office. Cleveland is about twenty miles north east of Chattanooga. The main office also was going to acquire a better vehicle for me to drive.

As instructed, one day I was told to drive the old Chevy Suburban to Nashville and turn it in. The supply chief really surprised me by taking me down to the Buick dealer, where we went out on the lot where several new Buick Skylarks were parked in a row. The supply chief told me to pick the one I liked. I could hardly believe it! I picked out a blue one, a Skylark, with a white vinyl top.

The Recruiting Station apparently had been told to get rid of the old vehicles, and they were going to lease new cars instead of purchasing new ones. Well, wasn't I the lucky one? I drove home in a brand new Buick Skylark. It was a beautiful car; quick and powerful, it was a dream to drive. Things were really looking up for me. I was being promoted to First Sergeant, I have my own one-man recruiting station, and I have a new Buick to drive! Maybe this helped to make up for those awful months when I served on mess duty years ago.

Yes, this was sure a long way from that sick, struggling Private First Class (PFC) at Camp Geiger in 1958, dragging a large bag like an old cotton sack, picking up trash on the base, and crawling through the mud in infantry training, sick with a cold that finally turned into pneumonia. Thank you, God, for all your blessings.

CHAPTER 44

LIVING IN KNOXVILLE, TENNESSEE

I was recruiting out of Cleveland for more than a year and enjoyed it very much. But, like the old adage, "all good things must come to an end," on December 11, 1972, I received orders to be transferred to Knoxville, Tennessee, to take charge of that office as the Non-Commissioned Officer in Charge. Getting promoted to First Sergeant was the reason for this assignment. Well, in spite of how much I liked what I was doing in Cleveland, this assignment to Knoxville, and being in charge of that office thrilled me. I was also happy that the orders hadn't been for an overseas assignment.

So, here we go again, with Delores preparing to move. But at least this should be a quick move, as Knoxville was little more than a two-hour drive north of us, and the government would deal with the actual move. The main thing we had to be concerned about was selling the house so soon after we had bought it. We again contacted the real estate sales representative who had helped us find this house. As it turned out, the current real estate market was good, and we had no trouble finding a buyer. The final contract included the buyer giving us some cash equity and taking over our housing mortgage payments. We thought that was a great deal, because that meant we'd have some cash for a down payment on a house in Knoxville.

Soon after receiving my orders, I called the Knoxville Recruiting office and spoke with the senior person there to inquire about the housing market and the availably of rental property. I learned that a Marine Corps Major and a First Sergeant from the Marine Corps Reserve Training Center both had good connections to real estate agents. How convenient! I called the First Sergeant and told him when I would be moving and what kind of housing I would need. He sounded very positive and told me that he looked forward to help us find a nice house.

In a few days, he called and said that he had a house for us to look at and wanted to know if we could come to Knoxville. I took the day off, and Delores and I drove to Knoxville. How fortunate we were! It was the perfect house in the perfect location. We immediately made an offer, which they accepted. And, just like that, our housing situation was resolved!

Our new home was located in the western edge of Knoxville and was near to all the important services. It had three bedrooms, plus a large recreation room, and was sitting on a large corner lot. The sliding back door in the kitchen opened to a small patio and large back yard. After we finalized the deal, we were very excited, and we were able to move just a couple of days before Christmas.

Of course, moving one's household is always a huge job, but getting the perfect house and a new job at the same time sure made it a lot easier. We moved into the house and put everything in its place in time for Christmas.

Now there was just one more important thing to do: shop for Christmas presents! The day before Christmas we received a ten-inch snowfall. So, quite unexpectedly, everything worked out to the effect that we had one of the best Christmases we'd ever had! On Christmas Eve, with the snow still coming down, we went to the huge shopping mall near us to shop for presents. Almost everything was on sale, and there was a joyous, excited feeling in the air, with the soft snowflakes still drifting down. We didn't have time to wrap the presents. We just left most of the kids' gifts in the car until they were all fast asleep, and then I brought everything in and put it under the tree.

On Christmas morning the kids were very excited, and so were we! Because our new house was seated on a little knoll, we had a great view of the community from our living room picture window! It was every bit as beautiful as any snowy scene on a Christmas card.

I had also run out on Christmas Eve and picked up a turkey and all the trimmings along with a large bottle of Irish Cream whiskey for Dad. So, we had our Christmas feast and enjoyed our new home. Looking back over the years, we remember our first Knoxville Christmas fondly as one of the very best ever.

After Christmas, when we got settled, I dressed in my dress blues, took my orders to the recruiting office, and checked in for duty. The recruiting office was among the other services' recruiting offices located in the U.S. Federal Building in the downtown area. It wasn't an ideal location, and I was happy to learn that there were plans to move all these offices from the Federal Building to a new location west of town in a suburban area near where we lived. But, for now, the Federal Building would suffice.

I checked in at the office and met several of the recruiters. I called the Nashville office and told them that I had officially returned from leave and was on the job. The Major called me later that day and said that he wanted to meet with all the recruiters, including me, the next morning at 08:00. He said that no one was excused. I sensed that there might be some kind of problem.

By asking around a bit, I begin to understand that the problem was probably because the Knoxville office hadn't met their quota during the past several months. Therefore, it was likely that we were all in for an ass-chewing.

At 08:00 the next day, the Major briskly walked in, sat down, and gathered everyone around him. His message was short and powerful. This office *must* start making quota, or he would request overseas orders for all of us and close the Knoxville office. He added, "And I mean it!" Then he asked if there were any questions. There were none. He got up, walked out, and went back to Nashville.

For a few minutes we just sat there, somewhat stunned by what he had said. He had driven all the way from Nashville to speak for less than a minute. Wow! I used the occasion to introduce myself to all the recruiters. I had to reiterate that it was my intention to make quota, as the Major had stressed. I told them that I would be as helpful as I could be, because I had no intention of receiving overseas orders right now. I told the recruiters that the first thing I intended to do was to meet with each of them separately to discuss exactly what they were doing or not doing in their area of recruiting, and to find out if there was some way that we could improve their efforts and success.

Time goes by so quickly! Our children were really growing up, and it was hard to keep up with all their activities. Looking back, I think that I was probably a bit negligent in my share of the duties. My job at the Recruiting Station kept me very busy, plus I had a lot of extra outside activities with musical events. There was no way that I could put my music on hold. I had to take whatever opportunities I could get to further my musical career chances.

It was amazing to realize how Bobbie had grown. In 1973, he had just finished the eleventh grade. He was working at Red Lobster and riding his new Harley Davidson motorcycle, and fighting all the temptations young people face at that age. He was an extremely handsome and cool guy and a "chick magnet." Trouble loomed.

After his birthday in July, Bobbie and I had a talk about these things, and his future. Being 17, he now could join the Marine Corps with written permission from one parent. I showed him all the opportunities available to him in the Corps. He thought about it for a few days and then came to me and said he wanted to join the Marine Corps if I would sign for him. I was very happy for him, so I did all the paper work involved and gave him the test. He passed the test and the physical and was sworn into the Marine Corps!

A couple of weeks before he was scheduled to leave, on sort of a spur-of-the-moment idea, we all drove to Parris Island and stayed over the weekend. It was a nice mini-vacation that we really enjoyed. We really loved touring the base and showing Bobbie some of the challenges he would face in boot camp. We all had, and still have, such fond memories of Beaufort. When we came back to Knoxville, Bobbie busied himself getting ready to go.

He left for boot camp, and now we found that we had to adjust to not having him as part of the family at home. We really missed him. Bobbie had had some emotional difficulties when he was a little boy and his biological mother and I were having our problems. Delores and I didn't know how, and if, his early life experiences might affect his adult development.

I believe our questions were all answered when Bobbie graduated from boot camp. He had made it! It's no small deal to graduate from Marine Corps Boot camp. We drove down to see his graduation. We were really proud of him, as he was of himself, when we watched his platoon pass in review at graduation. As it turned out, Bobbie liked the Marine Corps and stayed in, making it a career. He also met and married a woman who also was a career Marine. She retired with more than twenty years of service. Bobbie and his wife, Kay, gave us three wonderful grandchildren. He spent more than 22 years in the Corps, and is now retired and living in Southern California.

My son Bobbie graduates from boot camp, Marine Corps Recruit Depot, Parris Island, S.C., 1973. Pictured: Bobbie, Valerie, Delores, Quentin and Mark. All of my children in this photo would eventually enlist in the Marines, and I proudly attended each of their graduation ceremonies.

Rolling into the New Year, January 1973, I implemented numerous changes to increase the Recruiting Station's visibility and interactions with the community. Then, when we moved the station from the Post Office to the western shopping areas, there was more people traffic, all of which increased the number of recruits enlisted. Morale went up, and this made the Major happy. All the Recruiters made quota, and enjoyed working in the new office instead of the Federal Building.

To celebrate our success in making quota, I held a summer party at my house for all the recruiters. We had some hamburgers on the grill and plenty of the beverage that Marines everywhere love—beer. We enjoyed getting to know the recruiters and their families, and I think, overall, that this helped to increase the morale of the office. However, even though we were now meeting our quota, it was still really difficult to find qualified young men and women to join. Knoxville's unemployment rate was much lower than some other cities, like Memphis, where the unemployment rate was high and where they always met their quota.

This was only one of the factors that affected the availability of young people for a job. Knoxville was largely a tourist city, located at the foot of the Great Smoky Mountains. It was also the campus of the University of Tennessee. It was a beautiful area in which to live and travel. One of the fun things we did from time to time was to load up the car with some sodas, sandwiches, and snacks, and take a nice Sunday drive through the Smoky Mountains. One of our favorite drives was to head southeast of Knoxville to Gatlinburg, and Maryville, and back.

Well, our old Ford was beginning to be somewhat unreliable on long drives, and we began to think about purchasing a new car, or at least a later model. This was at the time when the Arab countries instituted an embargo on oil, which caused prices of oil to rise globally. The embargo forced the United States and Third World countries to develop plans for gasoline rationing. There were long lines at service stations, and everyone tried to keep their car's gas tank full.

These fears saw a lot of people getting rid of their large, gas-guzzling cars, in favor of smaller, more efficient vehicles. As I visited the car lots and car dealers looking for a suitable family car, I found that there were hardly any small cars available, and if one of them had a small car, the price was exorbitant!

One day I stopped by the Cadillac dealer thinking that perhaps there might be a small car there. The salesman who greeted me steered me to look at a 1970 Cadillac four-door sedan, with very low miles on it. I normally wouldn't even look at a Cadillac, because I knew that it would be way more than I could afford. In this instance, however, the salesman was so insistent that I thought, *Aw, what the heck. I might as well take a look at the Cadillac.* It was a beautiful car—a sparkling bronze color, leather seat covers, four doors, and plenty of room. The salesman wouldn't yet tell me the price. It was a Friday, and he said to me. "Why don't you just take it home this weekend, drive it wherever you want, and come back Monday, and I will tell you the price."

I remember thinking, *What have I got to lose?* So I took the car home for the weekend. Well, Delores and I fell in love with this vehicle and wished we could afford it. I took it back Monday and met with the salesman. Now it was time for the big question: how much does it cost? Honestly, although I can't remember the exact price, it was so low that I was shocked. I thought that maybe I had misunderstood what he said. I asked again, and he confirmed what I thought he'd said.

Incredibly, the price for this Cadillac was considerably less than what I had planned to pay for another family car. I bought the Cadillac. It was the first time I had ever owned one, and it still lives on in our memories as our family's favorite car. It was beautifully styled, powerful, comfortable, and with plenty of room. We kept it for twelve years and I sure wish I had another one just like it. The auto industry just doesn't make cars like that anymore.

Knoxville is an area where Bluegrass and country music thrive. Nearly everyone in those days played a stringed instrument of some sort, and "porch playing" was common. After church and dinner on Sunday afternoons, family members, friends, and neighbors would gather on somebody's front porch and play some old tunes. If you could play any instrument, you were welcome to join in.

Also, I learned that for many years Knoxville had been the home of "The Old Barn Dance," at the radio station WNOX auditorium. This is a stage show that showcased local artists and famous performers of the day every Saturday evening. I went by the building where the show was always held one afternoon. The building was open, so I stopped and went in.

There was a middle-aged man and his wife working there, cleaning the refreshment booth in the rear of the auditorium. They were friendly folks, and I had a nice conversation with them. They operated the refreshment stand and had worked with the people who owned and operated this music show for many years, going back to the 1940s. They knew all the country music stars and recalled when famous guitarist, Chet Atkins, came down from the hills north of Knoxville to play on the radio station WNOX and was also associated with the Barn Dance. When I told them about my musical history they said that I should come to the auditorium on a Thursday afternoon, as that was when there was a rehearsal for the next Saturday night show, and perhaps I could meet the manager.

I did as these folks suggested and, on a Thursday afternoon, I took the day off, picked up my guitar, and went to the auditorium. I went in and met and talked with the manager of the show. He asked about my history with music. Then he had me go up on the stage and do several songs. I took my guitar up to the stage and sang three or four Johnny Cash songs. He liked my singing and invited me to perform on the next Saturday Night show. Wow! This was exciting. Of course, I accepted.

I went to the next rehearsal and met the other people who were regulars on the show. It was exciting to meet these folks, as they had been around for a long time and either knew or were related to, some of the stars of the time. Delores and I were thrilled to meet a singer named Ava Barber, who was a regular on the "Barn Dance" and went on to become a regular on the Lawrence Welk Show. Mr. Welk would always introduce her as his "country singer, Ava Barber." She had the best voice in country music at the time, as far as I was concerned.

During the time when I was just coming onto the show, she and her husband, Roger, were leaving Knoxville and moving to California. However, at that same time, when I did a recording of a new soundtrack for my song "The Marine's Ballad," they were still in Knoxville. I hired Roger as the drummer on the recording, as he was the best around. While we were working on the recording in the studio, Delores sat and visited with Ava. Delores fondly recalls that visit and has stashed that memory in her mental footlocker. Ava was on the Lawrence Welk show for many years, and Delores and I always tried to make it a point every week to hear her sing. Roger sometimes played drums for her on the show.

I did a Saturday night performance on the "Old Barn Dance" for about six months. It was great fun and very exciting. I got to know quite a few people in the entertainment business, both artists and music business managers. One day, the manager of the show called and asked if I would take over as the Master of Ceremonies, in addition to my regular performances. Wow, this was great! I told him that I would be pleased to do so and began as the Master of Ceremonies in the upcoming show.

At first, I was anxious about whether or not I could pull this off. If I could, it would be a big step up for me and might possibly qualify me for a more prominent position and recognition in the Nashville music scene. Had I retired in Knoxville, which Delores and I had talked about, I know I would have been deeply involved in music. However, my Marine Corps career, and my plans to go to college, were much more important to me than even my music.

I never mentioned to any of the Marines I worked with that I was a performer on this show. I didn't want them to look upon me as anything but a Marine First Sergeant. It wasn't as if it was a top-secret piece of information, and, truthfully, I think they all probably knew, but we just didn't talk about it. During this time, when I was a performer on the show, I realized that it took a lot more time than one might expect. It meant much more than to just show up and perform every Saturday evening. Usually, on Wednesday evenings, all of us performers met in a local recording studio to practice our songs. I usually also went to the Thursday afternoon rehearsal at the auditorium, and then to the Saturday night performance. Yes, it took time, but it was time I really enjoyed. I look back and recall this as a very happy and exciting time in my life.

I also played and sang at other music venues while at Knoxville. Being as involved as I was, I met many people in the music business.

A couple of them worked as television hosts. They had a weekday TV talk show every morning. They would also invite certain performers as guests. I was invited and performed several times on their talk show, wearing my dress blue uniform. I was mostly there to talk about the Maine Corps and to explain what's involved in becoming a Marine.

They also recorded me on television singing my song "The Marine's Ballad" in my dress blues. This station kept the recording in their files, and, from time to time, they'd bring it out and play it when they were doing a program about the military or the Marines—and sometimes on a national holiday.

I also never knew when I was going to be on TV. One day at the recruiting office, I was at my desk in my uniform when a guy came in to talk about the Marine Corps. He began to look at me in a quizzical way. Then he paused and said, "Were you just on TV this morning?"

I said, "Well, maybe," and then he laughed. I told him what he saw was probably a recording. He went on to say that he could hardly believe that he had just been watching TV, had seen me on the program, got into his car and came down to the office—and there I was again! We had a good laugh. He sat down, and we completed the paperwork for him to join the Marines. Shortly thereafter, he was on his way to Parris Island, Marine Corps Recruit Depot.

The two hosts from the TV station also went to the state hospital in Knoxville once a month and sponsored a stage show in the auditorium for the patients and staff. They included me as a regular performer. It was a fun experience, and I continued to play on their monthly show until I left Knoxville. It was unusual in that sometimes there were patients in attendance, and some of those patients had emotional or mental problems. We were told to not act surprised or frightened if a patient came wandering up on the stage to look us while we were performing. They said to just continue our performance. And indeed, there were some rather funny things happened that weren't scheduled.

I was also booked and played for a music program called "The Tri-County Jamboree." This show was usually held in a former high school auditorium north of Knoxville. It was an area of Tennessee where at there was at least one member of the family who could play Bluegrass music at some skill level. During my recruiting activities, if there was a music store in town, I'd go in and get acquainted with the employees or owner. I would typically ask for a guitar to play and would sit down and begin playing. Soon others had joined me. It was typical for any music store in that area to have two or three people sitting around, playing some old Bluegrass songs, just for the fun of playing.

When I went to play at the Tri-County Jamboree, the place was packed, with standing room only along the inside walls. I think I did pretty well, but I could tell that some of my jokes didn't get much response, and I wondered why. Later, I think I realized why. These jokes and some of the things I talked about were developed in southern California, and for that audience. Some of these mountain people didn't pick up on those punch lines. I'd give myself a C+ grade for this performance. Instead of a good old belly laugh, I'd maybe only get a weak smile, a nod, or a blank stare. My music and this crowd just didn't click very well. Everyone was nice to me, but I didn't book another performance there. I'll just file this in my memory as a fun experience.

Since I was getting involved in the music scene in Knoxville, I decided it was time to do another recording of my songs, "The Marine's Ballad," and "Make a Marine," because I thought that the early recordings could be improved substantially.

There was a very nice recording studio named Handy Recording in Knoxville. Through this studio I was able to get in touch with a producer, John Taylor. I met with him, and we made a contract for him to be the producer of the recording. He would do everything to prepare for the recording session, such as hiring musicians, and so on.

I met with him one day at the studio, and we played the 45 RPM recordings of the songs, and I told him how I wanted to improve them. After making this contract with John Taylor, he did all the rest. All I had to do was sing the songs the way I wanted them to sound. Mr. Taylor made arrangements for the studio time. He had a long list of some of the top country stars who had recorded here, and he was very proud of those events.

The recording time was established for evening. Delores came with me to the studio. It was a memorable event—recording a song in an actual professional studio! I was very impressed with the way that John Taylor managed everything. I met and talked with the musicians he had hired. There was a drummer, Roger Barber, whom I've mentioned before. There was a bass guitar man, a lead guitar player, and a rhythm player, along with a trumpet player. All of them were very helpful with working out the "kinks" in the song.

When we thought that we had everything figured out, I went into the recording booth. This was the first time I had ever sung without playing the guitar. I didn't think I could do it, but I did! This booth was like a large telephone booth. There was a stool, and there was also a microphone hanging down and a set of earphones. John Taylor and the other musicians and I could all communicate with each other.

We began to work on "The Marine's Ballad." It took about two hours to get this song to the point where I was satisfied. I was very happy that Mr. Taylor made some changes from the first recording, which really improved the song. By the time we got it right, I sure was tired of singing it!

Next, we went to work on "Make a Marine." I worked with the lead guitar player to develop an intro. This song wasn't very complex, and it took us only an hour and a half to work it out and call it done. John Taylor kept the master tape and did more mixing of the sound before he determined that it was finished.

Over the years, many CDs and other recordings have been made of it. Recently, I've released the song as a music video. My youngest son, Dwight, also a musician and a computer expert, was able to create a music video of "The Marines Ballad," which can be seen on YouTube. Dwight was named an Honorary Marine in 1993 by order of the Commandant of the Marine Corps for courage he demonstrated in recovering from a devastating car accident, which left him totally disabled.

In the April 2011 issue of *Leatherneck Magazine,* there's a feature article about me, my family, all of whom have served in the Marine Corps, except for Delores and Dwight (officially), and my song.

In 2010, while living in Portland, Oregon, I again released the songs, creating a digital version made from the old master tape, improving the sound and quality. I also designed a new label and cover. I'm satisfied that the song will be around long after I'm gone.

As our Knoxville adventure rolled into 1974, we were thoroughly enjoying our life there. Being a college town, and also as the home of the University of Tennessee, it was a dynamic town and a great place to live. We'll always remember our Sunday afternoon drives through the foothills of the Great Smoky Mountains.

Delores and I must have had a memorable Valentine's Day in 1974, as not too long afterward she broke the news to me that she was pregnant. Wow! Here we go again, bringing a new life into this world. We were excited about this news.

Among other things that I really enjoyed while at Knoxville were the regularly scheduled staff meetings held in Nashville, our home regional office. All the recruiting sub-stations like ours at Knoxville, and others, such as Memphis, Chattanooga, Huntsville, Alabama, and Tupelo, Mississippi, would be required to send their senior person. We would all travel into Nashville the day before the meeting and stay at one of the Holiday Inns.

Our get-togethers on the evening before these meetings nearly always ended up as party time, and we had a lot of fun. The next day, seated at the table were some very hung-over Marines, trying to appear sober and attentive,

On November 10th of every year, the Marine Corps celebrates the birthday of the founding of the Marine Corps, on November 10, 1775. This is a celebration that takes place at all Marine Corps Commands in the States, as well as on overseas bases, no matter where they're located. The Marine Corps Command at Nashville sponsored the birthday celebration every year for our recruiting area.

In 1974, the Marine Corps Birthday fell on a Sunday. The Recruiting Office, therefore, held their Marine Corps Ball celebration on Saturday, November 9th. I attended the celebration, but Delores wasn't feeling up to going, as the baby was due. It was only a two-hour drive from Nashville to Knoxville, so Delores and I agreed that it would be okay for me to go to the ball. The hospital where she would deliver was only blocks away.

I attended the ball, and it was a memorable event. I stayed all night in Nashville and went to a brief staff meeting at the main office, heading home early Sunday afternoon.

I arrived at our house in the late afternoon and parked in our driveway, I got out of the car and saw Delores upstairs waving at me from the bedroom window. She was smiling and looked great. For a couple of months I'd been telling the recruiters and the major that I'd worked with that Delores and I had planned to have this baby born on the Marine Corps birthday. Of course, I was just joking around with them, and they knew it. It would be extraordinarily difficult, if at all possible, to pick a particular date on which to have a baby born. I had also carried it a step further and told the Major the same thing.

In a mostly joking tone, I said to Delores, "This is November 10th, the Marine Corps birthday. Are you about ready to go have that baby?"

To my astonishment, she said, "I think so. I've been having labor pains all day!"

Wow! "Really?"

"I'm not kidding!" she said. "You need to come on in and help me." What we had been joking about now seemed possible!

Delores's labor pains grew harder and closer together, and by about eight PM I took her to the hospital. I was with her when the nurse examined her. She was going to be admitted, as the delivery was close. As she was wheeled into the labor room, I told the nurse that today was the birthday of the Marine Corps, and I wanted the baby to be born before midnight.

The nurse looked at me like I was some kind of kook, and she said, "You'll have to talk to the doctor about that!" Well, there wasn't any time to do much, because they showed me a room where I could sit and wait for Delores.

I had barely gotten settled in the waiting area when I was called back into the labor room. Delores had just delivered a big, healthy baby boy. *Good girl, Delores!* Wow! I was so proud of her.

And, he was born before midnight, on the 199th birthday of the Marine Corps! How exciting! *Oorah!!* Now I *really* had bragging rights!

Delores and the baby were fine and were resting comfortably. I could hardly wait go to the office the next day to tell everyone and to call the Major personally to give him the news. I had stuck my neck out and told him that Delores would have this baby on the birthday of the Marine Corps, when we all knew it was virtually impossible to predict the exact date that woman give birth.

Because of this prediction and the result, it became a story that was brought up often at our monthly staff meetings. In our family circle of Marine friends, Dwight's birthday became a real celebrated event.

As we rolled into 1975, I knew that I was going to receive orders soon, as it was time for me to rotate overseas. I was surprised when in early January I received orders to Parris Island to attend First Sergeant's School! These orders were for (TAD) Temporary Assignment Duty, and I would return to Knoxville when the school ended. Of course, Delores and the children would just stay where they were in Knoxville. It's only about a four-drive from Knoxville to Parris Island.

On January 5th, I traveled to Parris Island and checked in to the First Sergeants School. I drove our old '64 Mercury, leaving the

Cadillac for Delores to drive. First Sergeants School focused on the personnel management system of a Marine Corps Unit and to also familiarize us with the new computer-based personnel reporting system. There were no personnel inspections and no scheduled physical fitness workouts. There was an exception that students be well groomed at all times and on a voluntary physical fitness program.

The school was interesting and enjoyable, especially because I ran into several of my old Marine Corps buddies, who had, like me, been promoted to First Sergeant. School was like a break for us from our regular duties back at our parent units. The course work wasn't difficult, and we all had time to relax a bit. We almost considered this assignment a vacation!

On two weekends, I drove back to Knoxville. I would leave Parris Island at about 17:00 and arrive in Knoxville before midnight. It was a fun trip, but I was pretty beat up by the time I got back to Parris Island around midnight Sunday evening. The time passed by quickly, and on March 5th I graduated and returned to Knoxville.

On March 7th, 1975, I received orders to the 3rd Marine Division, Okinawa, Japan. I knew this was going to a major assignment for at least thirteen months out of the country and away from my family. None of us were happy about it, but we had to accept it. Now, we had to figure out where Delores and the children were going to live while I was gone. This was always a difficult decision.

After considering several options, we decided to sell the house and move Delores and the children to eastern Kansas near my Mom and Dad. They were elderly and with major health problems. This may be the only chance for our children to live near and get to know their grandparents. In addition, I had always planned to go to college and get a degree when I retired from the Marine Corps, so there were several good options in eastern Kansas. We decided to sell our house in Knoxville and buy a house in Fort Scott, Kansas, which was only 11 miles from Fulton where their Grandma and Grandpa lived.

It seemed like a huge problem to make this all happen in the short amount of time we had. But we just dived in and operated with a positive attitude. As it turned out, we had no trouble selling our house and property, and we even made a profit on it! We would use the profit to buy a house in Kansas when I retired.

As it all worked out, we had to turn over the house to the new owners before I could pick up my orders and depart Knoxville. We had made arrangements with Mom and Dad to stay with them for a few days until we found a place to live. We released the house, and Delores went on ahead of me and took the children. I kissed them goodbye, sent them on their way, and then I checked into the local Holiday Inn. I would be there for about a week until I could officially pick up my orders at Nashville and head toward Kansas, which was just a stopover on my way to my ultimate destination, the "Western Pacific" area, with the Third Marine Division on the Island of Okinawa.

When I arrived at my folks' house in Fulton, it was so good to see Mom and Dad again! They lived in this wonderful old wood-framed house with one bedroom downstairs and three bedrooms upstairs. They could fit us in very comfortably, if for only a short period of time.

The next day, we began our house hunting in earnest and soon realized that there were almost no nice rental apartments or houses. We did, however, find a suitable small three-bedroom house for sale on the south edge of Fort Scott. It had a nice front and back yard. The real estate agent handling the house said that if we worked out a deal where the sellers would give it up in thirty days we could make them an offer. I told the agent that wasn't a satisfactory plan, as I was on orders to report to California in a lot less time than that. I told the agent to make them an offer. We would pay them their full asking price, with no quibbling, if they could get out of the house in ten days. The agent was skeptical, but he made the offer, and the owners accepted. We signed a contract. Hurray! Hurray! Housing problem resolved!

We had a lot to get done, because I was due to report for duty with the Third Marine Divisions on April 7, 1975. We soon took ownership of the house, had our furniture and belongings moved in, and began to get everything arranged the way we wanted it. There were several things I wanted to get done before I left. I was so busy that it kept me from being sad about leaving my family for at least thirteen months. That's a long time to be away from loved ones. Before I left, I hired a carpenter and had a garage built onto the house. We also had a four-foot high chain link fence built around the property. I also built a metal storage shed. I gave a shout out to my Uncle Raymond to come over and help me assemble it by installing hundreds and hundreds of metal screws. The rest of the things we needed would have to wait until I returned.

Time passed quickly and soon the day of my departure had arrived. Delores took me to the Kansas City airport to board my flight to California. Dwight and Quentin came along. On our way, we stopped briefly at Fulton to say goodbye to my Mom and Dad. As was usual when I left home, Mom teared up, which made me do the same. We decided to leave Dwight with Mom and Dad while we made the trip to the airport. They loved having him, and it would sure ease our burden. After some goodbye hugs, we were on our way again.

The trip went without difficulty, and, sooner than I wanted, we were in the airport and at the gate when there came the call for my boarding. It was time for that final hug. This hug would have to last for thirteen long months. I tried to squeeze Delores tightly so I could remember how she felt. I admit to some goodbye tears, mostly mine. I broke away and boarded the plane, which was filled to capacity, and soon we were on our way. To help overcome my sadness I began to talk to myself. *This is what Marines do*, I told myself. *They go away to war, or where it is imminent, or to help our allies, or to take action when the security of our country is threatened. This is what is expected of me; and I will go and do what my country tells me to do. Then, when I come home, I can perhaps consider retiring from the Corps and going to college.*

Too many things to think about. I pushed back the seat, leaned back, closed my eyes, and just let my mind wander. Again, a big transition was taking place in my life. How would it all work out?

CHAPTER 45

FINAL DEPLOYMENT, CAMP HANSEN, OKINAWA, THIRD MARINE DIVISION 1975

First Sergeant of a Marine Rifle Company, "Mike" Company, 3rd
Battalion, 4th Marines, 1975.

By the time the huge Continental Airlines jet touched down on the airstrip at Kadena AFB in Okinawa I was really ready to get off the plane. It had seemed like a long, long ride. My body was numb all over from sitting in that hard, crowded seat for seven hours. All I wanted was to get out of that airplane!

When the doors were finally opened, we were hit with a surge of hot, humid air that took my breath away. Kadena Air Force Base looked the same: endless runways simmering under a white-hot blistering sun. I was wearing my full dress-green uniform of the day, and I couldn't wait to get somewhere—anywhere—out of that sun.

A green bus was waiting to take us to an assignment center where we would be processed and sent to our assigned unit. Same old drill, same old process—some things in the Marine Corps never change. I checked in at the assignment center and was told by a guy to "Wait out there," as he pointed to some chairs, "until your name is called." As I said, some things never change.

I was in a really bad mood, so I told myself to just chill out and calm down. *You know the drill. Deal with it!* I was tempted to just go outside, grab a cab, and head over to the Rocker Club, the large Air Force service club nearby on the base. But wiser voices in my head prevailed.

When my name was finally called, I went into an office and took a seat. Soon a tired, scruffy-looking staff sergeant came to the desk, and we went through a hurried, forced introduction and handshake. He picked up a small sheaf of papers stapled together, looked at them, and said something like, "Okay, First Sergeant Lay, you are being assigned to the Third Battalion, Fourth Marines. That unit is stationed at Camp Hansen. There'll be a bus here in a few minutes to take you to that unit. Are there any questions?

"Yes, where can a guy get something to eat?"

"Over there is a snack bar," he said, pointing to a booth that sold sandwiches, chips, drinks, etc. I proceeded to the booth and picked up a sandwich and soda and gulped it down. I felt much better after that. *Those twelve-hour, non-stop airplane rides should be against the law*, I thought, still fighting to overcome the effects of the trip.

While waiting for the bus, I was shooting the breeze with three other First Sergeants who were waiting for the same bus. We all were from the same First Sergeants class that we had recently attended. Our rank of First Sergeant created a genuine closeness among us. We were happy to see each other and had fun speculating about what our new assignment might be. I think we all knew deep down that we were probably going to get Infantry assignments, but we were hoping instead that we might luck out and get something a little cushier.

One of the First Sergeants was dragging around a large bag of golf clubs along with all his other gear. We all teased him about it, asking him where did he think he was going—on vacation? We told him that he might as well get rid of those golf clubs, but he was still hoping that he'd get a good assignment where he could play golf. We laughed. "No way!" we told him. But he kept on holding out hope.

Our bus arrived, and we all grabbed our gear and climbed aboard. The bus made a couple stops and some people got off, but we First Sergeants remained on the bus. We were heading north, through Ishikawa Beach and beyond. We "old salts" knew, without vocalizing it, that continuing north would lead to Camp Hansen, and Camp Hansen meant Infantry, unless—just by the slightest chance— there was an easy, never before-heard-of job for a First Sergeant.

We had fallen silent as the bus proceeded through the main gate at Camp Hansen. It slowly made its way through the base and came to a stop in front of the Headquarters of the Third Battalion, Fourth Regiment, of the Third Marine Division. A very large sign in front of the building in bold yellow words on a dark crimson red background seemed to indicate that this was a proud unit.

Historically, it *was* a proud unit, with an impressive combat record. There was nothing subtle about it. As the bus slowed to a stop, the driver opened the door and said, "Last stop, everyone off!" Well, there was no doubt now. Any hopes of getting a quiet, cushy job were disintegrating like dust in the breeze. We now knew there was no such a thing.

At about 18:00 hours on April 16, 1975, we dragged our gear inside the building and were directed to the office of the Sergeant Major. He had waited up for us. How kind of him. The Sergeant Major told us to leave our gear in the hallway and come on into his office. I sat down in one of the chairs in front of his desk.

He was a squared-away-looking Marine, who wore the mantle of sergeant major very well. After some niceties about our flight here and where we were coming from, etc., he got down to the business at hand. He told the First Sergeant who had been dragging the huge bag of golf clubs that he may as well either store them or get rid of them, because he wasn't going to have any time to use them. He told us that we were going to be assigned to a rifle company. I was assigned to "M," Mike Company.

Well, there was no guessing anymore. I would be the First Sergeant of what was generally referred to in the Corps as a Rifle Company. This is it. This is what the Marine Corp is all about. These are the ones who must get close to the enemy and take him out, whether with a bullet, a bayonet, or in hand-to-hand combat. These are the men for whom all the rest of the Marines in the Corps are doing their jobs, to support them—to make sure they have the beans, bullets, and bandages they need, wherever they may need them. They are the ones who are awakened in the middle of the night to muster their weapons and fighting gear, ready and willing to go anywhere in the world to take out an enemy of our country.

The unit would be participating in training for amphibious assaults, and we would receive many alerts, but we would never know whether an alert was just for practice or if it was the real thing. And I am now realizing that I am one of these elite troops! It frightened me a bit. Was I ready? Could I do It? *I have never failed at any job the Marine Corps has given me,* I told myself. *I will not fail at this job.*

After the Sergeant Major gave us our assignments, he told us that this battalion was gearing up to "go afloat" in the Pacific and South Pacific area for six months. Going "afloat" means that a Marine Corps unit, often referred to as an "expeditionary" unit, is practicing amphibious landings from Naval ships throughout their area of operations. He went on to say that most of the companies were understrength, so we would have a lot of people joining our unit, and a lot of people leaving our unit, because many of them would be rotating back to the States.

We were told that we would be on a training schedule to ensure that this unit fully was trained and at full strength by the time we were to go afloat in September. He told us that the Colonel wanted us to be the best trained in the division, and that he, the Sgt. Major, supported the Colonel's goal.

Then he proceeded to expound on what he wanted from us until my eyelids were getting heavy and I was almost falling asleep. I was thinking, *Okay, okay, we all know all this. Let's end this bull session.* He finally wrapped things up and called his driver to take us to a barracks where we could get some sleep and then come back the next morning to the office to get checked in. Okay, great. Maybe now we could hurry and go get some chow and get settled for the evening.

The next couple of days I spent checking in, as was routine. I was billeted in a semi-private room and shared the head and shower with another First Sergeant. It was a pretty nice setup. The room had a single bed, a table, lamp, desk, chair, a lounge chair, and a TV.

Two of my First Sergeant buddies and I went to eat at the Staff NCO club. It was a nice club—large, with a stage and a lot tables and chairs. I had no more than gotten settled in with my meal in front of me, when my song "The Marine's Ballad" began playing on the large speakers from the jukebox. I hadn't expected that!

I later went up to the jukebox just to see my name in the listing. Sure enough, it was there! Probably most of the Marines in the club at that time had heard the song a lot but would never connect it to me that evening. To them, I was just another old First Sergeant eating his supper. I didn't plan to make them aware of this song and myself.

When it played again during our meal, one of my buddies recognized it and knew that it was my song. Both of the guys at the table with me gave me a quick handshake and congratulated me. But even though it was a bright spot in my day, having my song still being played and enjoyed by Marines, it wasn't going to make my assignment as First Sergeant of a rifle company any easier. Once again, it was time for me to live up to the inspiring words in my song.

After a couple of days I got word that the Sgt. Major wanted to see me. I went to the battalion office and met with him, along with the other First Sergeants. He asked us to sit down while he gave us a lecture on leadership and what he expected from his First Sergeants. I guess he owned us now.

He took us for a walk through the Battalion area, pointing out various buildings and company offices. Lastly, he went to the "M" Mike Company office with me. He took me to the First Sergeants' office and then we went to the Company Commander's office, where he introduced me to Captain Brown, the Company Commander, a tall, lean, somber guy.

As he walked outside to go, the Sgt. Major told me, "This is your company now, First Sergeant," and he turned and walked away. Well, I thought, *This is it, First Sergeant, get to work*! I turned and went back to the "Mike" company office.

I thought it best if I talked to the Captain as soon as I could about getting started. I knocked on the Captain's door. He told me to come in. I entered and had a good talk with Captain Brown. We discussed my role as the company First Sergeant and his expectations of me. He said that he was an Infantry Captain and liked it. He told me that he doesn't like paperwork and is strictly a field Marine. I told him of my leadership skills and management of an office and that I had recently graduated from the First Sergeants' school at Parris Island. I also told him that I had never before been in an Infantry unit, but I felt confident that I could handle the job.

Captain Brown told me that he would count on me to run the office, handle disciplinary problems, make sure that all personnel problems were addressed, make sure that the unit diary gets completed every day, and then said that he would take care of the company field training and field problems. He said he knew a lot about company tactics and looked forward to field training. This all sounded great to me, and it seemed like the Captain and I would get along very well together, as far as these matters were concerned.

That very afternoon, I plunged myself into the myriad of problems that the company office was having. First and foremost was an alert status regarding what was taking place in Vietnam. North Vietnam appeared to be starting military operations again, and that affected all military units in and around that area of the world. This alert status hung over our heads constantly. Everyone was required to have their weapon either on them or close by, and must be wearing the helmet, flack jacket, and field gear, and be ready to muster on short notice.

It was hot in Okinawa at this time of the year, and wearing all that combat gear made it especially miserable. My utility uniform was constantly wet with sweat. In this type of serious situation, my duties ran into much more than an eight-to-five job. Mostly, it was day on, stay on. The rifle company units were on a training schedule, and, upon completion, they would be deployed on float in an amphibious expeditionary unit.

Clearly, North Vietnamese forces were openly beginning their activities to overrun South Vietnam, breaking their treaty obligations of 1973. No one in our government, including even President Ford, knew exactly how far North Vietnam, in April 1975, would carry out their new aggression. All military units were trying to address this new threat to South Vietnam. Sometimes it seemed like there were conflicting orders that we were trying to fulfill.

Down at the unit level, we were busy trying to determine just who was in the company. At first there was an order issued to cancel the previous orders of those who had received them to rotate home. Then there were new people checking in to bring the company up to full strength. I found out that the new computerized personnel management system didn't work well in situations like this. It just crashed. For a little while, I didn't know who was in the company. It was my job to find out. I had to resort to the old 5 x 8 card-file system. I called a company formation and handed out a card to each person, asking them to fill it out, then get in line, alphabetically, and hand their cards in to me.

I found one of the old, wooden file boxes for 5 x 8 cards and set up a table outside the company office. When a Marine stepped forward with his card, I would do a quick review of the information on the card and then would take his card and place it in the box in alphabetically. This took about an hour, but at least for the present I knew who and how many people were in my company. This old system worked well for several days until the personnel people got the wrinkles ironed out with the new computer management system. It certainly made sense to me that before you take a unit of men into a combat situation in a foreign country, you need to be sure just whom they are.

Getting myself settled into my new job and getting the company's personnel and computer system operating took several very busy and frustrating days. During this time, from the day that I took over the company until the big day, April 29th (the day Saigon fell), I could say with confidence "Mike" Company was ready to carry out any orders a rifle company would be expected to do, anywhere in the world. It had pretty much been a day and night effort by all leaders in the company—platoon sergeants, platoon commanders, squad leaders, all the way down to the junior privates doing their jobs.

After many months of arduous training, and on constant alerts status regarding the developing situation in Vietnam, my unit is named "Honor Company."

Throughout the last two weeks of April 1975, nearly all of the military units in the Far Eastern command were constantly adapting to changing mission statements, because the North Vietnamese were now definitely taking over the South. The U.S. Congress refused to authorize more funds to support the war in South Vietnam. Consequently, the United States and its allies had to virtually stand by and watch as North Vietnamese military forces systematically overran the South, killing anyone and everyone who stood in their way and stealing their property.

As April slipped by, the United States forces continued to evacuate large numbers of people from Tan Son Nhat Airport in Saigon. Americans, and South Vietnamese people who had worked for the United States in South Vietnam were fleeing. Thousands of these people's lives were now in grave danger. Thus began a mass exodus to get out of South Vietnam, especially Saigon. It also became clear that we were not going to be able to evacuate everyone who was in danger. People fled in any way possible. They fled in small boats, large boats, aircraft, and through all the evacuation efforts of the United States from the airport. Meanwhile, the infantry units like mine on Okinawa were on high alert, ready to respond to any contingency.

The American Embassy became the focal point for evacuation during this time. On April 29th, the main evacuation efforts continued all day. Although a number of aircraft evacuated hundreds of people from the airport, Marine helicopters were evacuating people from the roof of the American Embassy! Hundreds of people, mostly Vietnamese, crowded the Embassy grounds, struggling to get over the walls and gates. They were met by U.S. Marines who held them back so that a wholesale attack and bloodshed could be averted.

This evacuation took place mostly all night and into the early morning of April 30th, when the last of the Marines left from atop the Embassy on the last helicopter to leave Vietnam. America's longest war, the Vietnam War, was over. The last American serviceman, a Marine, stepped off Vietnamese property and onto a United States helicopter from the roof of the American Embassy, thus ending America's involvement in the war.

During this period of time, while these evacuations were taking place, my company, as with many others, was kept on high alert in addition to carrying out the daily training schedule. In preparation for the potential deployment of our unit to South Vietnam, the company commanders, other battalion staff members, and first sergeants, attended several high level briefings. I attended one meeting that was held by Colonel Al Gray, Commanding Officer of the 4th Marine Regiment, in the middle of the night, as the situation was constantly changing. Colonel Gray later became Commandant of the Marine Corps. Then, late on April 30th, the high-alert standby was relaxed, as the evacuation was over. North Vietnam had taken control of South Vietnam.

After that, we continued to carry out our regular training schedule. Being on a certain level of alert was a normal part of being in the Third Marine Division in the Western Pacific area. Marine units were expected to be able to answer any call for military force anywhere in that area. Consequently, the life of any Marine serving in those commands was going to be very busy and subject to being always prepared to pick up your gear and go, ready for any action, at any time.

At this point in my career, I had more than twenty years service in the Marine Corps and was eligible to retire if I wanted. It was something I began to think about during the just-passed evacuation of Saigon and the uncertainty of where and when the next hot spot in that area of the world would flare up and our unit would be called. That is what Marines do.

However, I began to think about what this meant for me. I had been in Vietnam early in 1964, and again, another 13 months in 1968, and returned home safely each time, and now there was this evacuation in 1975.

Was I pushing my luck? It seemed that I had spent enough time in the war in Vietnam, or anywhere else for that matter. Maybe I had better retire before I get killed in one of these operations just when I become eligible to retire, leaving Delores and my children to fend for themselves.

I couldn't help but again recall the faces of those Marines whom I helped bury in Nebraska. I will never forget their faces and the grief of their loved ones when told of their death. Their dreams were all shattered, their lives turned upside down. These men never expected to die.

The sudden death of a loved one such as this shatters the immediate family and has a rippling effect throughout the extended family far into the future. I knew that I didn't want to die, nor did I expect to die; neither did I wish to treat my life carelessly. I thought about how my death would affect Delores and the children. It was an awful thought. I had dreams of another career and life after the Marine Corps. I had always wanted to go to college, get a degree, and never have to leave my family again.

Delores, may God bless her, has been the strongest person I have ever known. During those long separations in 1964 and 1968, and now again, in 1975, for fourteen months at a time, she had always stepped up and taken charge of the household and complete care of our children. She kept the bills paid, did all the shopping, and, on one separation, worked at a full-time job, even when she was sick, and I didn't want her to have to do that again.

Consequently, I decided to submit my request to retire. It seemed, considering all the options and the fact that I was in an overseas command, that the soonest and best possible time for me to retire would be effective September 30,1975, approximately three months away.

I submitted my request to retire effective that date. That would mean I would not go afloat in September. Rather, in August, I would be transferred to another Rifle Company that had just returned from being on an afloat assignment. Meanwhile, from May until late August, I served with my current unit getting them ready and trained for that assignment. It was a tough job, no doubt about it.

After my request to retire was submitted, I began an undetermined waiting period until my request was approved or disapproved. In the meantime, I would just carry on with my regular duties as First Sergeant of "M" Company. As the weeks passed by, I anxiously awaited the unit mail every day for a response to my request to retire.

With the exception of a couple periods of going on an alert status because of some possible military interaction or intervention, our unit was on a standard training schedule, to fully prepare them to be able to carry out any assignment. Their training included weapons training, getting them completely familiar and efficient with every weapon, such as machine guns, hand guns, mines, (both ours and our enemy's), infantry tactics, and survival skills in the jungle. This training is conducted regardless of weather conditions—whether in sheets of driving rain or under the blistering hot sun. War doesn't wait for perfect weather conditions. Infantry training is never cancelled due to the weather.

When we were not on an alert status, the troops were authorized liberty in the evenings and weekends. Being the kind of troops they were, fighters, essentially, they often got in trouble for fighting, both in the barracks and on liberty in the nearby villages. It is a well-known fact that infantry troops are more difficult to manage than perhaps engineers or troops with technical jobs. I have had the experience now of being First Sergeant of both types of troops, and I would agree. It requires that junior NCO's themselves be hard, tough men. Being an infantry Marine is certainly not a job for sissies. Being first sergeant of a rifle company requires a person to be someone they don't want to tangle with. But, far more important, you have to be a straight shooter, honest and fair with them. I wanted to be not only a person they had some fear of but also a resource person who would help them with some problem they may have. In a body of men like this, a phony will be easily discovered, and the same goes for a liar or an unfair person.

At any given time, I might have three or four men waiting, with charges leveled against them, to appear before the captain for a hearing. A lot of these infractions were related to fighting or drinking and destroying property.

In this unit, the Battalion Commander required two senior staff NCO's to be walking patrol in the evening in the nearby community, which was Kin Ville, right outside the main gate. The patrol was to be in the streets and clubs, in uniform, from 21:00 to 24:00. This was to help keep our troops from getting in trouble with the local police. It was believed that our presence alone would often prevent some actions that would get them in trouble, such as being intoxicated, which was the most common infraction. I decided to also place myself on this duty, even though as First Sergeant I was excused.

Then, one night, when I was walking patrol with another senior staff person, I became engaged in an incident that could have gotten me in serious trouble. I saw one of my men coming out of a bar and recognized him as someone who was restricted to the barracks as punishment for some earlier infraction of the rules. I approached him and took him into custody. He appeared so shocked at seeing me, and so remorseful, that I released him and sent him back to the barracks with direct orders to report to the Battalion office, and then to report to me the next morning.

He went on his way, and we continued our patrol. Less than an hour later I caught him again, this time going down an alleyway. I stopped him and questioned why he wasn't where he was supposed to be. He began to walk away from me. Then I did something that I shouldn't have done. My temper flared, and I grabbed him by the arm and spun him around. I wasn't authorized to physically touch a man to force him to do what I ordered. He jerked away and threw a punch at me. I don't even remember if he hit me, but I swung back at him. He came back at me, and now, here I was, fist fighting in an alleyway with one of my men. It's a good thing that some other Marines were there and broke up the fight.

I told the man to walk with me because I was taking him back to the base, or the police would be called. He obeyed, and I went with him to the Battalion office. I officially put him in the custody of the Battalion Guard until morning. The next morning I went to the office and had charges brought against him. He was then confined to the Brig, awaiting a hearing before the Battalion Commander and would likely face a court-martial.

This event reinforced my decision to retire. Dealing with these kinds of men and situations for more than another year—six months of it on a ship—put me even more in the possible position of getting killed in some military action, or getting into trouble and being unable to retire at my present rank. Yes, it was time to get out.

My daily routine over the next three months began with a short walk to the mess hall, then head back to my room, brush my teeth, and make the quarter-mile walk to the Company office. Now that my retirement request had been submitted, I was always anxious for the company mail to be picked up so I could see if it was going to be approved. I was in the office at 07:15 every day for a daily conference with the Captain and the platoon commanders to review the day's schedule. After the captain and I had completed the morning inspection of the barracks, I settled in at my desk to go through my mail and handle any new problems that may have come up overnight. The company office was always very busy with people coming and going, checking in, checking out, and some rotating back to the States. At any one time I would have the service record files of from half-a-dozen to a dozen troops who were waiting for a hearing before the captain for some violation of regulations. These troops were a rowdy bunch to manage.

In mid-July, after a particularly stressful day, the captain called me into his office and asked me how would I like to go on R&R to Taipei, Taiwan, for four or five days. I shrugged and told him that I couldn't—there was just too much going on here.

He said, "Well, there's a flight leaving this afternoon and one scheduled person has cancelled out, so you can have that slot." He went on to say that everything would be okay at the office, and he encouraged me to go.

I thought, *What the heck, I need a break.* "Okay, I'll go," I told him. He told me where I could get a ride to Kadina and handed me the paperwork that would get me on the flight.

I hurriedly shut down my office and left to grab a quick shower and a duffle bag of essentials. I checked in at Kadina Air Terminal and caught a C-130 Hercules to Taipei, Taiwan. There were about ten other Marines on the flight who were also going on R&R. It was an uneventful three-hour flight and a soft landing at Taipei International Airport. This must be a very common event, as there was already a ride standing by to take us to two different hotels—our choice. I didn't know anything about either one, so I chose to get off at the first stop. I climbed out of the van and found myself right in the middle of large, crowded, bustling modern city.

When I entered the hotel lobby, I was greeted like royalty, with one hotel employee grabbing my bags, and another one carrying a tray with a large glass of ice-cold beer. I went to pay for it, and he waved me off. "On the house," he said. Wow!

That cold beer really hit the spot. I sat down in the air-conditioned lobby to enjoy my beer and relax. The hotel employee took my name and checked me in without my even going to the desk. He just assumed that I was staying there and came and told me that my room was ready whenever I was ready. I had another one of those cold glasses of beer while I relaxed in the lobby observing the clientele coming and going. This was great! Just a few hours ago I was in my office, wet with sweat, trying to manage the daily chaos, and now I'm in Taipei having an ice-cold beer.

When I was ready to go to the room, I was ushered up by the same servant. He came on into the room, quickly turned down the bed, made sure the air conditioning was working, checked out the bathroom, and was ready to leave, but he lingered a bit, and I realized that he was waiting for a tip. I gave him five dollars, and he bowed gracefully and quickly disappeared.

As soon as he left, there was a soft knock on the door. I opened it, and there stood a middle-aged Chinese woman, often referred to in these Asian countries as a Mamasan, with two pretty, young women. They all bowed, and then the older woman asked if the gentleman would like a woman's company. I'll admit I was a bit surprised and taken aback. Both of the young women were attractive and perhaps in their early twenties. She told me their names and said that I could pick either one for a short period of time, or for a day, or to stay with me as long as I wanted.

I forced myself not to think about it, and said no. I knew I couldn't do that. I thanked them, and the older woman said that if I changed my mind to let her know, and she gave me a business card, bowed again, and they left. That last glass of beer was hitting me, so I got comfortable and lay down across that big large bed and took a well-deserved nap in air-conditioned comfort. It was bliss!

Now, *this* is one of the things I really loved about being a Marine. How else could I afford a free four-day vacation and air passage to one of the great vacation capital cities in the world?

After a relaxing four days in Taipei, sightseeing, eating great food, and sleeping, I returned to Okinawa and resumed my duties with "Mike" Company, anxiously waiting for the unit mail to learn if I had received an answer to my request to retire. I even persuaded one of the Battalion Officers (who happened to have a friend in the office in Headquarters Marine Corps, back in Quantico, where these requests are processed) to make a phone call to see if my request was being considered. This friend checked the files and was able to tell me that my request was there and was being processed. It was a relief for me to know this, but there was still nothing left for me to do but wait. I was becoming more and more worried that I wouldn't get my request approved before the unit was scheduled to go aboard ship at some point in late September.

Going "afloat" was a term used by most Marines in this command in this part of the world. It refers to one of the regiments of the Third Marine division going aboard ships for about six months. This unit is known as a Regimental Landing Team and cruises around the Southern and Western Pacific areas, visiting a number of ports such as Hong Kong, Singapore, Australia, and others. During this time, they're constantly training by making a number of mock landings at several places. This then becomes, in effect, the president's police force in that area. Sometimes this unit is even called upon to remove all Americans from an embassy where the political situation has become dangerous because of flooding or other natural disasters.

CHAPTER 46

GOING HOME

One blistering hot day, I was sitting in my office, drenched in sweat, wearing my helmet, flack jacket, and with my weapon strapped on, when the chief clerk, who was going through the mail, suddenly said, "Hey, First Sergeant! I think I have something here you're going to be happy to see." I hollered back, "Well, bring it in here for me to see!"

He brought me a message from Headquarters Marine, which read, in effect, that my retirement had been approved, effective date, September 30, 1975. Wow! I jumped up from my desk, kicked back my chair, which banged against the wall, stood up, and let out a holler of some sort. I read the letter over and over again. Then I received a phone call from the Division Sergeant Major, who was an old Marine buddy going back to my Drill Instructor days. He and I had gone through D. I. School together. He had also gotten a copy of my message. He said, "Well, so you're going to bail out on us. You're quitting!"

I told him, "Yeah, I guess you could look at it that way." I also said that I was I looking forward to going to college and doing something else with the rest of my life.

He wished me good luck, and said, "We'll talk again soon."

Well, it was now official. I would not be going on float in September. I would be going home! How exciting!

The message went on to say that I would be transferred to H & HS Company, a Naval air station in Millington, Tennessee, where my retirement would be processed and finalized, effective date September 30th. Meanwhile, our Battalion would find another First Sergeant to replace me in "M" Company as soon as possible so he could get to know the men in the Company before they went on float.

As for me, I soon received orders to "G" Company, 2nd Battalion, 4th Marines. This assignment didn't require that I move from my barracks. I would just go to work at another battalion area, perhaps an even shorter walk to work every morning.

I reported for duty at my new unit on August 12th. I occupied my new office and got a bit settled, met the office staff and the CO, a captain. I received a short briefing from the Admin Chief and settled in. There were no Marines awaiting office hours, nor other disciplinary matters pending, that I would have to deal with. The daily unit diary report was completed for the day. Great! It was so nice to be in a unit that was disciplined and functioning like a Company should. Perhaps this was because this unit had been operating together for nearly a year. All the troublemakers had been weeded out months ago. Back at "M" Company, I had still been in that process.

My job in this Company was pretty routine: a number of inspections and the daily training scheduling, which affected the troops and platoon commanders and not me. My job mainly consisted of making sure that all of the paperwork and the personnel reports had been made for handling a rare disciplinary problem.

As the time for me to carry out my retirement orders drew near, another First Sergeant reported in to take my place. After he had gotten checked in, I told him that I didn't see the need for two First Sergeants in a Company, and he agreed. I excused myself and went back to my room. It was during this short walk back to my room that I really felt free of all the weight of responsibility that goes with being a Company First Sergeant. I wasn't going afloat—I was going home!

For the first time in many years, I felt free. Even if a war started in this area, I already had my orders from Headquarters Marine Corps to retire. When I got back to my room, it was only mid-morning and I was without anything to do. Wow!

I opened my locker and took out a bottle of Johnnie Walker Black Label Scotch and enjoyed a couple of good shots. I took off my boots, lay down, and took a nap—the kind I had only dreamed about for a very long time. Some of the other first sergeants who were my longtime friends were at the barracks, and they were envious. I joked with them, telling them that while walking back from what had been my office to the barracks, my pack had slipped off, and I'd just kicked it into the weeds—trying to symbolize getting rid of all my military duties. They got the point. I told them, "Your day will come someday. Just *continue to march.*"

I later picked up my checkout sheet from the Battalion Office, and spent a couple of days turning in items and clearing myself from the Battalion. I turned in my .45 Cal. pistol, all my web gear, a couple of books from the library—books that I'd never found time to read.

Checking out with Medical wasn't as easy. I had to schedule and get a complete physical exam before they cleared me, which meant I had to take a base bus to the main medical facility on the far side of the island. One exam caught me by surprise. They said I had to have a colonoscopy. As I waited in line to get this horrible exam, I was visiting with several other guys who were also there waiting. One of these guys made the observation that he didn't know that a person had to be a perfect asshole to be eligible for retirement!

Within a day or so, I was free of my Battalion's obligation and picked up the orders that essentially told me to be at passenger check-in at Kadina Air Force base on a certain date. As I awaited my plane's departure, I began to feel a bit of nostalgia, having been through here so many times in the past years. The first leg of my long journey was from Kadina to Travis Air Force base in California and then two commuter flights to get to Memphis. Millington was a few miles north of Memphis. I found a bus to Millington and then the building where I was to check in.

I checked in, had my orders stamped, and was greeted enthusiastically by pretty woman Marine, a Lance Corporal. I was still standing at the counter getting my orders checked when she hollered from across the office, "First Sergeant Lay! First Sergeant Lay! It's good to see you!" She came running around the counter and gave me a big hug. She was one of the women Marines I had enlisted in Knoxville while on recruiting duty. I didn't recognize her at first, but then we had a brief gab session, each bringing the other up to date on our lives. She was happy and doing well, and glad to be a woman Marine.

I was assigned a room in a very nice barracks and went upstairs to check it out. It was a nice large room with a queen-sized bed, much better than what one might get at a local motel. After I got settled, I went down to the Headquarters Company office. The Company First Sergeant invited me in to his office to chat. He was familiar with processing people out and to retirement. Then he said, "Well, there's only room for one First Sergeant in a Company (indicating himself), and I don't have any other kind of work here for you to do, so you're on your own. Do as you please. Just keep me informed about where you are so I can get in touch with you if I need to. I'll need to see you the day before the scheduled retirement on September 30th. So, until the date of your retirement, almost a week, you can do whatever you want—just let this office know where you are and how you can be reached."

So, he just sort of dismissed me. My duties were whatever I wanted to do! I thought this might be a good time to go through all my clothing, throw away all the old, worn-out stuff, and clean and shine my shoes. There were plenty of activities to keep me busy until my retirement date.

My retirement consisted of only a simple formation of Marines and their Commanding Officer, a Colonel, reading my retirement order and then a dismissal of troops. Three other Marines were also retiring on that date. With that dismissal, I was on my own. I no longer had any duties. I no longer had any authority as a First Sergeant. I could do what I wanted! Surprisingly, this was a bit harder to accept than I had thought it would be. No longer was I Company First Sergeant, with all that weight on my shoulders and people jumping to obeying my every command. I was nothing now—nothing but an old retired First Sergeant. Never again would I be able to achieve and demand the respect I had before, up to even a few minutes ago. I was finished. All I had to do, and all I was expected to do, was to get off the base and go home. The very thought of it brought tears to my eyes and I had a lump in my throat. There was no going back now.

Retirement Ceremony, 1975.

One thing I needed to do was to find the best way to get from Millington, Tennessee, to Fort Scott, Kansas—a rather inconvenient destination. There was no way to fly into Fort Scott. A person had to either fly into Kansas City and find transportation south a hundred miles, or fly into Tulsa Oklahoma and come north, also nearly a hundred miles. I didn't want Delores to have to drive these distances, considering she had her hands full running the household and take care of the children. So, it seemed that the best alternative for me was to take a bus from Millington to Fort Scott. I bought a bus ticket for a bus departing in the afternoon on the date of my actual retirement, September 30th. It would take me through Memphis west and then north through Little Rock, Arkansas, and up through Joplin, Missouri, through Pittsburg, Kansas, and then north to Fort Scott. At first it didn't seem like a long journey, but as we rode into the night hours I began to feel extremely tired, and the hum of the tires on the road lulled me to sleep.

We rolled into Joplin just before midnight. As we pulled into the station, the driver announced that this was the end of the line for him and told us to check in with the office for connecting rides. Surprise, surprise! I went in and spoke with the ticketing agent, and he told me that the bus station closed at midnight and wouldn't open again until 7:00 AM.

It appeared that I was going to have to get a motel room where I could sleep. I hadn't planned on this. Add to this the fact that the bus station wasn't anywhere near the area where there were any motels. I hated to have to get a hotel room just from midnight till 7 AM. I spoke with the ticket agent who was trying to get me to leave the bus terminal because he was closing down in a few minutes. I decided to try and work something out with this guy. I mentioned that there was a sofa in the main terminal, and that there was no one else but me. I suggested that maybe I could just stay there in the terminal and sleep on that sofa until morning and then catch the 7 o'clock bus north to Fort Scott. I told him that he could just lock me in, and I would still be here when he got there to open up in the morning.

At first he told me that he couldn't do that. I pushed him a bit, and said, "Look at me. I'm a Marine First Sergeant. You can trust me, if you can trust anyone! In fact, it'll be like an having extra security for the bus station overnight." I told him, "I have everything I need here—a restroom, water, the sofa to sleep on, everything. I'm going home after retiring from the Marine Corps today."

He thought about it for a minute, with this new view of the situation. Finally, he said that regulations didn't permit it, but since it was me, a veteran, he would do it. He gave me his home phone number and asked me to call him if something unusual happened. I thanked him very much, and he turned out all the lights, locked the place up, and left. He said he'd see me about 6:30 in the morning.

Whew! This was going to work out okay. I hit the head, got a cup of ice water from the drinking fountain, took off my shoes, and lay down on the sofa. I had to dig around in my bag to find my old sweatshirt, which I rolled up for a pillow. I wished that I had a blanket, because it got a bit chilly in the early hours of the morning. But I had slept many, many times being much colder at Camp Pendleton and other places. Surprisingly, I got a fair amount of sleep. I guess I was really tired.

The next morning, I was already awake when the ticket agent came to open up. I'm sure he was relieved to see me and note that everything was fine.

I thanked him again for bending the rules for me. There was a snack bar that opened early, so I grabbed a quick cup of coffee and a donut for breakfast and was ready to catch that 7 A.M. bus.

When the bus left Joplin, I really began to get anxious but also excited knowing that I was going to be in Fort Scott before noon. I was very familiar with this road between Joplin and Pittsburg, having traveled it many times in the past. Soon we were in Pittsburg, where we made a brief stop at the station.

As we rolled out of there toward Fort Scott, I could hardly contain myself. I was so excited! It only took us about thirty minutes, and we were rolling into the south edge of Fort Scott. I moved up to the front seat by the driver. He asked me if I was familiar with Fort Scott and where the station was located. I told him that I did. He said that he hadn't ever driven this route before and asked if I could direct him. So, I told him how to get to the bus station.

Then, the thought hit me: I was going to be coming home by bus to the same old Trailways bus station on East Oak from which

I had departed twenty-two years earlier when I was leaving home. I remembered that Mom and Dad had brought me and had seen me off. How ironic. I could have never have foreseen this!

Well, here we were, pulling into the old station now. It looked very much like it had twenty-two years earlier. For me, a lot of life had been lived, passed under the bridge, so to speak, but the old bus station hadn't changed. And instead of Mom and Dad being there to greet me, there was my wonderful lady, Delores, and the kids! Wow! How long I had pictured this moment and had looked forward to it. And now I was there. I could hardly believe it.

I stepped down from the bus, and Delores greeted me with open arms and some very warm hugs and many kisses. I knelt down to give the kids some hugs. What a great homecoming!

I put my bags in the trunk, and we got into our old Cadillac. Could I drive? You bet! I loved our Cadillac. Within ten minutes we arrived at our house, and I pulled into the driveway. I stopped the car and turned off the key.

I was home—really and truly home! I told Delores, "I will never leave home again!" I gave her a big hug and a kiss. All was right with the world.

Continue to March!

EPILOGUE

Our father's life journey began with his upbringing in Bourbon County Kansas, on through his Marine Corps career, which concluded in 1975. His parents were solid, resilient farmers, whose strength and fortitude, tested by the beautiful, yet harsh plains of Kansas, instilled values of self-reliance, determination, faith, and hope as foundations of good moral character.

Dad and Mom's love story began in Miami Beach, Florida, and we never tire of listening to them relay to us their mutually shared fond memories of how they met. The way Dad tells the story, our family began due to a stoplight and a last-minute decision to turn left into the Sea Gull Hotel that fateful day. Mom credits her swimming skills with being able to snag this handsome Marine at the Sea Gull Hotel where she was vacationing.

Our parents embody the classic story of two very different people who fell in love and took off on a whirlwind of time, not knowing where it would take them. They were confident their love was lasting. Although they were both born in the depression era of WWII, they relay completely different experiences. Mom was a city girl whose brothers fought in WWII. She was accustomed to city life, radios, streetcars, television, electricity, and running water in the old immigrant brick homes of Braddock, Pennsylvania. Dad was a Kansas farm boy, raised by descendants of pioneers who lived a life of hardscrabble during the depression with farming and road crew jobs. They had no running water, used kerosene lanterns for light, and raised livestock, hunted, and grew their own food. He had very few connections to the outside world until he joined the Marines.

Dad could keep us fascinated for hours telling us stories about his childhood growing with his family on the Kansas farm, his Marine Corps life, his near-fatal illness at the lowest point of his life, stories of falling in love with Mom and their early days. He often spoke of his times of sadness when he had to go to Vietnam and leave us, his days of playing music in Da Nang, Vietnam, our adventures of military-ordered relocations, endless car troubles, and many loving stories of his parents and sisters. We pestered and encouraged him to please write a memoir. How could we ever remember all the stories he has told us?

Well, at last he did, and the completion of his memoir came unexpectedly as he sat at his computer recovering from multiple vertebral fractures. He was 83 years old and determined to write the memoir for which we so pleaded.

Our family is blessed with great storytellers. This was the way it was growing up during this period. Visiting our relatives on the farm, we kids would sit and listen as Grandpa Lay, Uncle Raymond, and Dad would "one up" each other with a better story or joke. We would giggle and laugh. Dad would then get his guitar, and we were enraptured listening to his rich, deep voice as he sang songs, and we all sing along.

When Dad was gone to Vietnam in the 1960s, we yearned for him. Gone were the times of lying in bed upstairs at our home in Omaha, Nebraska, listening as Dad sang and played guitar downstairs. Mom kept us stable. Our lives "carried on." We were loved, well cared for, life was idyllic. There was always Mom and the relatives near and far. A vivid and fond memory we share occurred one day when Mom gathered Bobbie, Mark, and Valerie in the living room of the large, white house. She had a reel-to-reel tape player. Mom started the tape and we watched it go around, and suddenly it was Dad's voice! He spoke to us and addressed each one of us individually, telling us to be good and listen to Mom, that he missed us, and assured us that he would be home soon. We wondered, where is he? Was he wearing his Marine Corps uniform with the brass buttons? Was he wearing his sequined cowboy suit and holding his guitar? Was he working? Maybe on a car somewhere? It was beyond our comprehension that Dad was in a far-off country, Vietnam.

Dad's return brought celebration and adventure. We were going to California! We didn't even know we were military brats until we moved and eventually landed on base in Tustin, California. The epic trip was one to remember, and Dad was a source of endless entertainment. We visited family, stayed at motels all the way across the country, sometimes ones with swimming pools! There were the unavoidable, seemingly predictable car troubles.

Dad was always calm when dealing with his children during our road trips. He had a way with direct discipline and was never one to shout in anger. He laid down the rules, and when we got out of hand with our squabbles, the car would pull over. Oh no! Bobbie and Mark would receive some gentle discipline, resulting in hurt feelings and possibly a wounded ego. Dad couldn't bring himself to inflict corporal punishment on his baby girl, and pretend spankings ensued at the rear of the station wagon as Dad clapped his hands and Valerie cried and played along. Our time in California was the best and was very exciting. We had many visits from distant Pennsylvania, Kansas, and Missouri relatives. We took a cross country road trip to Pennsylvania in our VW van, camping along the way. We spent days at the California beaches, made many trips to Disneyland, and enjoyed never-ending entertainment as only southern California can offer. And, we also had a new baby brother, Quentin! Dad, with his sense of humor and pranks, kept us on our toes as he challenged us to Halloween dares. We even watched astronauts land on the moon on TV! Life on Marine Corps Air Station, Tustin, was beautiful. Dad was a hard-charging Marine, commanding his unit, caring for his family, and performing music gigs on the weekends. Soon though, we had to move, as new orders arrived: Tennessee!

First stop, Chattanooga, Tennessee. What a difference from southern California. We adapted, tried making friends, but it was tough. These were not military kids, and we didn't relate well. But we soon picked up a southern accent, and shortly thereafter we moved to Knoxville, Tennessee. Once again we were the only military kids. Our family was the center of our world. And, we had a new baby brother, Dwight. He was born on the Marine Corps Birthday, just as had Dad predicted! Dad left for work early every morning in his dress blue uniform to recruit new Marines. He often performed at events on weekends, and sometimes we saw him on TV, in his uniform, talking about the Marine Corps and singing "The Marine's Ballad" or "Make a Marine." This gave us a sense of celebrity like no other kids we knew. We diligently prepared Dad's 45-RPM record covers, stuffing them with his record to ship to all those waiting Marines out there. We hoped that Bobbie might even get one while he was in Marine Corps boot camp!

All too soon, it was time to move, and Dad was going to take us to Kansas to live near Grandma and Grandpa Lay while he was stationed in Okinawa, Japan. This was exciting news. We were moving, but it was also bittersweet. The music would again pause, while our singing Marine father went away to a far off country. Would this Vietnam War never end? It seemed to forever dominate our childhood years. We settled in Fort Scott, Kansas, and rejoiced in seeing Grandma and Grandpa, and aunts, uncles and cousins. Mom was very busy with four children to care for. Her brother (and our favorite uncle), Uncle Abe, traveled from Pennsylvania as often as possible to help out. He was a spark in our lives. Mom instilled firm, motherly values and discipline. One disapproving look from Mom was all it took. We were expected to do chores, watch after each other, and Mark delivered newspapers by bicycle through heat and snowstorms to earn extra money. Times were tight, and not as joyful. Fort Scott, Kansas was a tough farming town, and we were the only military kids around. We were different. And, we missed Dad.

When Dad returned from Japan, he was the same Dad! The music was back, and our father would guide us to the next adventure. Dad said, "I'm not going to leave my family again." He never did.

Eventually, we were the ones to leave home, one by one, as we attended college and followed in our father's footsteps, with all of us becoming Marines ourselves. We wrote many a tearful letter home. Mom or Dad would write us back, encouraging us and listening to our woes. In his letters and emails to us we could count on one thing: Dad always signed off his letters to us with "Continue to March, Love Dad." When he proposed that the memoir he was writing would be titled "Continue to March," we instantly knew that this was the only title that would be appropriate.

Thank you, Dad, for your loving devotion to Mom, the example you set for family values, your mentorship, guidance, always reliable sage advice, and your desire to live a life of love, meaning, integrity, and honor.

Most of all, thank you for directing us to "Continue to March." Semper Fi from your loving children.

ACKNOWLEDGMENTS

This book is dedicated with love and gratitude to the many people who have encouraged and assisted me in writing this memoir.

To my loving wife, Delores. You have been an amazing partner, a devoted and caring mother to our children, and an example of strength and courage. You are a beautiful and classy woman. We celebrated life's good times, and comforted and supported each other during the difficult times. Your loving support and patience never faltered as I worked on the book. Your extraordinary memory was invaluable in recalling events and dates. Thank you for the many hours you dedicated to this endeavor. Love you, Delores.

To Barbara Lay, my daughter-in-law and editor, for your guidance and insightful suggestions. Your meticulous proofreading and edits are greatly appreciated. What a lucky guy I am to have you as my editor and family member.

To my son Mark, whose tenacious dedication to detail and word-by-word review exemplified patience and perseverance.

To my daughter, Valerie, for bringing light-hearted laughter and bonding camaraderie while working closely with Mark to create photo additions and craft an epilogue.

To my sons Bobbie and Quentin for their faithful support.

To my son Dwight and his family for their technical support.

To the Marines I served with, "those mighty gallant men with their rifles and their packs": Semper Fidelis!

ABOUT THE AUTHOR

In accordance with his disciplined, self-directed command, "Continue to March," First Sergeant Robert Lay did just that.

Following his retirement from the Marine Corps in 1975, Mr. Lay moved his family from Fort Scott, Kansas, to Pittsburg, Kansas, and enrolled in Pittsburg State University as a 40-year-old freshman. In 1978 he received a Bachelor of Science degree in Education, and continued his studies, earning his Master of Arts degree, with an emphasis in Communication. In 1979 he accepted a position in Topeka, Kansas, with the Kansas Commission of Civil Rights and settled the family in Hoyt, Kansas, north of Topeka, which was only a few hours from his parents' home in Fulton, Kansas, and his nearby sisters. He achieved promotions quickly and served as Investigator I, Investigator II, Field Supervisor, Assistant Director, and retired from the Commission in 1997 as Executive Director. After retirement he taught classes in Public Speaking and English Composition at Highland Community College. In August 1999, the Governor of Kansas, Bill Graves, appointed Mr. Lay as a Commissioner to the Kansas Commission of Civil Rights, representing Business & Industry. He moved to Oregon in September of 2000 to be close to and provide support and encouragement to his youngest son Dwight, who had a physically disabling injury and was attending Oregon State University in Corvallis. He and Delores settled in Hillsboro, Oregon, living near their sons Mark, Quentin, and Dwight. Their daughter, Valerie, and Bobbie live in California. Delores and Bob have been together 59 years. Mr. Lay never stopped playing guitar throughout the years he lived and worked in Kansas. He and his band performed at various venues. He continues to write music, and, to this day, his guitar is never far from reach.